Advance Praise for *Alone in the Ring*

'Coming on the heels of his masterpiece, *Kashmir Conundrum: The Quest for Peace in a Troubled Land*, General N.C. Vij has come out with another gripping narrative, *Alone in the Ring: Decision-making in Critical Times*. This book delves into the heart of challenges faced in various military operations and contemporary military issues, offers invaluable insights, captivating narratives and glimpses into the intricacies of decision-making, as seen through the eyes of the top rung military commanders. It provides a riveting account of some crucial conflicts and the strategic brilliance of decision-makers in the face of adversity. From the fog of war to the clarity of hindsight, the author navigates through the intricacies of military operations (Kargil, rescue in Sierra Leone, Operation Parakram), establishment of an anti-infiltration fence along the entire LOC and the formulation of some game-changing policies and measures focusing on morale and welfare of soldiers with a deft hand and authoritative narration. He has also masterfully discussed doctrinal issues such as cold start and military reforms including jointness, integration, theaterisation and complexities of modern-day warfare, all of which are essential for understanding the conflicts of today and the future. Decision-makers and bureaucrats exploring the nuances of security strategy can draw upon the rich real-world experiences presented by the author. In a world of uncertainty and an ever-changing geopolitical landscape, understanding the dynamics of decision-making is crucial for policymakers, civil society and academics alike, and hence this book must also be read widely outside the military circles. I compliment General Vij on this outstanding work.'

Dr Karan Singh
First Sadr-i-Riyasat of Jammu and Kashmir, Former Union Minister and Former Governor of Jammu and Kashmir

'These memoirs, of one who successively served as DGMO, Vice Chief and Chief of the Indian Army, contain a telling analysis of the ruinous delays and failures in the response of the military, defence apparatus and the polity to the Pakistanis' intrusion in the Kargil sector and, later, to the Pakistani terrorist attack on our Parliament. With certain reforms underway, the gargantuan challenge is to secure the operational integration of the defence services for achieving this objective. The author stresses on the pressing need for the promulgation of the National Security Policy, from which alone will flow the entire spectrum of joint war fighting doctrines, adherence to which would ensure against recurrence of past mistakes. This book is a must-read for military and political leaders and all policymakers.'

N.N. Vohra
Former Principal Secretary, Former Union Home Secretary, Former Union Defence Secretary and Former Governor of Jammu and Kashmir

'General Vij has thought deeply about his experiences leading one of the world's largest and most powerful militaries through an eventful and critical time of transformation. The Kargil war, the buildup on the LOC in Kashmir, rescuing Indian UN peacekeepers in Sierra Leone and securing India against terrorist infiltration from Pakistan are some of the operational experiences that he contributed to and drew broader lessons from. He also masterfully discusses doctrinal issues such as cold start and military reforms including jointness, integration and theaterisation, all of which are major concerns today. This honest and analytical examination of military decision-making in India is exemplary and highly relevant in its approach and conclusions. It deserves to be widely read outside military circles. It also reflects the Indian Army's ability to learn from good and bad experience and then to evolve. So long as the Indian Army has generals like N.C. Vij and continues this tradition, we can expect the best from our armed forces.'

Shivshankar Menon
Former Foreign Secretary and Former National Security Advisor

'This is a comprehensive narration of operations in which General Nirmal Vij participated as Principal Staff Officer, and other important strategic and administrative decisions in which he was involved as Chief of the Army Staff. General Vij's views on jointness, integration and theaterisation are noteworthy. His critical observation, based on experience, is that the political and bureaucratic tendency to keep the military leadership out of the information-sharing and strategic decision-making loop has an adverse effect on military preparedness and its contingency planning.'

General Ved Prakash Malik
Former Chief of the Army Staff

'A most absorbing and informative book by former Indian Army Chief General Vij which offers a first-hand account of how some major challenges to Indian security such as the Kargil war and Operation Parakram were addressed, the logic of the cold start doctrine and measures taken to tackle militancy in Jammu and Kashmir. He shares his thinking on complex issues of organisational reforms including jointness and theaterisation. As Foreign Secretary, during a part of General Vij's tenure, I had the occasion to observe the great clarity and firmness of his practical approach to our national security challenges. A very rewarding read.'

Kanwal Sibal
Former Foreign Secretary and Chancellor of JNU

'*Alone in the Ring* is a riveting and instructive read. Penned by a key player, it provides fresh and authentic insights into many developments that occurred on General Vij's watch, like the Kargil conflict, Operation Parakram and Operation Khukri. As the author of the cold start doctrine, which was long wrapped in mystery, and the driving force behind the LOC fencing, in the face of much scepticism, General Vij has dwelt in this book on their nature, rationale and evolution with unmatched authority. In addressing these and many other issues, ranging from the not-so-well-known heated behind-the-scenes debate on the possible induction of Indian forces into Iraq following the US attack, to questions of higher defence management, the book brings out our Army's ethos as well as the qualities which go into the making of a successful leader as exemplified in the author. In sum, this book is a must-have on the shelves of those interested in the Indian Army.'

Satish Chandra
Vice Chairperson, Vivekananda International Foundation, and Former Deputy National Security Advisor

'General N.C. Vij has written an excellent and engrossing account of his experiences during the final years of his illustrious career wherein he held highly coveted appointments before taking over the reins of the Indian Army. Having served very closely with him during this eventful period I find *Alone in the Ring* an authentic first-hand narration of important events and his role in decision-making and execution both at the national and army level such as the Kargil war, Operation Parakram, national security, modernisation and restructuring of the Army and major administrative reforms aimed at enhancing the motivation, morale and pride of the rank and file. The book is laced with striking anecdotal accounts too. This eminently readable book authored by an outstanding general with vast experience is a must-read not only for all military professionals and scholars but also the political elite and decision-makers at the national level.'

General J.J. Singh
Former Governor and Former Chief of the Army Staff

'Decision-making on national security requires foresight, precision and timeliness since it has long-term implications affecting the nation's destiny. The political class, more focused on day-to-day governance and quick electoral gains, tends to shy away from this vital subject because of inadequate knowledge. Consequent dependence on the bureaucracy with its limited exposure leaves a void, which this seminal work by General Vij has tried to fill. Covering a crucial period when Pakistan was ruled by an ambitious and vengeful military dictatorship in cahoots with a rising China, the book gives a deep insight into how the twin threats were handled at the highest levels and long-term measures instituted to safeguard national interest. A must-read for practitioners of national security as well as for our countrymen to appreciate decision dilemmas at leadership levels.'

General Deepak Kapoor
Former Chief of the Army Staff

'General N.C. Vij, PVSM, UYSM, AVSM, the former COAS, has lucidly highlighted the challenges of decision-making at the strategic leadership level in the Army. Having served as director under him when he was the DGMO, and later as the DDGPP (Strategy) and DDGMO (B) when he was the COAS, I vividly remember his extraordinary style of functioning. Being a visionary general, he consistently focused on bolstering and honing the Army's combat power and evolving ingenious doctrines and strategies for its application. Concurrently, he also implemented some notable welfare and administrative reforms to address the long-term aspirations of all ranks. *Alone in the Ring* offers profound insights into the General's multifarious strategic initiatives and the related decision-making challenges. Given its valuable content, the book is a premier asset for all those who wish to delve into the myriad facets it encompasses.'

General Bikram Singh
Former Chief of the Army Staff

'In his book *Alone in the Ring*, the former Army Chief General N.C. Vij provides rare insights into how decisions were taken in the highest military echelons at critical moments in the nation's history. Whether it was the Kargil war, the tense situation after the terrorist attack on the Parliament, the evacuation of Indian peacemakers in Sierra Leone or building a hi-tech fence on the LOC to stop cross-border infiltration of terrorists, General Vij was involved in decision-making in one way or the other. As national security challenges become even more complex in the third decade of the century, the book holds lessons for national security decision-makers and planners. One lesson is to keep the nation first, provide the necessary support to the armed forces and remain ever vigilant.'

Dr Arvind Gupta
Director, Vivekananda International Foundation, Former Deputy National Security Advisor and Former Secretary of National Security Council

'Decision-making especially in combat situations is a very complex process wherein the acumen and capacity of the commanders is tested to the hilt. I have known General Vij for more than five decades and can say it with conviction that he combines in himself the finest attributes of being a bold commander and a meticulous planner. He has an admirable trait of being resolute without being overbearing. As the DGMI, both of us worked alongside each other closely and it was a pleasure to see his cool nerves and ability to take critical decisions. Personally, I will give a good share of the credit for this victory to him, because of his deft handling and teammanship.'

Lieutenant General R.K. Sawhney
Former DGMI and Former Deputy Chief of the Army Staff

'As a very junior subordinate of General Nirmal Vij, I got the honour of highlighting some of his virtues and achievements as an Army Chief, all downplayed for far too long. Among his landmark decisions, I recall, were the orders to Northern Command to operationalise towards achieving a sub-1000 figure of terrorists in Jammu and Kashmir, the decision to construct the LOC fence against all odds of terrain, climate and adversary fire, raising of HQ South Western Command, bifurcating XVI Corps to create IX Corps, institution of the Ex-servicemen's Contributory Health Scheme and the setting up of the

Married Accommodation Project. This, despite facing all the challenges that the wake of Operation Parakram brought, was something phenomenal for a Chief's tenure. I am glad we are getting to read some of how all this was achieved by him in such a short tenure. A book for the leadership collection, to be quoted for many years.'

Lieutenant General Ata Hasnain
Former GOC XV Corps, Member of the National Disaster Management Authority and Former Chancellor of Central University of Kashmir

Alone in the Ring

ALONE IN THE RING

Decision-making in Critical Times

GENERAL N.C. VIJ

BLOOMSBURY

BLOOMSBURY INDIA
Bloomsbury Publishing India Pvt. Ltd
Second Floor, LSC Building No. 4, DDA Complex, Pocket C – 6 & 7,
Vasant Kunj, New Delhi, 110070

BLOOMSBURY, BLOOMSBURY INDIA and the Diana logo
are trademarks of Bloomsbury Publishing Plc

First published in India 2025

Copyright © General N.C. Vij, 2025
All photographs from the author's personal collection except if otherwise mentioned

General N.C. Vij has asserted his right under the Indian Copyright Act
to be identified as the Author of this work

The maps in this book are neither accurate nor drawn to scale and
the boundaries as shown neither purport to be correct nor authentic
as per the Survey of India guidelines

All rights reserved. No part of this publication may be: i) reproduced or transmitted in
any form, electronic or mechanical, including photocopying, recording or by
means of any information storage or retrieval system without prior permission
in writing from the publishers; or ii) used or reproduced in any way for the training,
development or operation of artificial intelligence (AI) technologies, including
generative AI technologies. The rights holders expressly reserve this publication
from the text and data mining exception as per Article 4(3) of the Digital Single
Market Directive (EU) 2019/790

Bloomsbury Publishing Plc does not have any control over, or responsibility for,
any third-party websites referred to in this book. All internet addresses given in this
book were correct at the time of going to press. The author and publisher regret any
inconvenience caused if addresses have changed or sites have ceased to exist, but can
accept no responsibility for any such changes

ISBN: HB: 978-93-56409-51-4; eBook: 978-93-56409-35-4
2 4 6 8 10 9 7 5 3 1

Typeset in Bembo Std by Manipal Technologies Limited
Printed and bound in India by Thomson Press India Ltd

To find out more about our authors and books visit www.bloomsbury.com and sign
up for our newsletters

To the brave officers, soldiers and families of our valiant Indian Army

Contents

Preface   xvii

1. The Kargil War: View from Its Nerve Centre   1
2. Operation Parakram: On the Brink and Back   48
3. Operation Khukri: Rescuing Indian Peacekeepers in Sierra Leone   75
4. The LOC Fence: A Novel Strategy to Control Infiltration in Jammu and Kashmir   95
5. Cold Start Doctrine: Securing India   116
6. Jointness, Integration and Theaterisation: Developing Cross-domain Cutting Edge   128
7. Advising against Participation in Iraq War: Nation First   161
8. Administrative Reforms: Welfare of the Men behind the Gun   173

Epilogue   201

Acknowledgements   205
Appendix A: Journey Highlights of My Tenure   207
Appendix B: Letter to All Officers of the Indian Army   209
Notes   223
References   233
Index   237
About the Author   245

Preface

'You must rise up to the need of the hour. You should fear nothing except deviating from your duties.'
                    Lord Krishna in the Bhagavad Gita

Why do we write? In all professions, it is necessary to keep oneself abreast of the latest developments and try to keep ahead of them. In the profession of arms, it is especially important to learn from the experiences of others and try to adopt their methods of overcoming adversity. While we should never fight historical wars again, we need to understand those events. The best way to do that is to read what has been written about those wars by those who fought them.

From 1999 to 2005, my last six years in the Indian Army, I was often in a position where I had to make decisions myself or help others to make them. Decision-making in complex environments – both within the army and externally with the government – became one of the most important parts of my job. This book is about decision-making in critical times.

The title of this book is inspired from Muhammed Ali's 'Rumble in the Jungle' bout against George Foreman. It was October 1974 and Ali was a massive underdog facing the reigning undisputed heavyweight boxing champion of the world. Ali was being given a lot of advice from his corner on how to tackle Foreman. However, he shut his mind to all that because he felt that his trainer's job had already been done. It was time for him to go by his own instincts and judgement. Ali decided that he was alone in the ring and only he could influence the final outcome. He delivered a spectacular knockout to win the bout. This analogy can be extended to the armed forces, where invariably the final decision rests with the commander, who has to trust his instincts and make the decision alone. Of course, the value of our field commanders and staff remains immense, as no war is fought alone, and I will remain ever obliged to them for their contributions.

Each chapter of the book is related to a particular decision made or influenced by me. As a result, the book runs thematically and not chronologically. The chapters on the Kargil war and Operation Parakram are based on my experiences as the director general of military operations (DGMO) and the vice chief of the army staff (VCOAS) respectively. I was most intimately involved with the operations in Sierra Leone as the DGMO. The 'anti-infiltration fence' was conceptualised and implemented during my tenure as the army chief.

The chapter on the 'cold start' doctrine is based on learnings from Operation Parakram. This doctrine still remains at the heart of the proposed restructuring in the army to prepare for the next war. The chapter on integration and 'jointness' is a result of my experience while in service as this concept was active when I was the army chief. The proposal of sending troops to Iraq was seriously considered at the time and I was involved in the institutional decision-making. The narration would have been incomplete without recollecting a few major reforms that were important for improving the welfare, self-esteem and honour of our soldiers.

Almost two decades have passed since my retirement and much of this book is based on recollections of my time in service. I have tried to fact-check as much as possible using public records and unclassified official histories, but there are instances – such as Iraq – where I had to depend on my memory alone. If there are any unintended inaccuracies, I alone am responsible.

During the course of writing this book, I received invaluable guidance and assistance from a close group of friends and colleagues who read the manuscript and offered advice as it developed. I am grateful to them all. I hope that this book will serve as a valuable resource for all interested in the events it covers.

I wish the brave officers, soldiers and families of our valiant Indian Army good luck for the challenging times ahead!

1

The Kargil War
View from Its Nerve Centre

'Kargil was an absolute disaster.'
Benazir Bhutto, June 2003[1]

'Kargil was Pakistan's biggest disaster after 1971.'
Nawaz Sharif, former Pakistani prime minister,
June 2000[2]

Introduction

IN JANUARY 1999, I was commanding IV Corps at Tezpur when General Ved Prakash Malik, the chief of the army staff (COAS), arrived on an operational visit and told me that I would shortly be moved to the Army Headquarters (Army HQ) as the director general military operations (DGMO). The transfer happened the next month. Little did I know then that soon I would closely be involved in a historical and critical war, forced on us by Pakistan's deceit.

The military operations (MO) directorate at the Army HQ becomes the centre of all operational activities at times of war. This is where all plans are coordinated and troops deployment initiated after discussion between army commanders and the chief. During war, all directorates at the Army HQ work wholly towards the enhancement of operational efforts and hence are virtually in support of the MO directorate. In the words of General Malik, 'Throughout the Kargil war, the MO directorate was an extension of the battlefield. Its officers and staff along with their counterparts from the air force and the navy worked with remorseless commitment to collate and analyse unfolding events in their correct perspective. They would obtain and communicate appropriate decisions. The MO directorate is the repository of such critical operational decisions.'

Strategic Backdrop

Pakistan has fought three major wars with India: 1947–48, 1965 and 1971. The liberation of Bangladesh in 1971 was a great humiliation for Pakistan. With the signing of the Simla Agreement, Pakistan had to abandon its quest to militarily annex Kashmir. It had to evolve another strategy and prepare for a long-drawn struggle. It came up with a plan based on two key strategies: one, to attain nuclear capability; and two, to launch a proxy war in the Kashmir Valley and other parts of Jammu and Kashmir. The second strategy aimed at instigating the locals to demand secession from India.

In 1984, General Zia-ul-Haq tasked Pakistan's Inter-Services Intelligence (ISI) with evolving a plan for exploiting the political space in the Valley. This was given the code name 'Operation Topac'. It commenced soon after the Soviet withdrawal from Afghanistan in February 1989, once Pakistan's commitments in Afghanistan had come to an end. The operation was launched in Kashmir by the end of that year.

Pakistan also tested a nuclear bomb in May 1998, within weeks of India doing so. This development of nuclear capability was to act as a deterrence against the superior conventional capability of India. From that point on, proxy war was carried out under the shadow of a nuclear threat. The strategy worked quite successfully for Pakistan.

What probably prompted General Zia-ul-Haq's plan to move even more aggressively against India was the loss of Siachen glacier in 1984 and the establishment of a new LOC in un-delineated areas in the glacier (now called the Actual Ground Position Line, or AGPL). Siachen glacier lies among a group of glaciers in the Karakoram Range to the north-east of the famous Pt NJ 9842. No formal delineation of a boundary has ever been carried out in this area. The 'ceasefire line' (CFL) drawn in the Karachi Agreement in 1949 and the 'Line of Control' (LOC) adopted after the 1972 Simla Agreement did not physically mark the LOC beyond Pt NJ 9842. The maps, as required under the Simla Agreement marking LOC, were initialled by Lieutenant General P.S. Bhagat (India) and Lieutenant General Abdul Hamid Khan (Pakistan) and exchanged in December 1972 in a formal ceremony at Suchetgarh. These maps, comprising seventeen mosaics, were later put up to the respective governments for ratification. However, when it came to describing the northern-most extremity of the LOC, the wording was left vague and the LOC was stated to be running to NJ 9842 and 'thence northwards to the glaciers'. To any military observer it is obvious that the boundary between two countries (LOC in this case) must follow natural geographical features, such as crestlines or watersheds. The natural delineation here would be the Saltoro Ridge, running NNW from the glacier snout to Indra Col, the Saser Kangri and the Sia Kangri peaks, crowning the Siachen Glacier. Therefore, India claims that this line should lie along Saltoro range. Thus much of the glacier falls on the Indian side of the LOC. Pakistan, on the other hand, claims that the LOC should run from Pt NJ 9842 to Karakoram Pass, at the Line of Actual Control between India and China. Till the early 1980s all expeditions to the glaciers were launched from the Pakistani side. The US Defense Mapping Agency added to the confusion when it published maps that showed a straight line from Pt NJ 9842 joining at the Karakoram Pass. The US has since removed this line from all its maps. The differing interpretations of the alignment of the LOC in this area has led to continued dispute. When Indian intelligence agencies gathered information that Pakistan, taking advantage of ambiguity in LOC delineation, was getting ready to occupy the area, the Indian Army pre-empted this by moving troops to the glacier in a brilliant operation (Operation Meghdoot) and occupied it on 13 April 1984. The new LOC was thus formed and termed AGPL. This loss of huge territory that Pakistan illegitimately claimed belonged to it caused great embarrassment to it, which it has kept hidden from its people.

Besides this incident, the situation along the LOC had remained largely peaceful in the 1970s and 1980s with only the occasional restrained exchange of fire. The Actual Ground Position Line, however, remained active right from the time of its inception, making it a virtual warzone. From 1990, the situation along the LOC too started to deteriorate due to the launch of a proxy war by Pakistan. As the years passed, the situation went from bad to worse and heavier calibre weapons began to be regularly employed.

The capture of Kashmir has always been an obsession with Pakistan and is deeply embedded in its national psyche. To gain political mileage, successive regimes in Pakistan have exploited the issue of Kashmir to whip up anti-Indian sentiments among Pakistani citizens as well as the people of Jammu and Kashmir. It also took the opportunity to internationalise the Kashmir issue at various international forums and in the United Nations (UN). By 1997, Pakistan's proxy war had expanded to an area known as 'South of Pir Panjal Range' (SPPR), which extends from Doda–Bhaderwah to Rajouri–Poonch–Kathua and Samba sectors.

By early 1999, the success of operations by the Indian security forces and the flourishing of the democratisation process in Jammu and Kashmir became a cause of great worry to the ISI and General Headquarters (GHQ) of the Pakistan Army. The planning of their

Kargil operation was likely influenced by the urgent need to draw away the bulk of the Indian Army from security and counterinsurgency operations in the Valley and thereby reduce pressure on the militants. This was necessary for them to reinvigorate the militancy and regain the initiative in the region.

As a result, after India had consolidated its gains in the Valley and quietened the insurgency, Pakistan suddenly began shelling across the LOC in an unprecedented manner. Its firing was aimed particularly at the Tithwal and Kargil sectors. There were signs of ammunition being dumped and new and improved defence posts being constructed, pointing to an increase in infiltration into the Valley.

There were also new launch pads opened for inducting militants across Zoji La in the Dras sector and reports of road-improvement work and the establishment of militant camps. However, despite all these indications, the Indian intelligence agencies – and to some extent our holding formations – failed to carry out a proper assessment of Pakistan's intentions.

Terrain, Geographical Location and Layout

Before moving further in the narrative, it is important to understand the location and terrain of the battlefield. The area of operations falls in the Ladakh region of the erstwhile state of Jammu and Kashmir. Ladakh comprises the twin districts of Leh and Kargil and stretches northeast beyond Kashmir Valley to the Karakoram Range, which forms its eastern boundary with China. It is a vast arid expanse dominated by four major mountain ranges. The Great Himalayan Range marks its southern periphery; while the Zanskar (or Zaskar) and Ladakh ranges, separated by the Indus River-cut across its centre. In the north and east, bordering China and Afghanistan, the Karakoram Range demarcates the northern extremity of both the region and the country.

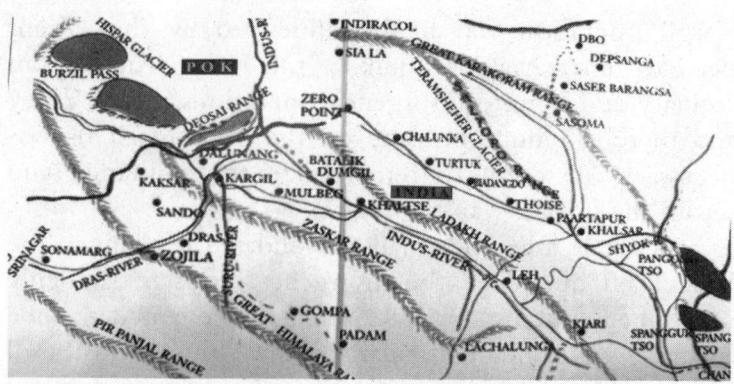

Map 1.1 Schematic layout of mountain ranges in Ladakh

Reproduced by permission from Lieutenant General Mohinder Puri, *Kargil: Turning the Tide* (Lancer Publishers, 2016)

The national highway NH-1D is one of the two road axes to Ladakh. Considered the lifeline of Ladakh, the highway starts from Srinagar and passes through Sonamarg before crossing Zoji La. From there it descends to the Gumri plains, traversing through Matayen, Dras, Kargil, Bodhkharbu and Khalsi before reaching Leh – covering a distance of approximately 430 kilometres. NH-1D remains closed between the end of November till the first week of May because of heavy snow between Sonamarg and Matayen.

The second axis to Ladakh originates at Manali, goes over Rohtang and Baralacha La passes and connects Leh, bypassing the Kashmir Valley and Kargil. This road stretches over a distance of approximately 425 kilometres. At the time of the Kargil operation, it used to be closed from November till May. Thus, the window for moving rations, military supplies and ammunition was only from May to November as both the axes remained closed during winter months. However, after the opening of a new tunnel over Rohtang Pass, this road now remains open throughout the year. This tunnel – named the 'Atal Tunnel' – is 9.02 kilometres long and gives great strategic advantage to India.

Kargil was carved out as a separate district along with Leh from the erstwhile Ladakh district on 10 April 1979. Situated on the banks of the Suru River facing the northern areas across the LOC at an altitude of 2575 metres, Kargil town is 60 kilometres from Dras and 205 kilometres from Srinagar. It is the second biggest town in Ladakh after Leh and has a population that is 90 per cent Shia of mixed Dard and Tibetan descent. The town is a prominent communication hub.

While NH-1D goes towards Leh, another metalled road starts at Kargil and runs north across the Hamboting La to Batalik. There, the road turns southeast along the Indus to Khalsi. The river flows in the opposite direction through numerous gorges before entering Pakistan-occupied Kashmir (PoK) at Marol near Batalik.

The main highway from Kargil towards Leh passes through the scenic villages of Mulbekh, Bodhkharbu and Lamayuru, which has a gompa with a uniquely beautiful statue of the Buddha made out of frozen butter. The road continues to descend through a series of hairpin bends – nicknamed the 'Jalebi Mor' – towards Khalsi and Nimu and then continues onward to Leh.

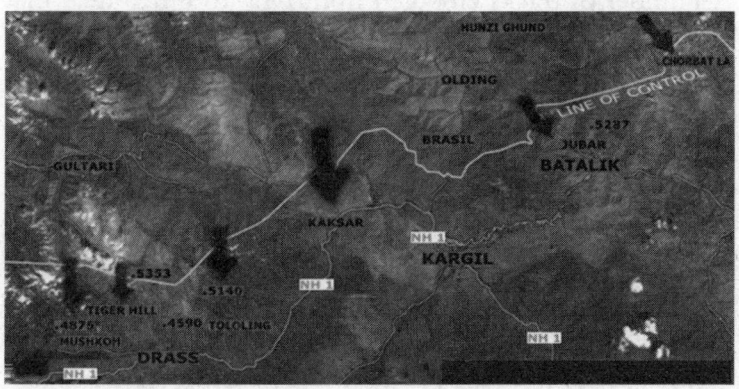

Map 1.2 Kargil: Area of Operation
Courtesy of World'sfact.com

Military Importance of Kargil and Dras Sectors

The military significance of Kargil for the enemy can be understood from three factors: first, it has the second-largest township in Ladakh with a predominantly Shia population; second, it is an important communication hub close to the LOC that also serves a dominating spot for observation and artillery fire; and third, the only road linking Srinagar to Leh passes through it. This area – approximately 229 kilometres long and overlooking the Srinagar–Leh road at altitudes of 4,800–5,500 metres is vulnerable to infiltration. For the purpose of operational narration, I will divide the area into subsectors.

Dras Subsector: Dras village is another important communication hub in the Kargil sector with a population comprising largely of Sunni Muslims. It is reputed to be the second-coldest inhabited place in the world outside the polar regions with icy winds and a recorded low of minus 60 degree Celsius.

In 1999, a fair-weather track ran westwards from Dras into Mushkoh Valley for approximately 10 to 12 kilometres, after which a mule track extended further west to Bakharwal. Another important motorable track ran from Dras to Sando. A number of tracks emerged from Dras to other areas that were scenes of action during the Kargil operation. Stretches of NH-1D around Dras, Kaksar and Harka Bahadur bridge – which is also the point closest to the LOC – remains susceptible to artillery fire from Pakistani posts.

The LOC in the Dras sector extends along the main ridgeline from Kaobal Gali in the west till Bhimbat in the east. The LOC runs along the watershed of this ridgeline, a total frontage of approximately 70 kilometres. In this area, there is no direct observation of the road from any of the Pakistani posts, except from an observation post at Pt 5353.

Mushkoh Valley: The Mushkoh Ridge is a smaller ridgeline that runs from Kaobal Gali towards Zoji La. This ridge runs parallel and south to the main Himalayan ridgeline. Mushkoh Valley lies between these two ridgelines. The entire Dras sector including Mushkoh is dominated by a series of heights along Marpola Ridge.

Dras Subsector: Other important heights in this area are Pt 5100 and Pt 4700, both of which dominate the highway and Dras town. Another feature is the Tololing ridgeline, which gained national fame during the Kargil war. Two formidable heights that provide excellent observation of NH-1D and the Bhimbat Valley to the east are Pt 5140, approximately 3 kilometres from the LOC, and Pt 4590, about 4 kilometres from the national highway. Marpola and Bhimbat are the two important passes on these ridgelines that provide avenues for offensive operations for either side. Hence, in spite of heavy snow, the bulk of the deployment on both sides is along these passes.

Tiger Hill is by far the most dominating height of the region. It towers above its surrounding peaks and dominates the entire Dras Valley and other adjoining areas. From Tiger Hill a spur runs southwest towards Pt 4875, which is another important military objective. Located 5 kilometres from the national highway, the height has complete visual domination over Matayen, Mushkoh and Dras Valley. Because of its location and domination, it assumes even greater tactical importance than Tiger Hill. Besides these, there are several other features that were also of tactical relevance during the Kargil operations.

Batalik Subsector: Here, the LOC cuts across the Indus between Batalik and Marol, which is to the west of Batalik and north of Kargil. The LOC then runs along the Shangruti and Chorbat La watershed on the Ladakh Range at heights that are well above 4,800 metres, before dipping towards Subsector Haneef (SSH) south of the Shyok river. There are four ridgelines that jut southwards along the Chorbat La watershed – Jubar, Kukarthang, Pt 5203 and Khalubar. These vary in heights from 4,500 to 4,800 metres.

SSH was the site of some of the toughest holding and eviction battles, as the terrain was almost unassailable and at very high altitudes.

Political Scene in Pakistan at the Time

Nawaz Sharif came to power in Pakistan for the second time in 1997. Despite his conflicts with his nation's president, judiciary and military, he was able to consolidate his power. Nawaz Sharif had fallen out with the COAS, General Jahangir Karamat, who had advocated the formation of a National Security Council which, with the representation therein of the three Chiefs of Staff and the Chairman Chiefs of Staff, would have given the Pakistan armed forces an institutionalised say in the country's governance on all security-related matters. Nawaz Sharif's dictatorial functioning finally culminated in the resignation of General Karamat.

The next chief was General Pervez Musharraf, a former commando. Sharif also made efforts to arrive at a peace agreement with India. Indian prime minister Atal Bihari Vajpayee reciprocated, travelling to Lahore by bus on 20 February 1999 with a big entourage comprising some famous personalities. This Indian initiative to bring about peace resulted in the 'Lahore Declaration' with the aim of building confidence in the nuclear and conventional fields and avoiding conflict. The pact also required both sides to resolve outstanding issues – including Jammu and Kashmir – through a composite and integrated dialogue. In hindsight, it is now apparent that the Lahore Declaration process was a facade behind which were already unfolding the Pakistani machinations that would lead to the Kargil misadventure.

The MO directorate examined the ground situation a number of times and came to the conclusion that infiltration through the LOC continued in full swing. The proxy war in Jammu and Kashmir showed no signs of letting up and the firing along the LOC had increased appreciably. Hence, the directorate was convinced that Pakistan's intents remained unchanged and it could not be trusted. General Malik stated in April 1999 that '[the] recent Lahore Declaration has not in any way changed the ground situation in Kashmir. If anything, the Pakistan Army and ISI are still active in aiding

The Kargil War

and abetting terrorism in the state'.[3] While the Lahore Declaration has been welcomed in India, Pakistan and all over the world, Pakistan has yet to translate the spirit of this into ground realities. This assessment was presented to the Government of India by the Army HQ that same month.

Little did we know that while these peace parleys were going on in Lahore, the Pakistan Army had already started moving into the Kargil sector to occupy the posts vacated for the winter by the Indian Army. It was a great fraud by Pakistan. The treachery was compounded by an insult when Musharraf appeared without his cap and did not salute the Indian prime minister at the official reception in Lahore.

Perfidy by Pakistan

Ever since the Kargil war, there has been lots of debate about who it was that conceived the war. Was Nawaz Sharif in the know and did the operation have his approval? Or was Musharraf alone responsible? In the revised edition of her book *Daughter of the East*, Benazir Bhutto talks of a presentation given to her by General Musharraf – who was then the Pakistani DMO – outlining his plans for capturing Srinagar. She asked him that should his plan be successful, what they would do after that. Musharraf is said to have responded, 'We will go to the United Nations and tell them that Srinagar is in our control ... and ask them to change the map of the world.'

Bhutto writes, 'If we did this, the Security Council will pass a resolution condemning Pakistan and demand Pakistan to unilaterally withdraw from Srinagar and we will have got nothing for our efforts, but humiliation and isolation.' She abruptly ended the meeting with Musharraf and left feeling very discouraged.[4] But Pakistan had a plan for the Kargil area since General Zia-ul-Haq's time. When Musharraf became the chief, he wanted to put it into effect. He was determined to settle the score for losing Siachen.

Najam Sethi is a renowned Pakistani journalist. In an interview titled 'Kargil War' that was aired on 23

November 2013, Sethi unravels the background of this operation in great detail.⁵ According to him, Musharraf organised a number of presentations for Nawaz Sharif but in a manner that kept the prime minister confused. In the final briefing on 16 May 1999, then Pakistani DMO Major General Tauqir Zia gave a briefing on a map on which the LOC was not even marked.

The DMO mainly talked of the gains that the Mujahideen had made and how they had destroyed the Indian ammunition dumps. No mention was made of the presence of Pakistani troops in Indian territory. He simply stated that they had some army support posts in the rear. Sharif was placated and told that it would be a great victory and he would go down in history as the liberator of Kashmir. This no doubt pleased the Pakistani prime minister.

However, Sharif was soon alerted by his foreign minister, Sartaj Aziz, and the minister for Kashmir affairs, Lieutenant General Abdul Mazeed Malik, that Pakistani troops had entered Indian territory. The prime minister realised that their own army had not apprised him of the full picture. This left Sharif quite worried. He asked for another meeting with the army, but by then the two countries were already at war.

On 24 May, Prime Minister Vajpayee called Sharif and questioned the presence of Pakistani Mujahideen and the Pakistan Army in the Kargil sector. He also told his Pakistani counterpart that India would take strong action to evict Pakistan army from its territory.⁶ As the DGMO, I called Major General Tauqir Zia, my counterpart across the border, and told him that we were aware of their full activities and we would initiate all actions under our command to throw them out.

We used to have weekly discussions every Tuesday. When I asked him why he did not attend the previous week's meeting, he hesitantly replied, '*Bachhe aa gaye the, unki tafrih mein lag gaye* (Our children had come, and we got busy looking after them).' I told him with a laugh, '*Apke bachhe to hamare pass aaye hue hein, aur aap yakin rakhiye ki ham unki achhi khatir tawajjo karenge* (Your children have now come to us, and you can be rest assured that we will take very good care of them).' He was left speechless.

Around the same time, world powers like the US, Russia, China, UK and others had also started calling the Pakistani prime minister about his country's intrusion into Indian territory. The Pakistanis were under diplomatic pressure and murmurs had already started in the Pakistan military about the operations going on in the Kargil sector. Perhaps it was the incredulousness of the whole affair that led Pakistani Air Commodore Abid Rao to famously quip, 'After this operation, it is going to be either a court martial or martial law in our country.'[7]

Lieutenant General Shahid Aziz was heading ISI's analysis wing during the conflict. Writing about it in a newspaper article more than a decade later, he said, 'the Kargil war with India was an unsound military plan based on invalid assumptions, launched with little preparation and in total disregard of the regional and international environment'.[8] In her book *From Kargil to Coup: Events That Shook Pakistan*, Pakistani national security expert Nasim Zehra writes that Pakistan's Kargil ploy was a blunder. She writes that one of the four planners of the Kargil infiltration lost his nerve and implored others to forgive him. 'I have made a big mistake,' he is quoted as saying. 'Now is the time for prayers!' Writing about the conflict for an Indian newspaper, she said it subverted the ongoing Pakistan–India dialogue.

On 26 and 29 May, Indian intelligence agencies managed to tape a conversation between the Pakistani chief of the general staff, Lieutenant General Mohammed Aziz, and Musharraf who was at that time in a hotel during a state visit to China. The conversation clearly revealed that Pakistan had deployed troops of their Northern Light Infantry (NLI) to dress like Mujahideen. In the conversation, Musharraf was most keen to know the reactions of the Indian DGMO and also of Nawaz Sharif.

Musharraf asked if the Indian DGMO threatened them. Aziz responded that the Indian DGMO was of the opinion that the infiltrators have Pakistan's help and artillery support, without which they could not have come to Jammu and Kashmir. 'This is not a very friendly act and is against the spirit of Lahore Declaration,' the Indian DGMO is quoted as saying. 'We will flush them out and we will not let them stay there.' Then Musharraf asked about Sharif. Aziz replied that both the prime minister and the foreign minister had said that any further escalation should be prevented as there may be a danger of war. Then Aziz self-incriminated himself and his country by saying that he told Sharif that 'there was no such fear as the *tooti* (scruff) of the militants' necks was in their hands' and could be regulated by the Pakistan Army.

The Indian foreign minister released the tapes of this conversation on 11 June – the eve of a visit by the Pakistani foreign minister.[9] The news created a storm and Pakistan's secret games stood exposed. Now the entire world had the real and complete picture of the developments in Kargil.

Operation Topac had been conceived during Zia-ul-Haq's time, when Musharraf was the Pakistani DMO. It continued as Operation Badr, launched in Kargil during Musharraf's time as the chief. Some Pakistani historians call the operation 'Koh-i-Paima'. Operation Badr had the aims of internationalising the Kashmir issue and changing the alignment of the LOC. Pakistan thought that a major reaction from their neighbour was unlikely as India was considered politically weak and unstable at the time with a caretaker government in Delhi.

As always, Pakistan was good at planning tactical operations but terrible with strategy as it did not realistically consider India's response. It has always underestimated Indian capabilities and determination. Pakistan thought that the Indian Army was tired of nine years of militancy in Jammu and Kashmir and that India would not have the stomach and political will to undertake a full-fledged operation against any threat from across the border. Pakistan assumed that this would enable it to negotiate from a position of strength. However, it was woefully wrong.

Pakistan was also counting on its nuclear capability acting as a deterrent to a strong Indian reaction. However, it is not militarily possible to have a nuclear weapon ready for deployment within one year of a test. Unfortunately, this is where India gave Pakistan too much credit and reacted with more restraint than necessary. No operation was allowed to be carried out across the LOC. Otherwise, the government gave the forces full latitude to respond strongly on our own side of the LOC in the Kargil sector. Despite all this restraint on the Indian side, Pakistan was still found wanting and was made to pay heavily for its strategic blunder.

The key element of the Pakistani operation was maintaining total surprise, which it managed to do. The operation was kept confined to a group of four generals. This secrecy was so well maintained that not even its DMO had any clue about it till 16 January 1999, when the plans were presented in the GHQ for the first time. By then, it was already in an advanced stage of operation and a few Pakistani elements had already intruded across the LOC. The chiefs of the air force and the navy were not taken into confidence because they would have no role to play.

Pakistan's main strategy was to have its forces occupy the posts vacated for winter by the Indian soldiers. From there, the Pakistanis would be in a position to interfere with NH-1D and cut Ladakh off from Kashmir. The terrain was tough and the Mujahideen were not trained for such operations. Therefore, the Pakistanis decided to use the NLI troops based in that area. The Pakistan Army had assessed that India would have no choice but to move troops from the Valley to counter this threat and that would leave the Valley open for Pakistani terrorists to regain the initiative there. They did not think any troops would be moved from the Indian hinterland because of Pakistan's nuclear deterrence.

Thus, Pakistan started the operation in January 1999 and occupied a number of vacated posts. However, it had made several miscalculations. Pakistan had counted on the international community to side with it, thinking that this action could be blamed on the Kashmir issue. However, the world sided with India because of its vigorous diplomacy that proved that Pakistan was the aggressor. Pakistan had also expected the Kashmiris to rise in revolt, which did not happen at all. Lastly, the Pakistan Army had hoped that their prime minister would support them, but because of the heavy pressure from the international community, Sharif panicked.

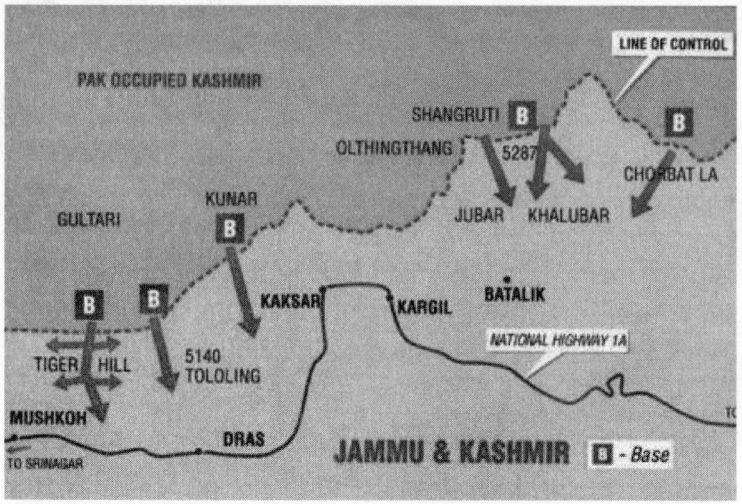

Map 1.3 Pakistan's intrusions plans in Kargil sector

Reproduced by permission from D.P. Ramachandran, 'Kargil: India's First Televised War', *Indian Defence Review* (17 July 2021)

During the operation, Pakistan was further hindered as it was unable to use its air force because it had told the world that no Pakistani soldiers were present in Kargil and it also could not induct more troops as Indian soldiers had not crossed the LOC.

India Swings into Action

In the first week of May 1999, I went on a familiarisation visit to the Kargil and Ladakh sectors. At Kargil, I was briefed by Brigadier Surinder Singh, who was commanding 121st (Independent) Infantry Brigade. Also present was Major General V.S. Budhwar, who was the general officer commanding (GOC) of 3rd Infantry Division. During the briefing, I was told about Pakistani small arms fire on NH-1D. I asked how Pakistani fire could reach the highway when it was well outside the range of their small arms when firing from the LOC. The brigade commander also mentioned that they were constructing a wall along the highway at places to prevent any interference by Pakistani fire on our convoys. Hearing this, I asked him if there was any possibility of Pakistani infiltration into our area. He replied confidently that they were very alert along the LOC. I was not convinced and was concerned about this development.

Next, I went to Batalik, where I was briefed by the commanding officer of 3 Punjab. He did not mention any infiltration attempts by Pakistan. Before leaving Kargil, I advised Budhwar to move his tactical headquarters to Kargil and personally monitor the ground situation because my professional instinct warned me that all was not well there. On my return to Delhi, I gave a detailed briefing to the chief and others.

On 3 May, a grazier named Tashi Namgyal of Gorkhum village reported some unidentified persons in Banjin in the Yaldor area of the Batalik subsector. The following day, a patrol attempted to reach the location but was unsuccessful due to heavy snow. On 5 May, a patrol under Lieutenant Siddharth Survey was sent to the same area. However, it was ambushed, resulting in four casualties. Then, on 7 May, a patrol under Major Desai of 3 Punjab reported the presence of people in black clothes. They also saw some *sangar* (temporary stone fortification) and antennae at Kukarthang and Pt 4821. XV Corps informed the MO directorate about these developments and casualties for the first time over the telephone on 8 May.

Notwithstanding these developments, XV Corps and the Northern Command assessed that it was only an infiltration and would be cleared in a few days. Based on this assessment, the COAS left on an official visit to Poland and Czech Republic on 10 May. However, we were not sure of the kind and degree of infiltration and wondered if it could be an intrusion. Certain precautionary moves were ordered by the MO directorate in consultation with XV Corps and the Northern Command.

1/11 Gorkha Rifles (GR) and 12 Jammu and Kashmir Light Infantry (JAKLI) while in transit after their tenure in Siachen were ordered to move to Yaldor (between Batalik and Chorbat La) with instructions to stabilise the situation and stop further infiltration. HQ 70th Infantry Brigade (which had moved from the Valley to Dras before closure of Zoji La) was ordered to assume operational responsibility of the Batalik subsector on 8 May, and 1 Naga of 56th Mountain Brigade and 8 Sikh of 28th Infantry Division (from the Valley) and 28 Rashtriya Rifles (RR) were ordered to move to the Dras subsector. Both battalions were in location by 14 May. Meanwhile, tactical headquarters of 3rd Infantry Division arrived in Kargil on 10 May and one battery from 4th Field Regiment of 3rd Artillery Brigade was moved from Nimu to Batalik on the same day. 10 Para less a team, a company of 5 Para from Southern Glacier and additional artillery from 315 Field Regiment of V Corps Artillery Brigade were inducted into Kargil on 12 May. On the same day, 56th Mountain Brigade (from the Valley) was told to move to Dras with 18 Grenadiers and 1 Bihar and take over operational command of Dras and Mushkoh by 22 May. Finally, 14 Jammu and Kashmir Rifles (JAKRIF) of 79th Mountain Brigade were inducted into the Dras sector from the Valley on 19 May.

Thus between 8 and 10 May, the equivalent of almost a division of troops was ordered to move into the Kargil sector from within the existing resources in the Valley and 3rd Infantry Division. Until then, 121st Infantry Brigade was holding the entire Kargil area with four battalions. As a result of readjustments and relocation, there were now a lot more troops in this area. This timely initiative paid off handsomely later.

Meanwhile, there were numerous reports of patrol clashes and an ammunition point of 121st Infantry Brigade was blown up. On 12 May, the Military Intelligence (MI) directorate demanded aerial photographs of the region during a Chiefs of Staff Committee (COSC) meeting. The following day, the defence minister visited the area with the army commander of the Northern Command and the

GOC of XV Corps. However, the assessment still remained that these were infiltration operations by Pakistan.

Between 15 and 20 May, 1/11 GR battalion was ordered to capture Pt 4812 in Jubar (Batalik) but they failed. On 22 May, a further attempt to capture Jubar by 1 Bihar also failed. Subsequent attempts to capture Pt 4268 in Batalik on 27 and 28 May also met the same fate. 1 Naga, which was to clear Pt 5140 in Dras, also suffered heavy casualties with no success. Similarly, 8 Sikh was tasked to capture Tiger Hill in Dras but took heavy casualties and stalled and did not progress as anticipated due to heavy resistance from enemy.

On 17 May, we received four sets of aerial photographs. Details of enemy locations in Mushkoh were revealed, including the existence of four helipads, tents and weapon emplacements. This went a long way to clear the gap in our information. We knew from years of fighting insurgency that no infiltration party ever pitches tents or makes helipads for their operations. These were operations by none other than the Pakistan Army.

We in the MO directorate were convinced that all this was a part of a bigger game and thus were not prepared to take any chances. That very day, we ordered a brigade from 6th Mountain Division (Army Headquarters reserve at Bareilly) to move to Kargil within two days, with the rest of the division to follow by 25 May. We were now preparing for a full-fledged war. However, the following day, during a Cabinet Committee on Security (CCS) meeting chaired by the prime minister, it was decided that the LOC will not be crossed as part of a national policy of restraint.

This decision had a direct bearing on the strategy at both the national and military levels. The chief of the air staff declined a request for attack helicopters to be deployed as he was afraid of escalation. He said that once the aircraft were in the air, it would be difficult for them to remain strictly behind the LOC, therefore the restriction of not crossing the LOC should be lifted before they were deployed. I think that somewhere at the back of their minds the government was worried that Pakistan would use its nuclear weapons.

On 20 May, the COAS returned from his foreign tour. By then the enemy presence had also been detected at Pt 5608, Bajrang Top and Spur Junction in Kaksar (Batalik subsector). It had become clear that the entire area from Dras to Batalik had been subject to Pakistani intrusion.

There used to be a daily discussion between the COAS, VCOAS and DGMO in the latter's office, on the ground situation of the day, during which our actions for the following days were also planned. In one such meeting, the discussion raised the following four suggestions that were to make a great impact later:

- We should immediately stop all the ad hoc attack operations as the troops that had been engaged in tackling the insurgency until then had lost touch with the tactics of conventional operations. We were wastefully accumulating casualties at the rate of about ten per day. As counterinsurgency operations and conventional warfare are entirely different, we should pause to train our troops in conventional attacks and only then recommence our operations.
- When 6th Mountain Division was fully inducted, we had to take a call on which division was to be employed in Kargil. It seemed to be a neater arrangement to put 6th Mountain Division in Kargil. However, I strongly recommended that 8th Mountain Division, which was deployed in the Valley, should move to Kargil because it had greater knowledge of the situation there and its troops were battle-hardened. The division's GOC, Major General Mohinder Puri, was a seasoned soldier knowledgeable about the area.
- In such difficult operations at a high altitude, casualties would be heavy. The attacks should be planned well for a final outcome of success, but we should be prepared to accept that the casualties inevitably and painfully would be high in such a terrain.
- We should induct maximum Bofors regiments from other commands to Kargil sector because they had a stronger impact during operations in the mountains.

The chief agreed to all these points except for the nomination of the division, which he wanted to decide after discussion with the corps commander, Lieutenant General Krishan Pal. On 26 May, he agreed to deploy 8th Mountain Division for operations in the Kargil sector.

Strategic Planning

The chief then visited Udhampur and Srinagar to get a full operational briefing and discuss plans with the commanders. It was confirmed by then that the intrusion extended from the Mushkoh subsector to the southern part of the Siachen Glacier. Our response at ground level was not of operational standard as dealing with the insurgency had led to a loss of the sharpness required for conventional operations. We were also short of the logistic support and artillery required to handle such difficult operations.

The aspect of exercising maximum restraint and not crossing the LOC posed multifarious problems. The terrain was difficult and we had to recapture our posts using frontal assaults at altitudes between 4,500 and 5,500 metres. We needed to open up other fronts, for which the preparation had to commence right away. It was agreed that in an emergency, the Indian Air Force (IAF) must be immediately allowed to operate, as it would convey a message of national resolve to the enemy. Until then, the air force had not been employed in offensive role due to the policy of restraint. The air chief had declared that attack helicopters could not fly at that altitude and the use of air power would lead to escalation of the conflict.

The decision to employ air power was approved in the CCS meeting on 24 May and the IAF commenced its strikes two days later. However, the request to lift the restriction on crossing the LOC received no immediate response from the prime minister. Later, the national security advisor (NSA), Brajesh Mishra, was quoted by a television channel saying that 'not crossing the border and the LOC holds good today, but we do not know what may happen tomorrow'.[10]

Preparations and planning for contingencies also began, in case there was need to escalate and activate the areas under the Western and the Southern commands. The army began a gradual build-up of their strategic reserves. About 500 special military trains rolled towards the western borders and dual-task formations from the east were moved to their assigned operational areas. Thousands of tonnes of ammunition was also moved from the depots.

6th Mountain Division was not employed in the Valley for counterinsurgency operations but retained as a threat in being for conventional warfare. Director general of the RR was moved from the Army HQ to Srinagar to take control of the counterinsurgency operations. All the RR battalions and other troops left in the Valley were placed under his command. They performed the task with commendable success. The GOC of XV Corps was relieved of counterinsurgency responsibilities and tasked with concentrating fully on the Kargil operation. The army also tightened up the rear area security to ensure smooth and safe induction of troops and ammunition. Overall, 8th Mountain Division was to take responsibility of Dras and Mushkoh sectors and 3rd Infantry Division was to handle operations in Batalik sector.

Enemy: As the operations progressed, we formed an accurate picture of Pakistani designs and force levels. In the Dras and Mushkoh sectors, five NLI battalions had been employed for the intrusion and a Frontier Force (FF) battalion was inducted as a replacement for the heavy casualties suffered by the NLI units. In Batalik sector, NLI troops had been deployed in the initial stages and were then reinforced by an additional battalion or two from outside the sector. In order to give the impression that the intrusion was by militants, these battalions were augmented and grouped with militants from various terrorist groups. Major General Puri was of the opinion that these jihadi militants were probably being used as porters.

The enemy was assessed to have amassed an additional ten or eleven fire units for their operations in addition to the twenty-two fire units already present. They also had air-defence

The Kargil War

artillery augmented by shoulder-fired missiles. In addition, they used helicopters for reconnaissance, reinforcements and replenishments. Scout subunits and support from the Special Service Group (SSG) were also made available to them. Overall, this was a sizeable force that confronted us.

Progress of War: This chapter is mainly a recapitulation of the major politico-military decision-making process during the Kargil war and the finer details thereof. Equally, it is the story of the unparalleled bravery of our men, young officers and commanding officers, and the quality of higher leadership. However, a brief outline of the major operations and their progress is essential to understand the overall context.

Until 6 June, there was a steady build-up of forces, artillery and ammunition on our side. Importantly, the time was also used for training the troops in conventional operations. We decided to concentrate on clearing the enemy from the Dras, Batalik, Mushkoh, Chorbat La and Kaksar areas in that order of priority. The enemy intrusion in the Dras area was of immediate concern as it was closest to NH-1D, which the enemy was effectively interdicting.

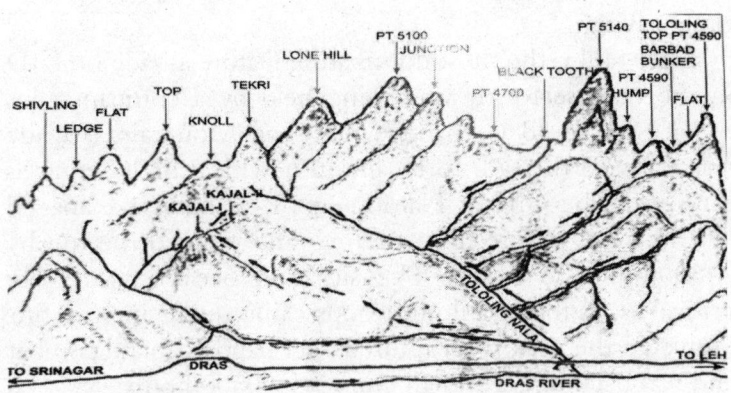

Map 1.4 Panoramic view of Dras sector

Reproduced by permission from Lieutenant General Mohinder Puri, *Kargil: Turning the Tide* (Lancer Publishers, 2016)

Dras Subsector: Tololing is located at a distance of approximately 5 kilometres as the crow flies from Dras. It was the deepest penetration made by Pakistan in the Dras sector. From there, they could dominate the Srinagar–Leh road both by observation and fire. Our initial attempts had failed, but a fresh operation with acclimatised troops and a massive concentration of artillery was launched on 12 June. An innovative 'direct firing role' was tried with eighteen Bofors guns and it proved to be a masterstroke. The Tololing complex was captured by 56th Mountain Brigade with 2 Rajasthan Rifles and 18 Grenadiers by 17 June.

The next objective was recapturing Pt 5140, which was an equally tough task. 1 Naga and two companies of 13 Jak Rif launched a multidirectional attack. The mission was accomplished on 20 June, but not before a bitter fight. Both these operations were indeed very difficult. These were also our first significant victories in the conflict and gave us confidence for subsequent missions.

I called the Pakistani DMO and told him that from the bodies of the Pakistani soldiers we had recovered identity cards and several maps with the LOC marked on them. When he refused to accept this, I faxed him the proof of our findings. He must have been very embarrassed, having been caught lying.

Tiger Hill is the most dominating feature astride NH-1D in the Dras sector. It was being held by a company plus of 12 NLI, so 18 Grenadiers of 192nd Mountain Brigade was assigned the task to recapture it with 8 Sikh acting as a reserve. The Ghatak Platoon of 18 Grenadiers managed to climb the feature from the rear and reached the top by 0430 hours on 4 July. The situation became extremely critical as all the assaulting troops came under intense fire. However, the peak was captured after hand-to-hand combat and was back under Indian control by 0500 hours.

The enemy launched two fierce counterattacks, but both were beaten back with heavy casualties to both sides. 8 Sikh interposed a reserve subunit on the reverse slope. Mopping-up operations were launched by 18 Grenadiers on the night of 7 July, forcing the enemy to flee from the area. The engineers subsequently removed several anti-personnel mines.

The capture of Tiger Hill was the most crucial of all the Kargil operations and delivered a severe psychological blow to the enemy. This defeat broke the back of the Pakistani resistance. In India, a wave of jubilation and relief overtook the people, who thought that it was the greatest victory of the Kargil war. I remember that the managing director of the Maurya Hotel in Delhi, Major Rehman (an ex-army officer), sent a ten-kilogram cake to the MO directorate to celebrate this great victory.

Batalik Subsector: Before the commencement of the Tiger Hill operation, I had, in consultation with corps commander, ordered additional Bofors regiments to be moved to the Batalik sector. This provided a great advantage in the offensive.

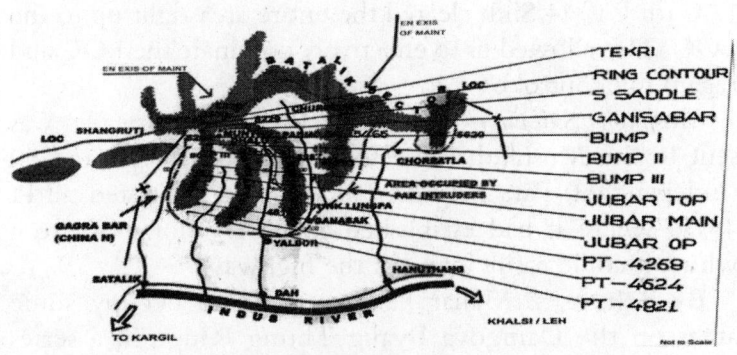

MAP 1.5 Batalik–Yaldor–Chorbat La

Reproduced by permission from Lieutenant General Mohinder Puri, *Kargil: Turning the Tide* (Lancer Publishers, 2016)

On the night of 7 June, two columns each of 5 Para and 12 JAKLI approached Pt 5203 from the south along four different paths. By first light, one column of 12 JAKLI succeeded in occupying the height. No further move could take place due to enemy's effective domination from neighbouring features. The fighting ensued over next few days until the main attack took place on 20 June. The entire feature was secured by 0700 hours on 21 June.

The hub of enemy defences in the Batalik subsector were at Padma-Go Ridge (Pt 5000, Dog Hill and Pt 5229) and Kalubhar Ridge (Pt 4812, Kalubhar and Pt 5287). Capturing this complex was essential for clearing intruders from Jubar and Kukarthang. After overcoming some stiff resistance and bloody fights, Ladakh scouts, 1/11GR, 12 JAKLI and 22 Grenadiers cleared the ridges by 7 July. Jubar is a dominating feature on the ridgeline emanating from the main Kukarthang Ridge. On 29 June, 1 Bihar commenced an attack on Jubar. They captured it by 7 July. It further enabled development of operations to cut off the enemy from the rear. 17 Garhwal Rifles (17 Garh Rif) also attacked and captured the remaining features by 9 July. The enemy ammunition dump at Jubar was hit by our artillery and destroyed.

Between 22 and 25 July, troops from 5 Para, 1/11 GR, 17 Garh Rif, 14 Sikh cleared the entire area right up to the LOC. This allowed us to effectively dominate the LOC and regain full control over it.

Mushkoh Subsector: The 79th Mountain Brigade was sent to the Mushkoh subsector along with 17 Jat and 50 (Independent) Para Brigade. Pakistan had infiltrated till Pt 4875, where it had established an observation post from which it could easily interdict the highway.

By 8 June, 2 Mahar had managed to occupy some areas on the Daingoya Byang Thung Ridge in a series of attacks. The main offensive to evict the intrusion commenced on 1 July and was completed by 12 July. However, we later had to launch attacks to clear Zulu Spur as Pakistan did not fully withdraw from the area as per the terms of the ceasefire.

Kaksar Area: Earlier on 14 May, a patrol led by Lieutenant Saurabh Kalia and five other ranks (ORs) of 4 Jat had left for the Bajrang post on the Southwest Spur, which was vacated for the winters. After communication with the patrol was lost, another patrol under Lieutenant Bhardwaj, sent to the same post was ambushed resulting in three fatal casualties. This confirmed that the post was occupied by the enemy. Between 20 May and 5 June, we had to resort to containing the enemy intrusions in other sectors by readjusting troops and sending reinforcements. The badly mutilated bodies of Lieutenant Kalia and five members of his patrol were returned by Pakistan on 8 June. This showed the inhuman face of the Pakistan Army. We immediately reported it to the diplomatic corps in Delhi, who severely condemned Pakistan's actions.

Devastating Role of Artillery: Besides the gallant role played by the infantry to physically attack, capture and hold various features, the most devastating role was played by artillery. The Pakistani military still talks about the pounding given to them by the Bofors guns. We had ensured that the maximum possible artillery was concentrated in Kargil by moving them out of various other commands. The Bofors were most innovatively utilised by dismantling them and moving them up the hill slopes to deploy them in a direct firing role. This was among the best innovations of the Kargil operations. A total of fifty fire units plus one rocket battery was deployed for the operations by 3rd Infantry and 8th Mountain divisions. Each artillery regiment fired between 15,000 and 20,000 rounds during the Kargil war and this greatly demoralised the Pakistanis.

Tiger Hill pounded by artillery before assault

The Role of the IAF

The code name for the IAF operations in Kargil was 'Safed Sagar'. It projected the national resolve. After political clearance was given for the deployment of air power, the IAF's core objective was to support the army in evicting the infiltrators. It did this by 'softening' the intruders' concentration in a dispersed mountainous area spread over 150 kilometres from west to east. Softening operations involve bombs, rockets and specialised ammunition. The IAF was also tasked with targeting the intruders' replenishment lines, bombing their ammunition points and choking them logistically. One of the air force's spectacular achievements was blowing up the Pakistani ammunition point at Muntho Dhalo.

Initially the IAF placed two fighter squadrons on high alert for possible strike operations in the Dras, Kargil and Batalik sectors. Two waves of strikes were carried out on 27 May and one on 28 May using rockets and guns. On the first day, an MiG was lost due to engine trouble and another was shot down by an enemy surface-to-air missile (SAM). The next day, an Mi-17 helicopter was hit by a SAM while attacking Tololing. These early losses led to the IAF reassessing their plans and methodology for attack. In the subsequent air campaign, the air force flew nearly 550 strike missions without any further loss. This was achieved by pulling out helicopters from offensive operations and using them only for air logistics, casualty evacuation and reconnaissance. Another tactic was operating the hi-tech Mirage fighters at heights of 9,000 metres, well out of the range of enemy missiles. The fighter jets would fire their weapons from a safe distance of 4 to 8 kilometres.

From 6 June onward, the IAF attacked with laser-guided bombs, which achieved good results. Mirages also dropped 250 kilogram of bombs in the medium altitude level release profile with a high degree of accuracy. Night operations were launched from 26 June. The air force flew over 6,500 sorties of all types. This included 1,200 sorties by fighter jets, out of which 550 were attack sorties. It was a great performance by the IAF that demoralised the Pakistani troops.

Maritime Dimensions: The Indian Navy was also put on high alert during this time. In line with our overall military strategy, the navy carried out strategic manoeuvres in the western theatre. The navy was well poised to control the sea line of communications and put an effective blockade of oil and vital routes to Pakistan. From 21 May, they also started pre-emptive deployment to prevent strikes by Pakistani Navy units on vulnerable areas on the western coast. The Naval HQ also made a presentation on amphibious operations on the Makran Coast to the Army HQ. However, the war did not extend to the Indian Ocean.

Other Preparations

The Northern Command was determined to win back the Kargil heights. However, should that not have been possible, we were ready to operationalise the Western and the Southern commands and launch a full-scale war. Only that would force Pakistan to vacate the areas occupied by them in Kargil. We were receiving reports that they had started to move their independent armed brigades. We had to be fully prepared by July to commence our operations should the need arise. All the offensive operations were drawn up in great secrecy by the army commanders with the chief in the MO room. This interlude was also utilised to get the equipment in good working order.

China Factor during Kargil Operations

Since 1998 there had been an overall increase in Chinese activities. Therefore, the Chinese ingress in 'Trig Heights' in June 1999 amid the Kargil war to alter the status quo in Ladakh and a provocative deployment in the Yangtse area (Tawang sector in Western Kameng) a month later came as no surprise. The Chinese deployed a company strength opposite our own post of equal strength there. This was perhaps with a view to demonstrate its support to Pakistan. However, we were not excessively disturbed by this incursion, especially in the MO Directorate as I had commanded a brigade (and later a corps) in this sector and knew that we were strong in this area. We held our ground, leaving the Chinese with no option but to withdraw.

Even as recently as December 2022, Chinese troops tried to do salami slicing (land grab) in the Yangtse area but were beaten back by Indian troops. There is no doubt today that Pakistan and China are in a collusive relationship. It is almost certain that should there be an operation by one country, the other will definitely join in. We must remain prepared for this contingency.

Political Parleys

In the midst of war, Pakistan expressed a desire for their foreign minister to visit India. Even though India knew that no purpose would be served by such a visit, the proposal was accepted as a normal diplomatic courtesy. Sartaj Aziz arrived in Delhi on 12 June via China, where he must have gone to discuss the Kargil situation. He offered a three-point formula: a ceasefire; a joint working group to review the LOC and its demarcation on the ground; and finally a reciprocal visit by the Indian foreign minister the following week.

This was a charade and Pakistan's effort to hold on to their gains – which were substantial at that stage, as we had not recaptured any major objective by then. India's external affairs minister, Jaswant Singh, made it clear to Aziz that India would not negotiate until the Pakistani intrusion was completely cleared. He stressed that the 'aggression had to be undone militarily or diplomatically, whichever was done first'. This point was reiterated by Prime Minister Vajpayee later in a press conferences.[11]

Meanwhile, international pressure was building on India to cease operations and negotiate with Pakistan. Our NSA, Brajesh Mishra, met his US counterpart, Sandy

Berger, in Europe on 16 June, where Mishra told Berger that 'India could not stay restrained for long; it would escalate if Pakistan did not withdraw behind the line of control'.[12] Berger in turn told US president Bill Clinton that the war threatened disaster. India was considering the option of extending operations to the entire international border (IB) and other parts of the LOC sector at any time because we had not met with any success with our operations in any sector of Kargil. Later we were told by the government that Mishra's message had been taken very seriously by the US administration.

India Clears Pakistan Intrusion

By 7 July we had captured almost all of the objectives, the last of these being Tiger Hill and Pt 4875. There were bodies of Pakistani soldiers all over. When we asked Pakistan to collect their dead, they refused to acknowledge and accept them. We then buried them with proper honours commensurate to their religious beliefs. Our own Muslim priests performed the rituals in a dignified manner.

In 2004, when I was the chief, the noted film lyricist Javed Akhtar visited me with his son Farhan to discuss some research for a film they were making about the Kargil war. We showed them the videos of the burials with full military honours of Pakistani soldiers by our maulvis. Javed Akhtar was greatly moved and said, *'Ye hi to farq hai Hindustan aur Pakistan mein* (This is the difference between India and Pakistan).' This line was prominently used in their movie, which was titled *Lakshaya*.

We had also captured documents and other evidence to confirm the involvement of the Pakistan Army in this operation. These were shown to the media and the defence attaches of several countries. Pakistan was panicking because the end of the war was in sight and its defeat was imminent. Nawaz Sharif first rushed to China and then sought a meeting with Clinton on 4 July (American Independence Day). It was clear that Pakistan did not know how to save face.

It is not known why Sharif went to the US. Some Pakistani generals claimed in interviews on local TV that it was Musharraf who begged his prime minister to bail them out. Lieutenant General Ali Kuli Khan Khattak, one of Pakistan's well-known generals, dubbed the Kargil war as the 'worst debacle' in Pakistan's history and went on record saying that the conception and planning at the highest level had been so poor that the only word that could adequately describe it was 'unprofessional'.

However, Clinton rejected Pakistan's plea to intervene in the Kargil dispute and told Sharif in clear terms that Pakistan would have to leave Kargil unconditionally. According to those in the know, there was no doubt in Clinton's mind that the Pakistan Army was fully involved in the operations and were the aggressors.

On 8 July 1999, General Malik was informed by Vajpayee that Pakistan had sought a ceasefire and withdrawal of forces. The chief's immediate reaction was that India should not accept such a withdrawal and allow Pakistan to escape. If we didn't throw them out ourselves, they would claim victory, he said. Vajpayee asked the chief how much more time would be needed to clear the remaining intrusions, and to this General Malik responded by requesting permission to consult his colleagues in the COSC.

That night, we discussed our course of action during an urgent meeting. Would allowing a withdrawal give Pakistan an excuse to claim victory, and if not, what method of withdrawal should we demand from them? We also talked about what contingencies could arise during such a withdrawal, as there was serious concern that the Pakistanis could lay mines in the vacated areas and along withdrawal routes to cause casualties to our troops.

After detailed discussions we decided that we should prioritise the areas from where Pakistani forces were to withdraw. We knew that we should not trust Pakistani troops and commanders under any circumstances. It was estimated that another week would be needed to clear the intrusions. The chief then explained our course of action to the prime minister, who responded that we needed to make a proper withdrawal plan in writing that would be enforced on Pakistan.

By 10 July, the Batalik and Dras intrusions had been all but cleared. In Mushkoh, 50th (Independent) Para Brigade and 79th Mountain Brigade were poised for a major victory. The morale of the Pakistani troops was low, as revealed by a Pakistan non-commissioned officer (NCO) captured by 50th (Independent) Para Brigade. He said that their areas were akin to a *gadristan* (that is, chaotic) and their officers never joined them at the front line unlike the Indian officers, who always led their soldiers from the front.

DGMO Meeting: That day, we were informed that Pakistan wanted to host a meeting between the two DGMOs to finalise the withdrawal plan. India agreed to the meeting, but only if it was held in India. The Pakistani DMO was asked to come to the Border Security Forces premises at Attari near Amritsar. The next day, I flew to Amritsar and then took a helicopter to Khasa. I was accompanied by Brigadier M.C. Bhandari and Colonel Ashok Sheoran. Major General Tauqir Zia, the Pakistani DMO, was accompanied by a colonel.

The talks went quite smoothly but we did not give the Pakistanis any leeway. Brushing aside all their protestations, we laid down a schedule for Pakistan's withdrawal. They were to leave Mushkoh by 0600 hours on 14 July, Dras by 0600 hours on 15 July and Batalik (up to Turtuk) by 0600 hours on 16 July. By these times, Pakistani troops must be well on their side of the LOC. There should be no new posts within 1,000 metres of the LOC in areas that were not held earlier. No misinterpretation of the alignment of the LOC would be accepted. After the stipulated time, our troops would move from south to north and anyone left on our side of the LOC would be removed in the way we deemed suitable.

The Pakistani DMO requested that more time should be given for withdrawal, to which I allowed one more day for clearing Mushkoh. He then asked for a simultaneous ceasefire in all sectors. This was firmly rejected by us. We instead agreed to a ceasefire only in the sectors where withdrawal was to take place as per the schedule we outlined. After this agreement, the question of missing personnel was raised. We told him that there was only one prisoner with us: Naik Inayat Ali of 5 NLI. The Pakistanis said that there were no Indian prisoners with them.

When I told Major General Zia that we had photographs of the burials of their soldiers, he refused to accept that they were from the Pakistan Army and instead insisted that they were Mujahideen. I then showed him the proof such as documents and identity cards, to which he responded with embarrassment and called the dead soldiers *ahmaks* (fools). However, during the tea break, he took me aside and said, 'You know the truth, sir, *aap hamein sharminda kyon kar rahe hein* (why are you embarrassing us)?' I agreed to his request that copies of all the documents and videos be handed over to them. I must say that Major General Zia was a fine soldier. However, lying is perhaps a second nature or maybe even a compulsion in the Pakistan Army.

Immediately after the meeting, I flew back to Delhi and went straight to the prime minister's house, where the CCS had assembled to be briefed. They were satisfied with the proceedings of the meeting, and the stage was set for Pakistan's withdrawal. Pakistan honoured their commitments but requested a delay of twenty-four hours in Batalik. India agreed to this. However, Pakistan continued to hold three pockets adjacent to the LOC – at Zulu Ridge in Mushkoh, Saddle in Dras and Ring Contour in Batalik. India cleared these last areas on 25 July through well-planned attacks.

A relevant aspect is that during war, communications between the two countries close down and only the official channel of communication between the DGMOs remain functional. So, this becomes a very important means of interaction. Currently, sector-level communications have also been set up and are functional.

While war is a grim affair, it also leaves space for human dealings and light-hearted conversations. I distinctly remember that there was a cricket match between England and India during the Kargil war with Pakistani cricket umpires. We won that match. In our next telephone conversation, Major General Tauqir Zia told me, 'Dekha, hamare umpire ne aapko jita diya (See, our umpire helped your team win).' I told him, 'I knew that in daily life you people are prone to cheating, but I did not know that your umpires and sportsmen also carry this trait.'

Mission Accomplished: The following day, I declared during a press conference that all intrusions by Pakistani troops had been cleared: 'With this, the mission assigned to the armed forces by the Government of India had been fully accomplished.' This was received by loud cheering from the media contingent and all others present in room number 102 of South Block.

On 27 July, the prime minister and his colleagues visited the MO directorate to meet senior officers of the three services and have a cup of tea with them. We were congratulated for bringing glory to India.

Strategic Lessons

Every war throws up some very important strategic lessons which must be examined meticulously. To ensure that we fight the next conflict much better prepared, we have to apply the lessons learnt from previous ones. In this section, I will discuss some of the more important lessons gained from the Kargil war.

Politico–Military–Diplomatic Cooperation: Essential to any successful war is a deep understanding between the politico–diplomatic and the military leaderships of the country. Firm resolve on the part of the political leadership is imperative. It is to India's credit that even though we had a caretaker government at the time of the Kargil conflict, there was no wavering of determination. The war was fought with the firm resolve of throwing the Pakistanis out of our territory. This understanding also helped in quick decision-making at the highest level. The military aim was quite clear and most of the CCS meetings were held in the MO directorate room because of the confidence and trust placed in the armed forces.

National Security Doctrine (NSD) and National Security Strategy (NSS): National security concerns the ability of a country's government to protect its citizens, economy and other institutions during both peace and war. While most developed nations have already drawn up an NSD or an NSS and formalised them, India unfortunately does not have any such official doctrine or strategy. An NSD guides various policies and plans related to both internal and external security. When formulated, it would fill a huge void in the higher defence management of our country.

Having an NSD or NSS is also necessary to tailor our defence doctrine and to formulate long-term measures towards a strategy based on severe retribution. This will guide the armed forces to prepare, equip and train in accordance with the outlined military aim. A draft National Security Policy was prepared by Shyam Sharan, a former chairman of the National Security Advisory Board (NSAB). The policy covers domestic security, external security, military preparedness, economic security and ecological security. The government has received the draft and it is in the process of being formalised.

Safeguarding Our Borders: One of the biggest lessons of the Kargil war was that even if the army has to allocate resources for counterinsurgency or other similar operations, it must never be at the cost of preparations for conventional operations for safeguarding our borders. The national policy remains that we must not lose an inch of our territory. We had slipped up and put the bulk of our resources and focus on the proxy war. It cost us dearly in the initial stages of the conflict.

Preparation for War: It is my firm belief borne out of forty-three years' service in the army that war can be prevented only if one is fully prepared for war at all times. The preparation includes training, equipment and modern weapons. This belief was proved true in Kargil, where we had to pause in the midst of war to refresh tactics for conventional operations. In the process we lost over a month. Therefore, we need to optimally utilise peacetime to train and prepare for war.

Good preparedness is augmented by good intelligence, which is one of the most critical parts of operational preparation. We need to have the latest information about the enemy at all times. Unfortunately, our Winter Aerial Surveillance Operation (WASO) was not effective during the Kargil war as the helicopters employed were not fitted with surveillance equipment. Our ground troops also remained ignorant because the patrolling was perhaps not intense and information from across the LOC was very limited.

In the third week of May 1999, we received an aerial photograph of a Pakistani helicopter flying on our side close to the LOC. When I told Major General Tauqir Zia that this was a serious violation of the Simla Agreement, he feigned ignorance and asked me to talk to the Kashmiri freedom fighters. In those days we did not have unmanned aerial vehicle (UAVs). Local surveillance radars had not been introduced into the service. Our intelligence, surveillance and reconnaissance (ISR) was a weakness and it continues to be so – it needs to be upgraded appreciably. India is presently in the process of upgrading its ISR capabilities in a big way at a fast pace.

Political Restraint: The Government of India could not have anticipated the possibility of a war so soon after the Lahore Declaration. Vajpayee kept trying to find ways to peace through the track-2 interlocutor R.K. Mishra, a respected journalist and political leader. Eventually, this dialogue also stopped. The military was not in the loop at that stage. We had gone wrong in judging Pakistan's intentions.

As India had only recently tested a nuclear weapon, we had to convince the world that we were a responsible nation that did not resort to unnecessary warmongering. We wanted international opinion in our favour and therefore were looking for irrefutable proof of the Pakistan Army's involvement. Subsequently we did manage to show to the international community various kinds of evidence, including documents and marked maps. Whatever the reason, this approach of restraint greatly restricted the armed forces. But for this approach, we could have inflicted even heavier punishments on Pakistan with much fewer casualties to ourselves.

Integrated Operations: When the IAF joined the battle, it was a big setback for Pakistan as it could not bring in its own air force without admitting that it had its regular troops operating in Kargil. The IAF aircraft stuck to our side of the LOC and this gave Pakistan no excuse to react. Should the war have expanded, the army, the navy and the air force would have shared the responsibilities for battle. However, it is desirable to have a formalised system of integration that would result in greater operational efficiency. That would prove more cost-effective. With the introduction of the post of chief of defence staff (CDS) and the concept of theaterisation, we are now moving in that direction.

Intelligence Failure: Surprise is an important principle of war and one of the major factors for success. There is no doubt that we were surprised by the Pakistan Army at the beginning and it gave them the advantage. India was caught unaware due to an intelligence failure. Not only was the intrusion detected late, but our intelligence agencies were also unable to assess if the intrusion was by militants or the Pakistan Army. In fairness to the intelligence agencies, there was an acute shortage of high-quality surveillance equipment at the time. The army was particularly poorly equipped for surveillance operations.

One could say that it was also militarily difficult to anticipate that Pakistan would launch such a risky operation at high altitudes in extreme weather with little possibility of big gains. However, the intelligence agencies gravely failed to detect the large purchases of winter fighting equipment from international weapons markets by Pakistan. The assessment of the Research and Analysis Wing (R&AW) was categorically that 'there was no possibility of a war with Pakistan in the current year'. This inaccurate assessment resulted in a strategic failure.

Setting Up of the Kargil Review Committee: The mandate of the Kargil Review Committee (KRC) was to review the events leading to the conflict and to make recommendations for safeguarding national security against such armed intrusions in the future. The operations during the actual conflict – that is, events from 26 May 1999 onward – were excluded from its remit. The committee noted that stealth, secrecy and deception were key to the Pakistani intrusions in Kargil. There had been virtually no movement from outside the sector nor any extraordinary dumping of stores and ammunition. This had made the detection of the operations more difficult.

Despite this, the KRC opined that there had been an intelligence failure and laid the primary responsibility for it on the R&AW. They had failed to detect a change in the deployment of battalions in the area and also the addition of one battalion to the force level normally deployed there. The committee also held military intelligence responsible to a lesser extent for not detecting the intrusion on the ground. We should have been able to pick up the forward moves undertaken by Pakistan as our troops were deployed on the ground.

Lack of information sharing and coordination among intelligence agencies was another flaw identified by the KRC after they found that hardly any out of the forty-five Kargil-related intelligence inputs were shared with the army or other intelligence agencies. The KRC concluded that intelligence failure was the single major factor leading to the Kargil conflict. The intelligence system has now been improved substantially. A military-specific defence intelligence agency has also been established.

National Security System: The most important recommendation made by the KRC was to undertake a thorough review of the national security system by an independent body of credible experts. This recommendation was accepted immediately by the government. In April 2000, a Group of Ministers (GoM) chaired by the home minister, L.K. Advani, was tasked with a review of the national security system. The GoM created four task forces to study different aspects of the security system. N.N.Vohra led the task force for Internal Security, Dr Madhav Godbole for Border Management, Arun Singh for Higher Management of Defence and Girish Saxena for Intelligence.

In May 2001, the GoM presented its report. Among its many recommendations was the creation of the post of chief of defence staff. This recommendation was hotly debated and was contentious, but I feel it was a very wise one. The prime minister accepted all the recommendations except for the one for a CDS, for which he wanted a political consensus. It was finally accepted much later, with the first CDS appointed only on 30 December 2019.

The GoM also strongly recommended the principle of 'One Border One Force' for better accountability. If implemented, it would put command and control of the Central Armed Police Forces (CAPF) under the army. The KRC had also recommended that the CAPF be deployed on the border under command of the army. However, these suggestions have not been implemented despite adverse ramifications for border security.

The army has long been requesting that the Indo-Tibetan Border Police (ITBP) be placed under its operational control for better border management. It would provide the cohesion, coordination and synergy required to counter China's offensive posture. Unfortunately, power games have prevented this from becoming a reality. The sooner it is resolved, the better it would be for national security.

Notification of Emergency/Mobilisation: In a limited war context, no formal precautionary telegram may be issued by the government. This was the case in the Kargil war. In the absence of such a notification of emergency, problems occur with many areas of logistical support such as impressment of civil transport and requisitioning the railways. It is therefore essential that the MO directorate or the military wing of the Cabinet Secretariat get the requisite notifications for partial mobilisations in contingencies. Orders and instructions need to be revised to enable preparation of wherewithal for war even without the declaration of a full emergency.

Leadership: Alexander the Great supposedly said that an army of sheep led by a lion is better than an army of lions led by a sheep. Leadership is indeed key to success. In the Kargil war, our young officers led from the front by displaying exemplary leadership and a burning desire to attain victory. They upheld the prestige and honour of their battalions, regiments and the country. Their example inspired the junior commissioned officers (JCOs) and the non-commissioned officers (NCOs) to follow their leaders in fearlessly exhibiting raw courage.

During the Kargil war, 26 officers were killed and 66 injured, while 523 soldiers were killed and 1363 injured. The fatality ratio of officers to soldiers was very high because our officers were always at the front. Most of the commanding officers too displayed exemplary leadership and motivated their command to victory. The ones lacking imagination and physical toughness were quickly replaced.

While the generals were not necessarily always at the forefront of the fighting, they too had major roles to play in motivating the force, drawing out comprehensive operational plans, ensuring availability of necessary resources and reacting rationally to any contingencies. Battle management is an art that needs experience and nerves of steel. No war has ever been won without good planning and astute direction by generals. While leadership at all levels is equally important, the Kargil war is a shining example of the value of junior leadership in winning a war.

Role of the Media in War: During the Kargil war, the media was successful in bringing the war into the nation's living rooms and building up patriotic fervour across the country. The electronic and print media was full of stories about the heroism of the officers and troops and as a result the last rites of the martyred soldiers were attended by thousands of people. Initially, however, there were some teething problems as the media was not well-trained in war reporting and sometimes resorted to exaggerations and even erroneous reporting under pressure. Gradually, the briefings to the media became more refined.

In the MO directorate, we framed a briefing system that worked very well throughout the war. In the morning our spokesperson (Colonel Bikram Singh, Director MO2, who later rose to become the Chief) was briefed by the DGMO and given one or two important battle events to be covered in detail, besides touching upon other general developments. The director general of military intelligence

(DGMI) then gave him additional inputs. After preparing his brief, the spokesman met the minister of external affairs to get his approval and directions if any, especially on diplomatic issues. Only then was the media briefed by the spokesman and that too with the help of maps. This method established the credibility of our briefing both nationally and internationally.

There were some important lessons gained from our interactions with the media. We learnt that the briefing must be factually correct and honest, be for a specific issue each day and be easily understandable. Our officers in the field must also be clear and precise about what they should say and also the media should be trained on how to write reports on military matters so that the context is not lost. Such training courses for the media (war correspondents) were indeed run by the army for a while and should be resumed.

There should be designated, trained and well-informed spokespeople who act as a link between the military and the media to ensure that reporting remains correct and any doubts are cleared. With proper media policies and systems, reporting standards would greatly improve. The media is undoubtedly a great force multiplier in building the image of the armed forces and the country.

Infrastructure Development: There are many types of infrastructure but I will focus only on border roads, railways, airports and telecommunications. India has well-developed infrastructure along our western borders with Pakistan. But in the present 'two-front' scenario, China – with whom we share 3,488 kilometres of an un-demarcated 'Line of Actual Control' (LAC) – becomes even more important. China has put in massive efforts to develop its western, central and eastern highways, the Beijing–Lhasa railway line and the Golmud–Lhasa–Beijing fuel pipeline.

China has extended its road and rail networks right up to the LAC in most areas. This gives it the ability to launch operations there within three or four weeks. Since its intrusions in eastern Ladakh in May 2020, it has further quickened its pace in infrastructure development in the area and now have seven or eight airfields in the region that are capable of night operations by fighter aircrafts. It has even built a bridge over the Pangong Tso.

For a while, India had followed a deliberate policy of non-development of infrastructure in eastern border areas under the rationale that any future offensive by China would get delayed due to the lack of infrastructure in our forward areas, and in the process give us vital time to prepare and move troops to counter the threat. This was also done keeping in mind that we would have fewer troops compared to the enemy. This policy changed after November 1975, when India established a China Study Group (CSG), initially headed by K.R. Narayanan (who went on to become president of India) and comprising the secretaries of external affairs, defence and home. The group in 2020 comprised the Cabinet secretary, foreign secretary, home secretary, defence secretary, vice chief of the army staff, vice chief of the naval staff, vice chief of the air staff, director of the Intelligence Bureau and director of the R&AW.

The CSG is now headed by the NSA and has identified 73 strategically important roads of 3,323 kilometres in length to be established as part of Phase 1 of the India–China Border Roads (ICBR) project. The plans were sanctioned by the government in 2005, and as of March 2022, connectivity had been achieved in 63 out of the 73 roads. In addition, 104 more roads over 6,700 kilometres in length have been sanctioned and approved in Phase 2 of the project in 2020. The construction of the roads are being funded by the Border Infrastructure and Management Fund, which has an allocation of around ₹13,020 crore from 2021–22 to 2025–26.

In January 2023, the defence minister unveiled 27 further border infrastructure projects including at Umling La in southern Ladakh at an altitude of 5,800 metres. Also, the Border Area Development Programme (BADP) – which had been initiated in 1986 with the aim of saturating the border areas with essential infrastructure – allocated ₹784 crore in 2020–21. Besides this, plans for more border airports and Advance Landing Grounds (ALG) are progressing on schedule. As of September 2021, India is constructing 31 road tunnels – 20 in Jammu and Kashmir and 11 in Ladakh – at the cost of ₹1.4 lakh crore. Improvement of mobile and internet connectivity is happening rapidly.

There are 14 ongoing projects for strategic rail lines running along the China, Nepal and Pakistan borders. In the first phase, four of these lines were to run along the LAC: the Missamari–Tenga–Tawang line, the Bilaspur–Manali–Leh line, the Pasighat–Tezu–Rupai line and the North Lakhimpur–Bame–Silapathar line. The final location survey – which maps the terrain, route alignment and sections of the route – was meant to have been completed by 2019 but it is lagging behind.

Besides strategic railway lines, there is an urgent need to upgrade the rail infrastructure to create adequate number of railway sidings at critical stations and enough serviceable ramps at entraining and detraining stations. More camping and marshalling areas would also be needed in the future. While the government is working on this, given the events of the recent standoff with China, the momentum must be maintained and all necessary budgetary support provided. India is already far behind the critical threshold at our borders with China, who is becoming more belligerent by the day.

Fallacies: There is a definite need for us to understand the nature of future conflicts. For a while, there had been a growing belief in the world that moving forward there was little or no possibility of a conventional war. A war, if any happened at all, would be a 'no-contact' war. This belief was shattered by the ongoing Russia–Ukraine war. I strongly disagree with this philosophy of 'limited' war. We in India should never fall into the trap of such thinking given that our two hostile neighbours are in active collusion. Diplomacy does not appear to be producing positive results.

Wars are always unpredictable and therefore we must always be prepared for a war on two fronts. Once started, a war can expand and escalate to any extent subject to the strategic aims of both the attacker and the defender.

In Kargil, it did not expand only because we succeeded in recapturing the entire area within two months. While limited local conflicts may still take place, there is no guarantee that they will remain limited.

Technology: Every country is trying to reduce manpower in the armed forces to cut down on recurring and ever-increasing defence revenue expenditure. In principle, I agree with the concept of taking advantage of ever-advancing technology to replace soldiers where feasible. However, I feel that the dictating factors have to be country-terrain specific. They must take into consideration the degree and possibility of threat, the expected intensity of conflict and also the terrain over which the operations are likely to be carried out.

In India's case, there is a definite threat and the conflict is likely to be over mountainous terrain. The requirements for mountain battles are a lot more demanding than those fought in the plains. The ability to use technology is greatly limited in such regions. Also, nuclear weapons do not have the same impact as a deterrence for us as both hostile nations in our vicinity are also nuclear powers. It is clear that any moves in that direction would be equally damaging for us. Nuclear capability also does not help us consider a reduction of troops as it is a weapon of last resort and not for fighting wars.

The Russia–Ukraine war has established that irrespective of technology, the combat soldier will continue to have his role as before. This raises the very serious question of whether a reduction in troops is possible, and if so, by how much? This debate can be settled only by a group of military experts and diplomats after a dispassionate and holistic study of the entire operational area. Only then should a decision be formalised. Of course, it is better to try to settle any border disputes diplomatically to reduce the extent of threat and only then look at a reduction of troops to keep defence expenditures low.

Ammunition and Equipment: In India, ammunition and equipment of foreign origin is sometimes not available in required quantities at short notice. Even indigenous ammunition production can be inadequate. Our government's self-reliance schemes may prove to be useful in the future but when it comes to modernisation of ordinance production, we still have some way to go. During the Kargil war, some emergent purchases that the government had sanctioned never arrived till much after the war. Therefore, we need to understand that emergent purchases do not work, are non-productive and come at prohibitive costs.

In future wars, the expenditure of ammunition is likely to be very heavy. While no specific figures are available for the Russia–Ukraine war, the reports indicate that both countries have almost exhausted their supplies. The ammunition expenditure on both sides is going beyond the production capacities of even their allies. It is believed that Russia is firing approximately 20,000 artillery shells daily, whereas Ukraine is expending between 5,000 to 8,000 rounds a day.

While Russia has ramped up its production considerably and is managing the current expenditure, Ukraine is heavily dependent on the support of the US and the European Union. The US government has authorised approximately $ 175 billion in assistance to Ukraine, out of which $ 69.8 billion have gone towards weapons, equipment, ammunition and training. Ukraine has received a further € 73.1 billion in aid from Europe. India has to draw a lesson about the scale of ammunition expenditure from the Russia–Ukraine war.

Conclusion

The Kargil war was the first one that captured the imagination of the entire country, with extensive coverage on television from newspaper correspondents present in the warzone. While this created a lot of enthusiasm and zeal that united the country, it was not a war that any of us wanted. Nevertheless, when war was thrust upon us, the nation responded with a firm resolve and daring that few believed was possible – least of all Pakistan.

Yes, we were taken by surprise because of Pakistan's deceit. We cannot be sure whether Nawaz Sharif was ignorant of the operation or if it was a politico-military collusion. But what went wrong for Pakistan? According to then director general of Pakistan ISI, General Sahid Aziz, the operation in Kargil was a failure and Pakistan lost badly to the Indian Army. General Aziz says that the Pakistani military leadership failed to anticipate the Indian reaction and visualise the exit strategy, as well as the international pressure.[13]

One major factor in our success was the strength of our regimental system and the battlefield leadership of our commanding officers. Every unit was prepared to make sacrifices to ensure victory and uphold the prestige of their regiment or battalion. It speaks volumes of our military leadership at all levels that we overcame our shortcomings in the quantity and quality of arms, ammunition and maintenance of our equipment. However, the hard-won lessons from Kargil must be applied and we should always remain fully prepared at all times. The frequent attempts of intrusion by the Chinese – especially since May 2020 – and Pakistan's continued support of insurgency in Kashmir are constant reminders to us that modernisation of our armed forces is of utmost importance.

I may not have been on the battlefield, but I frequently visited the operational area and thus was uniquely placed to witness the unfolding of events during the Kargil war while also being involved in the decision-making process at the Army HQ and the government. Of course, I cannot end this chapter without a special mention of the great efficiency and alacrity with which every officer at the MO directorate worked during those twelve weeks of war.

2

Operation Parakram
On the Brink and Back

> 'The Parliament is the highest representative of democracy, and they chose Parliament deliberately as their target. The attack was not on the Parliament, but on the entire nation…'
> — Atal Bihari Vajpayee, then prime minister of India, 13 December 2001

THE MORNING OF 13 December 2001 had been like any other until a staff officer burst into my room without explanation and switched on the television. The news channels were showing live coverage of what seemed to be a terrorist attack under way at Parliament House. I was serving as the VCOAS at the time and my office was just a kilometre away. I realised the noise outside that I thought had come from crackers was actually gunfire. It was already on TV as journalists were present at the venue to report on the winter session of the Parliament.

It was a chilling moment and time stood still as I watched the images on the screen. I knew that once again Indian sovereignty had been violated by a hostile attack – and this time on the very temple of our democracy. The COAS, General S. Padmanabhan, was in Chennai that day. I called the DGMO and asked him to mobilise two quick reaction teams (QRTs) to reach the Parliament House immediately. I told him that detailed instructions would follow, but we should place our formations on notice for mobilising at a short notice and also enhance security around military installations in Delhi. After these initial instructions, I tried to understand what exactly was going on.

Backdrop

After Pakistan was forced to face the ignominy of defeat in Kargil, Musharraf toppled a democratically elected government in a coup. Smarting under international backlash, he subverted the domestic agenda by diverting the attention of the Pakistani public to the Kashmir issue. Inevitably, militancy in the garb of jihad followed, and Pakistan-supported militant organisations continued to operate in Jammu and Kashmir. The militants targeted sensitive targets to draw headlines and keep their cadres motivated.

First, an Indian Airlines flight to Kandahar was hijacked in December 1999. India had to agree to the release of three dreaded terrorists in exchange for the 176 passengers. Then, on 22 December 2000, two militants attacked the Indian Army outpost at Red Fort in Delhi. It was not the scale of the attack that was worrying but the sinister symbolism of attacking a national heritage site from where the prime minister addresses the nation on Independence Day. Then came a major attack. On 1 October 2001, three militants from the terrorist group Jaish-e-Mohammed (JeM) rammed a vehicle packed with explosives into the Jammu and Kashmir State Legislative Assembly building in Srinagar. The suicide bombing mission killed thirty-eight people.

These attacks had made it clear that despite the security measures that had kept the militancy in check, isolated events, though unfortunate, could still happen. This attack on the Parliament was another such event. It was a direct and blatant attack on Indian sovereignty and was aimed at wiping off the national leadership. When the Parliament is in session, most senior political leaders are present in the Parliament House.

In this chapter, my aim is to put in correct perspective the events that followed and analyse the overall context of the massive and unprecedented build-up and deployment of forces that ensued. Many call India's show of military might a coercion, while some judge it as a missed opportunity and a strategic blunder. Proponents of each theory insist that they have valid supporting arguments.

After the Attack

The nation was aghast. India had reached a stage of no return. No more concessions could be made to the continued provocations by Pakistan. The public opinion was strongly in favour of India responding swiftly to punish our neighbours and teach them a lesson. What followed was the divisive Operation Parakram, even as political leaders around the world tried to dissuade the two nuclear-armed nations from heading to an outright war.

Prime Minister Atal Bihari Vajpayee issued a short statement on the same day of the attack, declaring that the fight against terrorism had reached its last phase and would be fought in a decisive manner. 'We are with the families of the people who laid down their lives fighting against the terrorist attack on Parliament,' Vajpayee said.[1] The next day, in a speech delivered at the platinum jubilee celebrations of the Union Public Service Commission (UPSC), the prime minister labelled the attack as an act of war against India and promised to take decisive action. 'Yesterday's terrorist attack on our Parliament was unprecedented not only in the history of India,' said Vajpayee, 'but also in the annals of democracy the world over.'[2]

A few hours later, Foreign Secretary Chokila Iyer issued a demarche to Pakistan's High Commissioner to India, Ashraf Jehangir Qazi, calling for action against the extremist outfits operating from Pakistan's territory. The demands included stopping of all support to the extremist outfits involved in the attack, disbanding them and seizing all their financial assets. India also wanted the masterminds of the attack to be handed over to them. These demands were expanded later to include the closure of facilities, training camps, arms supply routes, funding channels and all direct and indirect assistance to terrorists operating from Pakistani soil. It also called for a 'categorical and unambiguous renunciation of terrorism in all its manifestations'.[3]

Among the nations strongly condemning the attack on the Indian Parliament was, surprisingly, Pakistan – probably because it found itself on the wrong side of international diplomatic opinion. The statement from Pakistan came with a caveat that it would only act on credible proof of the involvement of militant groups based on their soil – a promise that none in India believed.

The five terrorists who had participated in the attack were gunned down inside the Parliament premises on the day of the attack. Within four days, four people were arrested and charged as the masterminds of the attack by Delhi Police. The perpetrators belonged to the Pakistan-raised terrorist organisations JeM and Lashkar-e-Taiba (LeT). Despite India providing adequate proof to Pakistan, our neighbours took no substantive action to reign in these groups.

On 21 December, for the first time since 1971 India recalled their High Commissioner to Pakistan. Nirupama Rao, spokesperson for India's Ministry of External Affairs, said in a statement, 'Since the attack on the Parliament, we have seen no attempt on the part of Pakistan to take action against the organisations involved'.[4] India then severed all air, rail and road links with Pakistan and banned flights over its airspace.

Mobilisation of Armed Forces

On the evening of the day of the attack on Parliament, the prime minister called the chiefs of the army, navy and air force for a meeting to discuss options for a response. NSA Brajesh Mishra was also present at the meeting, which I attended on behalf of the army chief. The IAF chief estimated a response time of two days while the naval chief said that one week would be required. I informed them that as per the existing operational plans, the defensive formations could be readied for limited offensive actions in three to four days. However, our strike corps would need three weeks to be ready for offensive operations.

I added that till the strike corps were in operational readiness, anything more than small-scale offensives by the holding corps could be risky. Pakistan required much less time than us for mobilising its offensive formations because its troops had to cover shorter distances to the border. The time advantage for deployment gave Pakistan the upper hand. I recall Air Chief Marshal A.Y. Tipnis telling me after the meeting that the political leadership was more excited for action than at any other time he could remember. However, no firm decision on action was conveyed by the government at that time.

A CCS meeting was called on 15 December 2001 with the armed forces chiefs again in attendance. By then General Padmanabhan had returned and he attended the meeting and found that the leadership was still in the process of making up their mind. The politicians favoured limited action restricted to Jammu and Kashmir. However, the area south of Pir Panjal was partially covered by snow and the valley had much more snow, which would grossly restrict ground operations. The outcome was unlikely to be commensurate with the effort and would not produce the desired results.

Therefore, the army chief insisted on full-scale mobilisation to cater for escalation and a possible nuclear standoff. Finally, it was decided that the military must mobilise and prepare to take necessary action. The chiefs were asked to give the prime minister a firm timeline for an offensive, should it be required. However, it was emphasised to them that the final decision on whether to go to war or not would be taken only by the government.

General Padmanabhan told me later that the nuclear threat was not discussed during the CCS meeting. More importantly, no political goals or aims of a military mobilisation were clearly defined. Admiral Sushil Kumar, the navy chief at the time, later stated on record in an interview that he specifically asked for the political aim of the actions to derive the military aims and objectives. However, no such aims were laid down. When the chiefs asked for the rules of engagement post-mobilisation, the prime minister asked them to mobilise for present, rest will follow.[5] However, no other specific formal directions followed and the instructions given later were only in the form of sketchy signals.

India's Options for a Response

It was essential for national security agencies such as the NSAB and the National Security Council (NSC) to share with the armed forces the collated multiagency intelligence inputs on possible Pakistani responses and their capabilities. We needed their threat assessment analysis but did not receive any. No assessments of levels of possible escalation under the nuclear overhang were provided. It was therefore not possible to derive the military aim of the operation.

It appears that the first reaction by the Indian government was to attack terrorist camps located across the LOC in Pakistan-occupied Kashmir (PoK). But this mood changed after a debate in Parliament on 18 December, during which even Home Minister Advani counselled restraint. The army chief had already mentioned to the prime minister in an earlier meeting that strikes against terrorist camps would not serve any useful purpose given that these camps could easily be relocated or reassembled. This was reiterated by the armed forces chiefs to the CCS during a subsequent meeting and intelligence reports corroborated this assessment.

There was a temporary decline in cross-border infiltration and terrorist violence linked to it from January to March 2002 while 'jehadi' cadres were advised to lie low. However, cross-border infiltration and terrorist violence continued and increased as the measures were relaxed with time.[6] The psychological impact of the proposed strikes on militant camps had to be weighed against the military escalation for which India was still getting ready. If limited strikes were to serve no useful purpose, a general war was also not desirable until we were prepared. Further, any military effort could also be impeded by the presence of US-led coalition forces operating from, around and through Pakistani territory in their fight against the Taliban in Afghanistan. For example, the strategic sea space available for the Indian Navy was considerably restricted by the massive US naval presence in the northern reaches of the Arabian Sea, which would have made it difficult for our navy to carry out even routine or surveillance missions. However, Foreign Minister Jaswant Singh dismissed the presence of US forces as an inhibiting factor in policy determinations because India did not have the option of using force.[7]

As early as 16 December, the US had started advocating restraint. I recall the NSA calling almost every day to say that he was under a lot of pressure from his American counterpart, Condoleezza Rice. Given such diplomatic pressures, use of military force was becoming a difficult option. The other option with the government was to generate some crisis on the ground in order to bring upon Islamabad direct military and diplomatic pressure from the international community. In other words, military mobilisation could be used as an integral part of a politico-diplomatic strategy to pressurise Pakistan into ceasing support for anti-India terrorists from within its territory.

Threat Assessment at Army HQ

Immediately after the CCS meeting, the army chief held a discussion with the army commanders to take stock of the situation and assess the threat. The MI directorate provided the following inputs, which had a great bearing on our war planning:

- Pakistani reserves XI and XII Corps were tied down with the US-led Operation Enduring Freedom against the Taliban, and hence it would take time for them to be redeployed in their own operational areas. The US resisted the moving of these two corps because it would affect its operations in Afghanistan.
- Pakistani build-up had not reduced since its winter exercise, which had commenced in October 2001. Around 20,000 troops from the strike corps – Mangla-based I Corps, Karachi-based V Corps and Bahawalpur-based XXXI Corps – together with an armoured brigade and an infantry division still remained in the sensitive Jhelum–Chenab and Chenab–Ravi corridors close to the LOC.
- The time needed for Pakistan to move forces to border areas was much less than India as it had to cover shorter distances. The Indian forces first needed to attain operational balance on the ground before any major offensive could be launched.
- Despite having a numerical disadvantage, Pakistan had a qualitative edge in certain equipment, notably tanks and anti-tank missiles.
- Although India had numerical superiority in almost all respects, the serviceability of our military equipment was down to around 64 per cent. There was an acute deficiency of force multipliers such as handheld thermal imagers, battlefield surveillance radars, disposable rocket launchers and flamethrowers. Tank ammunition supplies were also low. There was a 90 per cent deficiency in fuses of mines and ad hoc innovations to fuses resulted in many avoidable fatal casualties during laying and recovery operations.
- Dual-tasked formations were lacking in artillery, engineers and signals.

With the institution of the post of CDS, established in 2020, the anomaly of lack of coordination on the nuclear aspect has been resolved.

The Army Mobilises

The army's first task was to galvanise holding formations and move them to the operational locations for active patrolling in no-man's land. We had to then commence laying mines – both anti-personnel and anti-tank – along likely ingress routes. All units were instructed to recall their personnel from leave. War-like equipment and manpower were moved to forward locations, besides dumping of ammunition and other stores. Since specific orders on escalation and crossing the LOC or IB were not given by the political leadership, formations were asked to ensure that none of the patrols or surveillance parties cross the borders.

Three strike corps from the hinterland and dual-tasked formations from the east were given orders to move to their respective concentration areas and be ready to go to war within two weeks. Such a move needs more than 1,500 special military trains as roads cannot support the massive movement of more than 5,00,000 troops and vehicles. The MO directorate became the hub and coordinator of all the activities and also provided daily briefs to the COAS, the VCOAS and the COSC.

The Army HQ began to coordinate all logistics support, providing equipment to the field formations from existing reserve stocks or expediting purchases for fresh stores. Its responsibilities included coordination with the states for requisitioning land for deployment, traffic control during convoy movements and impressment of civil transport. Allocation of railway rakes and special trains was secured and they were moved on priority while railway sidings were cleared for the movement of tanks, guns, ammunition, heavy equipment and fuel.

The ordnance factories were told to produce ammunition and explosives at a war footing not only to make up for deficiencies but also to build on war wastage reserves. Procurement of critical warlike equipment was expedited using the national emergency procedures. By the first week of January 2002, the army chief had declared that the Indian army mobilisation was complete and it was ready for war. This led the NSA also to confirm that India was ready to cross the IB or the LOC.

The declaration sent ripples across the international community. The US asked India to hold off on its offensive as Musharraf was expected to make an important announcement. Bruce Pannier, a Central Asia analyst, wrote that many in Pakistan felt that the possibility of war between India and Pakistan rests on Musharraf's statement.[8] However, some were extremely cynical about the Pakistani leader's upcoming speech, saying the content had been written by the West.

The navy and the air force also declared their operational readiness and we were now waiting for the green signal. However, it never came. On 2 January, even as our troops were getting poised to strike, the Indian defence minister, George Fernandes, had told reporters that 'efforts were being made to defuse the situation through diplomatic intervention'.[9] On the same day, Musharraf reminded Indian leaders of the stakes, issuing a thinly veiled nuclear threat when he said that Pakistan's contingency plans reflected its capacity of responding to aggression.[10]

Following Musharraf's sabre-rattling, Prime Minister Vajpayee responded in kind, stating that 'no weapon would be spared in self-defence'. He declared that whatever weapon was available, it would be used 'no matter how it wounded the enemy'.[11] At Pakistan's GHQ the view grew increasingly bleak. Along Pakistan's western borders, the US operation aimed at rooting out Al-Qaeda and the Taliban from Afghanistan was in high gear, and now along their eastern border half a million Indian troops were being mobilised for war.

A SAARC summit took place in Nepal a few days later. Musharraf addressed the gathering on 5 January 2002 before resorting to theatrics. He said, 'As I step down from this podium, I will extend a genuine and sincere hand of friendship to Prime Minister Vajpayee.'[12] Our prime minister got up and shook hands with Musharraf. Then, in his speech, Vajpayee said that Musharraf should follow his gesture by 'not permitting any activity in Pakistan or any territory it controls today that enables terrorists to perpetrate mindless violence in India'.[13]

Strangely, while on one hand the armed forces of both countries were almost fully deployed and confronting each other, on the other hand these shallow peace gestures were being made. However, the Government of India was still debating its options, for the reasons explained subsequently in this chapter. Hence, no specific political or military objectives were laid down by the national political leadership and therefore the armed forces were forced to draw their own strategies from minimal inputs during the period of build-up.

The navy had mobilised to effectively dominate the sea, the air force had already selected some high-value targets for itself and the army had its strike corps balanced at places from where decisive offensives could be launched in the plains. The time taken by the strike corps to concentrate was not entirely due to a lack of vision by the army. The positioning of these corps in the hinterland during peacetime was in accordance with the war doctrine of 'strategic defence' in effect at the time.

Due to snow and limits on employability of forces, the options along the LOC were restricted and decisive victory could not be visualised at this stage. However, it was certain that now with our forces poised, even an early limited action in the plains within the capabilities of our holding corps would have been successful because Pakistan was sluggish with their preparations. If the military aim was to cripple Pakistan's war-waging potential and force them to desist from indulging in terrorism, there was an opportunity in early January 2002, once the forces had confirmed readiness.

General Padmanabhan responded to criticism that a slow mobilisation of troops 'gifted' Pakistan time to prepare its defences. He emphasised that significant military gains could have been achieved in January 2002 had politicians made the decision to go to war. These objectives, he said, could have included 'degradation of the other force, and perhaps the capture of disputed territory' in Jammu and Kashmir. The military objectives were achievable in January but not as much by the next month, and even less achievable in March. 'By then,' lamented Padmanabhan, 'the balance of forces had changed.'[14] The lack of understanding between the forces and the government was due to the issuance of ambiguous guidelines and the absence of clarity.

In early January 2002, the misplaced enthusiasm of the GOC of II Corps, Lieutenant General Kapil Vij, led to reconnaissance patrols being permitted beyond his corps concentration area in the Thar desert. This activity was picked up by US satellites and was assessed as a likely flashpoint. The Indian government too felt that it could prematurely lead to war, and this led to Vij's immediate recall. This reaction of the government could lead one to believe that ab initio our leaders never wanted to go to war despite the full-scale mobilisation. This ambivalent situation remained throughout the deployment period of Operation Parakram.

Some have argued that at least the air strikes against terror training camps could have been carried out in the early days while the army still needed time to prepare for the escalatory consequences of such attacks. However, the futility of such actions was confirmed by the army chief, who said, 'If you really want to punish someone for something very terrible he has done, you smash him. You destroy his weapons and capture his territory.'[15] Since our offensive formations were still not in position, said Padmanabhan, it could have 'ended up starting a war from which we would have gained very little, and that too at great cost'.

On 12 January, ostensibly under American pressure, Musharraf made his much-awaited statement. It was an ambiguous speech denouncing terrorism. He announced bans on six terrorist organisations including JeM and LeT and promised to arrest terrorists in his country. However, he refused to hand over the twenty terrorists that India had demanded. The Indian political leadership was torn between going forward with a possibly ruinous war or accepting Musharraf's statement at face value. A relieved Indian government claimed that our 'coercive strategy had worked'. This was another indication that the whole mobilisation exercise was an effort at coercion. If that was true, this detail was not shared with the armed forces at any stage.

Jaswant Singh writes in his book *A Call to Honour*, 'the Government, outraged, ordered a troop mobilisation; a near year-long standoff between India and Pakistan followed.' He goes on to declare that it was 'an example of coercive diplomacy, combining aggressive diplomatic action internationally with firm military positioning that contained the potential of pushing consequences should recalcitrance persist'.[16] Throughout this deployment, differing statements were being issued by important leaders. This created further confusion in the minds of the military leadership.

Mishra said in an interview that the major objective of the mass mobilisation was to tell Pakistan that if it did not stop this terrorist activity, then we would have no choice except to attack.[17] Mishra also recalled in the same interview that 'there was a unanimous decision to let Pakistan know this kind of thing would not be tolerated'. He also said that the decisions to mobilise and to cross the LOC and the border were all unanimous. When asked about Mishra's statements, Jaswant Singh cited an oath of secrecy and said, 'I do not disagree with what Brajesh has said but I cannot add to it nor subtract from it.'[18]

In his book, Jaswant Singh writes that 'the objectives of India's mobilisation were to defeat cross-border infiltration/terrorism without conflict, to contain the national mood of "teaching Pakistan a lesson" and, in the event of war, to destroy and degrade Pakistan's warfighting capabilities'.[19] However, he surprisingly adds that his 'most taxing challenge during the confrontation was to get India's military chiefs to recognise restraint as a strategic asset for avoiding conflict'.[20]

The statements of these leaders illustrate the military dilemma during Operation Parakram and the lack of clarity about the purpose of deployment. Coercion to compel an erring nation can be productive only if political statements are followed by actions. I feel that we left a lot to be desired in terms of clarity of our intentions at the political level. The government decided not only to hold off on an offensive but also to not remove troops from the border. This dichotomous and economically unviable approach seemed to lack clear aim and purpose.

Musharraf was also besieged at home. After 9/11, supporting US activities had become tremendously unpopular in Pakistan. A defeat at the hand of India would have proven to be politically disastrous for him. Therefore, Musharraf reneged on his promise. The arrested terrorists were soon let off, and LeT and other terror groups were allowed to operate as before. India watched these events with mounting anger. But the opportunity to attack had passed. The uneasy standoff continued.

While Indian forces used the time to train, Pakistan consolidated its positions to become strongly fortified. General Padmanabhan said that 'it remains unclear, however, just why the politicians who ordered the buildup finally chose not to use the military machine they had assembled'. He added that though there was a feeling that the US held us back, he was not clear if they did so or not. However, there had been great consternation among the American leadership about the huge Indian build-up. 'Finally, it was a decision that had to be made by our political leadership,' concluded Padmanabhan.[21]

The Second Peak

The crisis came to another boil quickly. On 14 May 2002, three terrorists dressed in Indian Army uniforms infiltrated an army camp in Kaluchak near Jammu and killed thirty-four sleeping soldiers. India exploded with outrage. Preparations for war were resumed. On 22 May, Vajpayee announced at a military base in Kashmir: 'The time has come for a decisive battle, and we will have a sure victory in this battle.'[22]

This led to a game of rhetoric brinkmanship with threatening statements being issued by leaders on both sides. Faced with the threat of an all-out war, Pakistan brought back its nuclear card. Lieutenant General Hamid Gul, a former ISI director-general, reportedly said, 'If it ever came to the annihilation of Pakistan, then what is this damned nuclear option for? As they say, if I am going down the ditch, I will also take my enemy with me.' Immediately afterwards, Pakistan began testing its nuclear missiles as a threat.

On 6 April, the 'Ghauri' missile – with a range of 1,500 kilometres – was tested, followed on 22 July by a test of 'Abdali' – a short-range missile capable of hitting targets 200 kilometres away. In response, George Fernandes reiterated what he had said during the Kargil war in 1999: 'Pakistan can't think of using nuclear weapons, because we could take a strike, survive, and then hit back. Pakistan would be finished.'

These developments shocked the USA. On 31 May, it began evacuating non-essential personnel from its embassies in India and Pakistan and warned its citizens not to travel to the region. Other Western countries immediately followed suit. These travel advisories came as a rude shock to India because foreign businesspeople began to leave the country. The order was interpreted in New Delhi as an indirect way to punish India economically and apparently it softened the Indian position considerably. It was a typical case of the victim being punished.

By then Pakistan had become more confident as the preceding months had given it time to strengthen its defences and mobilise the full strength of its army. To counter this, the Indian Army decided to concentrate all three of its strike corps on a single point at the Rajasthan border, which was the most threating posture. They also started reorganising troops for an offensive in Jammu and Kashmir as the weather had improved. This meant that some more time was needed before the beginning of the offensive. It was this precious breathing space that the US used to defuse the situation.

De-escalation

Richard Armitage, the US deputy secretary of state, met with Musharraf on 6 June and extracted a vague promise from the Pakistani president to cease all terrorist activities. Armitage then flew to New Delhi and presented this promise as a hard pledge from Musharraf. The Indian leadership decided to hold back its troops for the moment. The war bugles fell silent again.

According to the Indian government, the following months saw a perceptible drop in the rate of insurgent infiltration from the Pakistani side. This statistic was used by the government as evidence of Pakistani goodwill. Because our neighbour were sticking to its promise, the Indian government decided to pull back its troops. Finally, on 16 October 2002, the crisis was declared to be over, bringing the curtain down on one of the most dangerous periods in India–Pakistan relations. However, the government declared that troops were being 'strategically relocated' and constant vigil would be maintained, especially in Jammu and Kashmir.

The decision to mobilise at such a grand scale had come at a heavy cost as decisive opportunities were frittered away. What factors were responsible for this fiasco? Was it a lack of strategic vision from the government? Was it international pressure? Was it the nuclear threat? Or was it perhaps an ill-prepared military? I strongly believe that our deficiency in weapons and equipment was not the reason, as the army was prepared to go to war with what it had – and it would have definitely delivered.

Was Operation Parakram Coercive Diplomacy?

Diplomacy is the skill of managing international relations, typically by a country's representatives abroad. It aims to seek mutually acceptable outcomes as well as to convey a nation's stand on global issues. Conversely, coercive diplomacy is a strategy that employs a combination of diplomatic and military measures to achieve political or national goals by pressurising an adversary into making certain concessions or submitting to demands. Therefore, coercive diplomacy typically involves a credible threat of force, with the aim of compelling the adversary to change their behaviour without actually resorting to military action.

The Indian military mobilisation during Operation Parakram was designed to meet some of the key elements of coercive diplomacy. These include:

- Compellence: India utilised threats of force to compel Pakistan to take a specific action as demanded in a demarche – that is to stop any further activity inimical to the security environment of India. The objective of compellence was thus to induce change in Pakistan's behaviour by threatening to obliterate its war-waging potential if it did not comply with Indian demands.
- Deterrence: This is a policy of using threats to prevent an adversary from taking a particular course of action. The expressed willingness to go to war by Indian statesmen along with the turning of international opinion against Pakistan was all aimed at deterring our neighbour from further precipitating the situation.

India has a nuclear doctrine of 'no first use', therefore the nuclear threat did not contribute much to India's coercive diplomacy. However, we did adopt active measures of coercion that involved military mobilisation, laying of minefields, simulated moves towards naval blockades and selecting high-value targets for air strikes. These served to inform Pakistan about our intentions to strike and aimed to demonstrate the Indian resolve to go to war if required.

India's moves also showcased our ability to inflict significant damage on Pakistan if our demands were not met. Simultaneously, we also carried out passive measures of coercion through economic tactics such as cutting off all trade relations and transport links with our neighbour. In addition, we made use of political and diplomatic pressure to convince the international community to condemn Pakistan.

Coercive diplomacy is a complex and often risky strategy that on one hand can be effective in achieving policy goals, but on the other can carry significant risks of escalation and unintended consequences. The success of coercive diplomacy depends on credibility of the threat and coherence of strategy, which India displayed without a doubt. The willingness of the adversary to make concessions is also essential. Pakistan did make some insincere efforts under international pressure, but it never intended to follow through with those promises, given its pronounced position on Kashmir and an all-consuming desire to gain control of the whole of Jammu and Kashmir.

Therefore, it was crucial for the government to carefully consider the costs and benefits as well as Pakistan's motivation to comply before deciding to pursue coercive diplomacy. India had to project a credible threat of devastating punitive action in case of non-compliance. Did India try to enforce compellence through massive military mobilisation? Or was it a politico-military show aimed to induce a change in Pakistan's tactics of continued provocation? No official answer shall ever be available – at least not from the armed forces, because they were not privy to the government's real thinking.

Did Coercion Work?

NSA Mishra and some analysts believe that we were able to compel Pakistan to behave because India did not see a high level of terrorism from 2002 till the 2008 terrorist attacks in Mumbai. This assessment is not very correct and is not supported by the facts. The infiltration and militancy had shown a small decline after Operation Parakram, but it continued even after that. Pakistan never fully stopped it and kept the pot boiling.

The Indian government was apparently satisfied with the belief that 'a nation should not stumble into war – however limited – to assuage bruised public sentiment'.[23] Pakistan, however, did not keep any of the terms of promises it made. The terror financing was never stopped, militant organisations continued to enjoy politico-military patronage, efforts to escalate proxy war against India kept showing an upswing and nuclear capability – especially in tactical nuclear weapons – was further developed by Pakistan. As General Malik puts it, 'Despite speeches and international commitments, Musharraf's efforts to rein in jihadi groups remained cosmetic and tactical. Infiltration across the LOC and other ISI operations continued. There was no let-up in terrorist acts.'[24]

While India's belief in its conventional superiority and second-strike nuclear capability gave it confidence that Pakistan would submit to its demands and would take a step back, Pakistan relied on its first-strike threat and tactical conventional parity with India, which allowed it to act in contrast to Indian expectations. India evidently failed to convince Pakistan that its escalatory actions were for real, which is an essential element for a successful coercive diplomacy. Therefore, it may be reasonable to conclude that the massive mobilisation was not really to go to war but was instead intended to assuage domestic anger.

Noted strategic expert Brahma Chellaney thinks that the government took a huge risk by authorising the military mobilisation without a clear idea of how to follow through on the initial action. According to Chellaney, the Indian government failed to recognise that if the mobilisation was seen by Pakistan as a bluff, India's credibility would be severely dented, creating adverse strategic consequences for years to come. He further adds that 'when a nation enjoys credibility, it can usually achieve its objectives with a mere threat to use force'. However, he cautions that when there are 'serious credibility problems, even modest objectives are difficult to accomplish'. Chellaney opines that 'Vajpayee ended up practicing coercive non-diplomacy'.[25]

Indecisive Political Leadership

During the Kargil war, India demonstrated resolute politico-diplomatic leadership. Therefore, it was surprising to find a lack of dynamism and clarity during Operation Parakram. The government was politically weak due to several internal factors, including economic ones. The cost of the operation was in billions of dollars. The American threat of economic restrictions and the departure of international businesspeople from India made the standoff unpopular with the business community.

Whatever the reasons for India turning away from a war it was committed to start, the leadership dithered, delayed and lacked clarity on how to proceed even when the armed forces were battle-ready. No nation can afford such a wavering approach after such a large mobilisation. If the whole charade was only a coercion, the armed forces should have been taken into confidence. Many a casualty that inevitably accrued at the cost of expediency could then have been avoided.

The war hysteria persisted for ten long months, but the army did not march forward as it kept waiting for the directive from the government. Having failed to dissuade Pakistan to stop its proxy war for over a decade – including the limited yet costly conflict in Kargil – the logical political aim should have been to force compellence on Pakistan by punitive strikes on their territory and by liberating as much of PoK as possible.

If the main objective of the operation was to destroy Pakistan's military machine or to degrade its war-waging capability, then it was a total failure at a cost of billions of dollars – not to mention that we suffered more casualties than in the Kargil war. If the objectives were to stop the proxy war in Jammu and Kashmir as well as nullify the Pakistan Army's capability to export terrorism, then also it was a failure because it did not achieve them. The militancy supported by Pakistan continued unabated, albeit at a lower scale because of stronger security measures implemented by India. If the objectives were to draw global attention to the dastardly attack on the Indian Parliament and display Indian resolve for self-defence, then the operation was successful – but at a prohibitive cost.

The leadership was just not sure what to do and looked indecisive at critical points. They pulled back even when a decisive victory over Pakistan was assured. Jaswant Singh writes in his book that Prime Minister Vajpayee has expressed regret at not going to war with Pakistan after the terror attack on 13 December 2001, admitting that it was a mistake.[26] This is a most revealing comment.

The Military Perspective

The statements of the three military chiefs at the time bear ample testimony to their discomfort at the lack of a decision by the political leadership. When asked whether the deployment was aimed at attacking Pakistan, General Padmanabhan replied that there were many aims that were fulfilled but whenever there is a situation calling for the army's help, its role should be clearly defined to avoid confusion.[27]

Admiral Sushil Kumar of the Indian Navy has been more critical. He has stated that the government lacked any political aim or objective for deploying the army along the India–Pakistan border and has been quoted as saying that Operation Parakram was 'the most punishing mistake' for the Indian armed forces.[28] The air chief, Tipnis, had echoed similar sentiments at the time. 'We have shown enormous patience, now it is time to show we have resolve too,' he said. 'Inaction is damaging our credibility; people have begun to believe India is incapable of taking any action.'[29]

None of them can be faulted for their strong professional assessments because the government exhibited political control to the point of being oblivious to strategic military considerations. In his book *Operation Parakram: The War Unfinished*, former army vice chief Lieutenant General V.K. Sood rues that the government did not inform the military the reasons for the mobilisation and laments 'the surreal events surrounding the dismissal of a strike corps commander for overstepping his non-existent brief'.

Military leadership should be taken into confidence during national security policymaking, especially for times of war and when policies for border areas are being discussed. As a positive step, the CDS has now been placed as a member of the NSC as well as the nuclear command authority – which is tasked with decisions regarding nuclear weapons. The creation of a Department of Military Affairs (DMA) in the Ministry of Defence (MoD) seems to be another step in the right direction. However, in case of war or for its preparation, it is still desirable that the political leadership issues a written directive to the military leadership stating unambiguously what it wants of the armed forces.

Nuclear and Chemical Warfare

In his book, Jaswant Singh writes that the nuclear war alarm raised by the US and the UK was odd and that he found it entirely unnecessary. 'Why cause a deliberate scare by raising alarms about the possibility of a "nuclear conflict" or of this troops mobilisation acquiring any kind of uncontrollable autonomy?' he writes. 'This scare was incomprehensible, for a nuclear dimension just did not exist.'[30] This is further confirmation that the mobilisation of troops only served coercive diplomacy purposes. As there was little possibility of war, the question of nuclear warfare did not arise.

However, Pakistan is not known for stable governments and pragmatic decision-making. There were indications that the use of chemical weapons by Pakistan could not be ruled out. Irrespective of the likelihood of nuclear weapons being deployed, if one's adversary possesses the capability to do so, one must ensure that one's troops are prepared for their use. Protection equipment for nuclear, biological and chemical warfare must be provisioned far well ahead of time and be available for quick deployment in the field should the need arise.

Coercion vs Diplomacy

Coercive diplomacy remains an important tool to safeguard and promote the core interests of a country. During the standoff in early 2002, though the global community urged Pakistan to not allow terrorist activities on its territory, several countries also urged India to exercise restraint. India did get some support for greater escalatory action and created an international climate favourable towards coercive diplomacy. We have now seemingly come around to the views propagated by Thomas Schelling in his book *Arms and Influence* and Robert Jervis in his article 'Coercion and the Balance of Power', which state that 'the effectiveness of coercive action depends on the perceived proportionality of the response to the provocation'. The Indian policy based on conventional mobilisations was apparently disproportionate to the Pakistan-backed cross-border terrorism.

However, Indian surgical strikes in response to the Uri attacks in 2016 and the Balakot air strikes in response to the Pulwama attack in 2019 led to good gains while conveying India's resolve to defend itself. It would seem then that instead of coercion or threats, actual military action such as selective strikes may prove to produce better results. Yet, in the prevailing security environment, a military option could only be a last resort. Therefore, we need to consider a mix of measures to throw our adversaries off balance. These could include a public relations or diplomatic offensive along with covert operations to foment internal ethnic and sectarian conflicts to give Pakistan a taste of its own medicine.

Deficiencies in Equipment

Additional time was required not only to train the troops but also for making up the deficiencies in war stores. The Indian Armed Forces were still sure of causing substantial damage to Pakistan war machinery despite our own deficiencies as brought out earlier in the chapter also. The cost of going in with haste was heavy and there were large casualties even in the preparations. The defence minister reportedly stated in Parliament that as of July 2003, the army had suffered 798 fatal casualties during Operation Parakram – in contrast, there had been 527 fatal casualties during the Kargil war. The casualties happened predominantly during mining and demining operations. These were primarily because of the faulty fuses of the obsolete mines.

When the mobilisation began, Vijayanta tanks of 1970s vintage along with artillery guns that were even older were still in frontline service. It is clear that India did not have absolute conventional superiority. Analysts have pegged the overall combat force ratio of India and Pakistan during the operation at approximately 1.15:1 in India's favour. Speaking as an MP in the Rajya Sabha less than a week after mobilisation began, former army chief General Shankar Roychowdhury blamed the 'recurrent political controversies on military procurement in the last 15 years' for having 'crippled the army's modernisation programme.[31] In the kind of security paradigm that exists for us, it is most essential to always remain in a state of full preparedness and war-worthiness. We cannot afford to look for time for preparation in an event of crisis. This issue has to be addressed, irrespective of the additional expenditure that we may have to incur.

The Cost of War

While exact estimates are not available, the cost of sustaining Operation Parakram as per NSAB was ₹7 crore a day – or approximately ₹2,100 crore over 10 months. Presumably, this does not include the cost of mobilisation and de-induction nor the ₹300 crore paid in compensation to the border states where troops were deployed. Nor does it account for damage to equipment sustained in the process. Overall, the figure seems to be grossly understated.

As per estimates given by Aditi Phadnis, analyst and political editor with the *Business Standard*, in an article in Rediff.com[32] dated 16 January 2003, the cost is closer to ₹6,500 crore – while still not counting the induction and de-induction costs. In another estimate by Rajat Pandit, senior editor, *Times of India*, in 2003, the operation cost India nearly $ 4 billion but Pakistan only $ 1.4 billion.[33] The figures are varying because there is no official data available anywhere. Whatever the actual figures, the leadership should have taken the costs into consideration before commencing mobilisation. This further strengthens the point I made in the chapter on the Kargil war about India needing a comprehensive NSD or NSS, which would have prevented any knee-jerk decisions.

Conclusion

Operation Parakram has been dubbed 'the unfinished war', and many consider it to have been a lost opportunity. Even after two decades, I cannot disagree with that opinion. There were a combination of factors that prevented us from going to war, including international pressure, a lack of strategic vision, political dithering and perhaps even slow mobilisation by the armed forces. However, I am certain that a reasonably effective punishment could still have been inflicted on Pakistan.

The indecisive outcome of Operation Parakram perhaps lay in its genesis. The reaction to the terrorist attacks on the Parliament seemed to be more for assuaging the anger of the nation than any other purpose. Even the coercive diplomacy angle seemed to be an afterthought. We definitely lost the last opportunity to achieve our political aims through a decisive conventional war.

A part of the planning by the army was to capture parts of PoK to stop the terrorism for good rather than leave it to the empty promises of Pakistan. However, after the Kaluchak attack, the army wanted to go for an all-out war to solve the Pakistan problem once and for all. The concentration of all the strike corps in the Thar desert was a sure indication of that resolve. But that was not to be, despite the government making some feeble attempts to assure the military that it was serious about its objectives.

I recall that the vice chiefs of the army, navy and air force were called for a meeting with Defence Minister Fernandes at that time. We were given a two-page disjointed operational instruction document that was not really convincing. After I returned to my office, I told the army chief that the meeting was more like a process being gone through rather than a serious plan by the government.

A limited gain that Indian polity can claim is the international acknowledgement of India's position that Pakistan supporting terrorist activities is the main reason behind the troubles in Kashmir. This impelled the US and other major powers to exert pressure on Musharraf to crack down on Pakistan-based terrorist groups targeting India. However, Pakistan's stake in Kashmir is extremely high. Consequently, its motivation to persist with the policy of providing support to the jihadis is also very high. Therefore, Pakistan conceding to the Indian demand that it completely stop supporting the jihadi militants is improbable unless it is crippled militarily and financially.

Back in 2002, it knew that India did not have the option of going to war because of international pressure. The US needed Pakistan in its campaign against Al-Qaeda in Afghanistan. The Pakistanis knew that the Americans would be able to dissuade India from precipitating any aggressive action. However, it is most unlikely that India would succumb to any such pressure now or in the future, with the firm foreign policy we have presently.

New Delhi's decision to recall its high commissioner from Islamabad was rather premature. It did nothing except perhaps giving the general public some satisfaction. Instead of cutting off all contact, it is better to strike a bargain through talks combined with military pressure. India's actions seems to have been influenced by domestic and electoral calculations. However, when we should have reacted strongly to subsequent terrorist provocations such as the attack on the Kaluchak army camp, we did not. On the contrary, when this crisis erupted, international focus shifted away from Pakistan-sponsored terrorism and towards efforts to prevent the outbreak of war between the two nuclear-armed adversaries. It was an operation in which we lost nearly 800 troops with thousands wounded – casualties that in no way were commensurate to the gains. We are left wondering what the real aim and objective of Operation Parakram was.

What still remains a great concern is the risk of a nuclear war. Pakistan today is using the threat of a nuclear response against the use of conventional forces by India with reasonably good effect. It has developed tactical nuclear weapons and, as per its advocated policy, is likely to use them even against any shallow Indian gains in Pakistan. With the advent of Babur, a submarine-launched cruise missile, it is now assessed that Pakistan is also in a position to strike again after taking a retaliatory response from India to its first strike. India on the other hand is depending on a 'no first use' policy. We seriously need to consider a tweak to this policy now that Pakistan has attained second-strike capability.

However, India now does seem to be less uncertain in dealing with our neighbours. The surgical and air strikes after the Uri and Balakot incidents have sent an unambiguous message to Pakistan that India retain the right to strike anytime and anywhere should our national interests be threatened. This has also enhanced the confidence of the citizens that the Indian government will not compromise on national security.

3

Operation Khukri
Rescuing Indian Peacekeepers in Sierra Leone

> 'Peacekeeping is not a job for soldiers, but only soldiers can do it.'
> Dag Hammarskjold, former secretary general of the United Nations

IN MID-2000, the attention of the nation was on the aftermath of the Kargil war. Little was known about an unsavoury situation that was unfolding several thousand kilometres away in Sierra Leone, a small country in western Africa. Indian peacekeepers were deployed there as part of the United Nations Mission in Sierra Leone (UNAMSIL) under Major General Vijay Kumar Jetley of the Indian Army. The information we were receiving in India was that the multinational forces in the African nation were fulfilling their role reasonably successfully despite a few challenges to manage the mandate given by the United Nations Security Council (UNSC). The situation reports emerging from the UN headquarters were sketchy at best, with little indication of the events that were to follow.

In May 2000, 223 Indian soldiers and eleven military observers of the UN peacekeeping mission were held hostage in their garrison by the Revolutionary United Front (RUF), a rebel guerrilla group in Sierra Leone. Nobody in India seemed to be deeply concerned until the impasse stretched on till July, when the rebels cut off the rations supply to the garrison. That was when an operational plan had to be put into motion to rescue our soldiers. This needed an effort unprecedented in the history of the Indian armed forces.

UN peacekeepers were not allowed to open fire under the UN charter. Besides, the ragtag rebel group did not have an established commander and could not be relied upon in negotiations. The situation was further complicated by India being unable to take a unilateral decision on action because the forces were under the command of the UN, which showed little urgency to react to the situation. We had to take all these factors into account during our preparations. When diplomacy failed, we were left with no option but to break the siege and carry out a rescue mission. It was code named Operation Khukri and is best remembered for the bold decisions that led to victory.

India's Role in UN Peacekeeping Missions

UN peacekeeping missions aim to assist host countries to transition from situations of conflict to peace. Peacekeeping is distinct from peacebuilding, peacemaking and peace enforcement, although the UN acknowledges that all these activities are 'mutually reinforcing' and that overlap between them is frequent in practice. The activities are done in various ways, including confidence-building measures, power-sharing arrangements, electoral support, strengthening the rule of law and economic and social development.

The UNSC has the power and responsibility to take collective action to maintain international peace and security. As of 2022, the UN has undertaken 71 peacekeeping missions with 119 countries contributing military and police personnel to the missions. Where does India stand in this gambit of peacekeeping under the UN charter? We are one of the founder members of the UN and our policy since the very beginning has been to help this organisation and the international community to restore peace and security in troubled states across the globe. India has a long history of service in UN peacekeeping efforts, having contributed more personnel than any other country. More than 2,87,000 Indian soldiers have served in forty-nine peacekeeping missions since 1948. Unfortunately, India has lost 160 of its gallant soldiers during these missions.

We all understand that the basic role of any nation's armed forces is to defend the country against external aggression and protect it from internal threats when its national security is jeopardised. However, national interest is not limited to security alone. A country like India must aspire to have a larger say in global matters and have greater influence and control over global geostrategic and geopolitical matters. To this end, India has been vying for a permanent seat in the UNSC. This cannot be achieved by merely being a spectator to world events.

Therefore, the Indian government has been willing to send troops for UN missions while keeping in mind our strategic interests. There are distinct advantages for India to participate in such missions. It projects an image of our country as a capable and willing nation, thereby improving our chances to become a permanent member of the UNSC. It also gives exposure to our military leadership and troops to other armies of the world, giving us an opportunity to learn from them and gain experience. Despite these advantages, there are also problems that raise doubts about the purpose of sending our troops abroad. The most prominent example is the incident at Sierra Leone, where over 3,000 Indian troops were in service as peacekeepers.

Geography and Terrain of Sierra Leone

Sierra Leone is located on the west coast of the African continent. It is roughly circular in shape and has an area of approximately 72,000 square kilometres, stretching 332 kilometres from north to south and about 328 kilometres from east to west. It is bounded on the west by the Atlantic Ocean and shares borders with Guinea and Liberia.

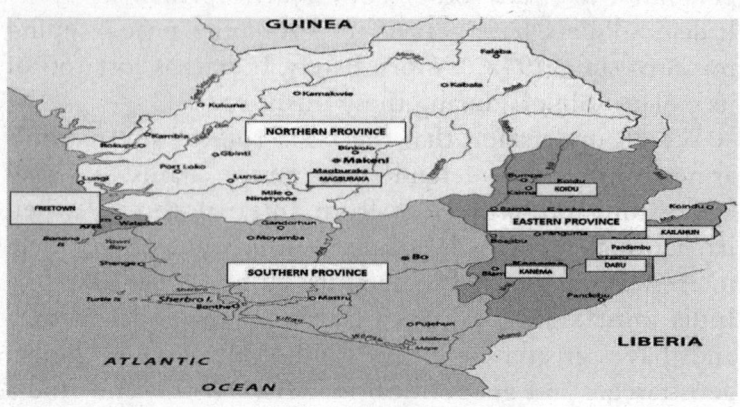

MAP 3.1 Layout of Sierra Leone
Adapted from 'Sierra Leone Maps & Facts', World Atlas. Highlights by author.

5/8 Gorkha Rifles (GR) were deployed for peacekeeping in the Eastern Province of Sierra Leone. The area is densely wooded with jungles crisscrossed by swamps and rivers, making cross-country movement extremely difficult. Swamps and rivers can only be crossed at specific spots, making it easier for ambushes to be laid by the RUF. The dense undergrowth also lends itself to sneak attacks by the rebels. There was only one unmetalled road connecting Kenewa with Daru, where 5/8 GR had their headquarters. From Daru the road further led to Kailahun, where our troops were held hostage.

This road had three concrete bridges, with the rest being log bridges – which were all potential bottlenecks and suitable for rebels to lay ambushes. The Kenewa–Daru road was around 70 kilometres long, but could not be used as it was under RUF control. Hence all movement in this area was in helicopters. Even from Daru to Kailahun, a distance of another 70 kilometres, the road was dominated by the RUF.

Civil War in Sierra Leone

The armed conflict in Sierra Leone began in 1991, but has roots dating back to the time the country was still a part of the British Empire. The UK founded the capital, Freetown, as a colony for freed slaves. Eventually, the rest of the country became a protectorate under British rule. Sierra Leone looked to have a secure future at the time. The best universities in Africa were founded in the country during the British era.

The slide to war began soon after the UK granted independence to Sierra Leone in 1961. Since social development was confined to a small ruling elite, inequality became rife in the country. Eventually, former army corporal Foday Sankoh and his RUF cadre began a campaign against President Momoh in 1991, capturing towns on the border with Liberia.

After many coups and changes of power, Ahmad Tejan Kabbah was elected president in February 1996. He signed a peace accord with Sankoh's rebels in November that year. However, that too did not last long. In 1997, the UNSC imposed sanctions barring the supply of arms and petroleum to Sierra Leone. Despite this, a British company by the name of Sandline – which was founded by ex-military officers – continued to offer military training, operational and logistics support, equipment and arms to the rebels for commercial gains.

In February 1998, a Kenyan-led intervention force from the Economic Community of West African States Monitoring Group stormed Freetown and drove the rebels out. However, fighting continued until the UN intervened. A peace agreement was signed in July 1999. It was greeted with cautious optimism that eight years of civil war may soon be over.

The Establishment of UNAMSIL

On 22 October 1999, the UNSC established a new and much larger mission after disbanding an existing group that comprised only military observers. The new mission, UNAMSIL, would have a maximum of 6,000 military personnel – including 260 military observers – to assist the government and the warring parties in carrying out the provisions of the Lomé Peace Agreement. On 7 February 2000, the UNSC revised the mandate of UNAMSIL to expand the military component to 11,100 personnel including the military observers already deployed. The mission was also tasked with greater responsibilities in civil affairs, policing and administration. The strength of UNAMSIL was increased numerous times after that, eventually going up to 17,500 military personnel including the 260 military observers.

UNAMSIL's initial mandate included the implementation of the peace agreement, disarmament, demobilisation and the reintegration of rebels. Further, it needed to ensure the security and freedom of movement of UN personnel and monitor adherence to the ceasefire. The mandate also included encouraging confidence-building mechanisms and supporting their functioning, facilitating the delivery of humanitarian assistance, supporting human rights operations and civil affairs and enabling elections.

When the mandate was enhanced, the responsibilities increased to include providing security to key locations; facilitating the free flow of people, goods and humanitarian assistance along specified thoroughfares; guarding weapons, ammunition and other military equipment collected from ex-combatants; and assisting in their subsequent disposal or destruction. The UNSC explicitly mandated the mission to 'take the necessary action within its capabilities and areas of deployment to afford protection to civilians under imminent threat of physical violence'.

The mission had troops from Nigeria (3,200), Jordan (1,800), Ghana (500), Guinea (500), Bangladesh (2,000),

Kenya (2,000), Russia (2,000), Ukraine (450) and India (3,660). The Indian contingent also had an engineer company, a field hospital, a field workshop and an aviation unit. Additionally, the IAF contributed a full-fledged, self-contained contingent comprising 212 personnel (including 33 aircrew), four Chetaks, three Mi-8 helicopters and three Mi-35 gunships.

The Indian troops were tasked with providing a guard company for the security of the UNMASIL HQ and formed a quick reaction company (QRC) for escorting convoys moving from Freetown to Port Loko and to deal with emergencies. The IAF contingent provided reconnaissance, casualty evacuation, communication, troop deployment, search and rescue air patrol and provision of air support to ground forces. Gradually Indian troops became involved in almost all mission activities. They were deployed in all parts of the country, even near the remote eastern borders with Liberia. Major General Jetley of India was appointed the first force commander of UNAMSIL.

The RUF saw the deployment of UNAMSIL troops as a threat. This should not have been the case as the rebels themselves were part of the 'Government of National Unity' of Sierra Leone as per the Lomé Agreement, which granted blanket amnesty to RUF fighters and invited them into the government. However, the rebels had a poor record of honouring agreements. The Disarmament, Demobilisation and Reintegration (DDR) program for ex-rebel combatants was central to peace resolution in Sierra Leone. Nearly 19,000 combatants were disarmed during the period before the May 2000 disturbances.

Disarmament required coordination with the warring groups and leaders. UNAMSIL secured disarmament centres and facilitated the registration of ex-combatants into the DDR program. The mission had set up five DDR Camps, with a sixth to be established in the diamond-rich areas of Koidu. This move caused considerable consternation among the rebels as it would cut off their finances and would mean the end of the road for their activities.

The deployment of UN peacekeepers to Sierra Leone had little effect on restoration and maintenance of peace. The RUF leaders were ill at ease with the growing popularity of UNAMSIL and displayed resistance to the DDR efforts in the northern and eastern provinces. Sankoh was still the leader of the RUF and also a minister in the government, having a post equivalent to vice president. He ordered the RUF rebels to renege on their commitment to the agreement.

The RUF Attacks

The situation became a flash point on 1 May 2000, when the RUF demanded that ten rebels from their cadre – who had willingly surrendered at a DDR camp at Makeni – be returned to the rebel group. This camp was under the jurisdiction of the Kenyan troops. When their demand was not met, the RUF attacked the DDR camp and the Kenyan positions at Makeni and Magburaka. They succeeded in capturing and taking hostage a number of military observers and some peacekeepers. They also laid siege to both Makeni and Magburaka, complicating the movement of supplies and the evacuation of casualties.

An ensuing military operation failed when Zambian troops were misled and captured. The rebels took about 500 peacekeepers in the Makeni and Magburaka areas as hostages. Through President Charles Taylor of Liberia, the UN entered into a protracted diplomatic discussion with the rebels. Taylor had influence over the rebels and was later said to be their de facto leader after Sankoh was imprisoned. The talks led to the UN securing the release of most of the hostages.

Targeting of Indian Peacekeepers

Even as they attacked Makeni and Magburaka, the rebels also surrounded the Indian peacekeepers tactically deployed at Kailahun. The garrison at Kailahun was targeted because its civic action programme had weakened the control and popularity of the RUF in the area. Where earlier there had been no semblance of governance in Kailahun, the Indian contingent laid a military bridge, opened medical camps, arranged clean drinking water, shared food and medicines and even evacuated civilian patients to Freetown.

However, due to the professional competence of the Indian troops, the rebels could not muster the courage to attack them. Major (later Major General) Rajat Puniya was commanding the company of 5/8 GR that was surrounded. He negotiated over fifteen times with the local RUF brigade commander but refused to agree to their demands to lay down arms. Despite being unable to force a surrender, the rebels continued with their standoff as it was the only bargaining chip that they had for future negotiations. The continued tension of being surrounded impacted on the morale of the beleaguered garrison at Kailahun.

The standoff continued for 75 days and even President Taylor failed to secure the release of the peacekeepers and military observers at Kailahun, who were mostly Indian. By July 2000, the rebels started blocking the supply of food and even casualty evacuation by road and air to Kailahun. It was necessary to end the stalemate. With diplomatic efforts having failed, the only option remaining was to resort to military action. This needed to be done as soon as possible because the impending rainy season would have made operations impossible due to the terrain constraints.

India Move into Action

By now it was quite clear to the Indian government that the situation in Sierra Leone was rapidly getting out of hand and no amount of effort by the local government or the UN would be able to secure the release of our soldiers. We had to do it ourselves. It was under these circumstances that I, as the DGMO, was instructed to lead a delegation to Sierra Leone. In the meantime, a patrol party of 5/8 GR comprising twenty-three soldiers were also held hostage at Kuiva, where they had gone to negotiate the release of our troops at Kailahun.

On 5 June 2000, I left for Freetown accompanied by B.S. Lalli, joint secretary of the defence ministry, and D.P. Srivastava, joint secretary of the UN. Enroute, our delegation visited the British Army HQ at London, the UN HQ at New York and the Foreign Office in Washington D.C. In these discussions, a few things became very clear to us:

- The operation would need the go-ahead from the UN secretary general because our troops were not allowed to open fire under the UN Mandate Clause VI under which they were deployed. However, we assumed that this should not be difficult as the UN themselves were in no position to help secure the release of Indian peacekeepers.
- The UK and the US were advising restraint but not offering any active help. These countries had no troops involved in operations on the ground in Sierra Leone and were thus not directly affected. Our delegation pointed out this hypocritical attitude to them and also told them that if they were not keen to help, we would go ahead on our own. We were disappointed by the stance of both these countries.
- We should never deploy any troops in countries where such situations could develop because our troops would get exposed to unwarranted risks. This was especially so for the areas where we had no specific strategic interests.
- Details of our operational plans should not be shared with UN officials or any other nation. The UN secretary general kept distancing himself from the problem and when he did engage, he insisted that the rescue force should be multinational, which had its own difficulties. Relationships between multinational troops were not very smooth due to conflicts in command and control and mismatched perceptions of strategic interests.

- Additional troops and resources were needed to augment the Indian contingent as there were approximately 1,800 RUF soldiers in the area around the Kailahun garrison.
- The list of required additional resources specifically included helicopters that could attack, fly at night and lift heavy loads. We also needed more artillery and engineers.

After arriving at Freetown, we had a detailed discussion with Major General Jetley and also met the commanders of other multinational garrisons. With a reconnaissance of the area of operations, we understood the topography and finalised the operational plans after exhaustive discussions. After reassuring Jetley that India would be handling the operations itself, I returned to India.

Back in Delhi, I briefed the army chief General Ved Prakash Malik and the defence minister, George Fernandes, of the grim reality in Sierra Leone. Fernandes understood the gravity of the situation and quickly agreed to the military action. He then briefed Jaswant Singh, the external affairs minister, who gave us a lecture on the geopolitical and geostrategic implications of such a military action. Both ministers were very concerned about possible casualties.

I again explained that options such as diplomatic pressure were unworkable mainly because of the lack of interest and concern from the UN and other countries. Military action was thus the only option at that stage. Of course, casualties were inevitable in any military operation – but given the condition of the RUF cadres, I did not expect there to be many. Jaswant Singh was finally convinced and said that the next step was to brief the prime minister, Atal Bihari Vajpayee. The prime minister heard us out and then said that it would be best to take the leaders of all political parties into confidence.

An all-party meeting was held in South Block in early July and among the attendees were Sonia Gandhi and Dr

Manmohan Singh, then leader of the Opposition in the Rajya Sabha. Jaswant Singh explained the political aspects of the operation and I added the military perspective. Although no operational details were given, the broad contours of the military plan were shared. The political leaders repeatedly asked about the number of casualties expected in the operation. My reply was consistent that no guarantee could be given but they were likely to be minimal considering the quality of training and equipment of the rebels.

I stated that the army was confident of successfully carrying out the rescue mission. The time had come for the humiliation and captivity of our soldiers to be ended and for them to be brought back home. The hour-long discussion was concluded with the unanimous approval of the plan. The die for the operations was thus cast. However, before the session ended, a question was asked by Dr Manmohan Singh. It was to have far-reaching consequences. He asked, 'What strategic interest of ours does it serve to have our troops there in Sierra Leone in the first place?' We had no answer to that. However, that question played a major role in our decision-making about where to send our contingents from that point onward.

Operation Khukri Begins

The Army HQ ordered an elite team of 2 Para Commandos, 18 Grenadiers, a mechanised company and an engineer company to move to Sierra Leone accompanied by attack helicopters. This was quite a sizeable force. In the meantime, Jetley used unique methods to gain intelligence about RUF deployment, strength and weapons. In one instance, a soldier from 5/8 GR pretended to be the driver of a RUF commander and gathered digital photos of areas traversed by them.

Intelligence was also gathered during the transportation of food supplies and air evacuation sorties provided opportunities to take aerial photographs. These helped not only to learn about the rebel deployments but also to find open areas that could serve as landing zones for helicopters during the operation. Therefore, by the time the additional Indian troops arrived, there was a very clear picture of enemy deployment and the terrain.

The UN still preferred to end the standoff through diplomatic means, so Jetley was asked to get the go-ahead from UN Secretary General Kofi Annan, who was visiting the capital of nearby Togo. Annan diplomatically said that the final decision to use military means rested with Jetley as he was the force commander,[1] but also insisted that any such operation must also include troops from countries other than India. The arrangement seemed to suggest that if the mission was successful the UN would take credit, but any failure would be blamed on the force commander.

The stage was finally set to launch Operation Khukri. Changes to the operation plans had to be made at the last minute to accommodate the UN secretary general's directive to make it a multinational force. Two companies each of Nigerian and Ghanaian troops were added as the multinational dimension. To maintain secrecy, final operational orders were only issued on 12 July 2000, one day before the start of operations.

The RUF had an approximate cadre strength of 1,800 rebels in this sector, while we had a total strength of about 2,000 troops. We also had an edge over the rebels with our attack and transport helicopters, artillery, mechanised infantry and special forces. The UK's Royal Air Force (RAF) agreed to work together because they wanted to rescue an observer from their country. Their Chinook helicopters heli-dropped the para commandos close to Kailahun and their C-130 Hercules aircraft blocked rebel communications. They also shared essential equipments such as digital cameras, GPS trackers and coloured smoke grenades. In addition, attack helicopters of the Sierra Leone Army were armed with 700 rockets provided by India and were flown by South African mercenaries along with other helicopters chartered from the UN.

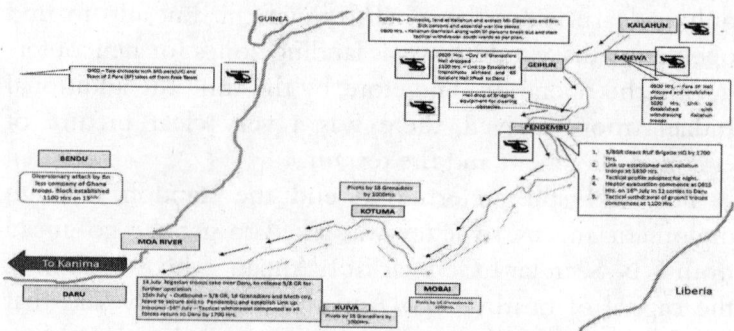

MAP 3.2 Schematic layout of the progress of Operation Khukri in Sierra Leone

Stages of the Operation

The plan was to carry out the entire operations in five phases.

Phase 1: During this phase, troops and equipment were moved from Freetown to Kenewa, the nearest airfield to Daru. Then they were transported to Daru by helicopter on 13 and 14 July. The Nigerian troops were to relieve 5/8 GR of their defensive responsibilities at Daru by the evening of 14 July. Artillery ammunition was initially dumped at Kenewa as much as possible using the available road and the rest was transported by helicopters. In order to maintain secrecy and surprise, the moves were done at the last moment.

Phase 2: It was initially planned to commence the operation on 15 July with a pre-emptive strike by artillery and attack helicopters at the RUF HQ at Pendembu and at the garrison at Kailahun. However, the RAF was reluctant to fly their Chinooks to Kailahun after such a strike and the plan had to be modified at the last minute. Artillery strikes were rescheduled to start only after the Chinooks had left Kailahun. The Chinooks, which had the ability to operate in bad weather, first dropped a team of 2 Para (SF) in the Kanewa area to act as pivot (pivot, incidentally, are troops deployed tactically around an area through which moving

Operation Khukri

columns can safely pass) and then landed at Kailahun and evacuated military observers and unwell peacekeepers. However, after rescuing their observer, the British military had no intention to participate further.

This was followed by a pre-emptive strike at Kailahun using artillery and other heavy weapons. This bombardment also used smoke at rebel positions to warn innocent civilians to evacuate from the area and thereby prevent collateral damage. At around 0800 hours, helicopters of the IAF landed one company-sized force (comprising around 120 men) of 18 Grenadiers to act as a pivot at Geihun. Simultaneously, another company-sized pivot of the QRC was landed at the three concrete bridges to secure them and prevent any response from the rebels.

At around the same time, the besieged troops at Kailahun broke out of captivity and linked up with a small team of 2 Para that was dropped by the Chinooks earlier. The RUF went berserk when they realised that their hostages were getting away. They began the chase and had to be suppressed with heavy firing, including rocket launchers, automatic grenade launchers, 51mm mortars and medium machine guns. At around 0930 hours the attack helicopters finally arrived and started strafing the rebels. It gave the escaping column some respite but the rebels kept reorganising themselves and continuously sniped at the troops bringing up the rear of the column.

However, the escapees managed to move south and reach the eighteen Grenadiers pivot at Geihun by 1100 hours. Jetley landed at Geihun and an impromptu air head (tactically secured area where helicopters could land) was established to lift sixty five personnel out to Daru. Meanwhile, the Ghanaian battalion created a diversion on the road from Kenewa to Daru in order to keep the RUF cadres in this sector tied down. They secured Bendu Junction by 1200 hours. All the while, the extricated troops column from Kailahun continued to move further south amid heavy firing by the rebels. The terrain was slushy and, in some areas, north of Pendembu bridging equipment was required. This was dropped by helicopters in the affected areas.

Earlier that day, the rest of 18 Grenadiers, 5/8 GR and a mechanised company had moved out from Daru to capture Pendembu. 18 Grenadiers moved from the south of Pendembu and cleared Kotuma, Kuiva and Mobai by 1000 hours, thereby securing the route between Pendembu to Daru as per the plan. However, the advance of the 5/8 GR troops moving to the north of Pendembu did not progress as per schedule because of stiff opposition from the rebels.

After heavy fighting, they could eventually clear the RUF HQ by 1900 hours. That meant that they could only reach the Kailahun column at 1930 hours. By then it was growing dark and the Mi-26 helicopters could not fly at night. As a consequence, the planned extraction by helicopter had to be postponed to the next day. Temporary defences for the night were prepared and were fired upon throughout the night by the RUF. However, the rebels were accurately engaged by small arms fire and 105mm light field guns and could not penetrate our defences.

Phases 3 and 4: By 0700 hours the next day, a helipad was prepared at Pendembu and troops moved from defensive positions to prepare for heli-lift. The helicopters started arriving by 0815 hours. A total of twelve sorties were flown, with the last helicopter taking off at 1030 hours. However, the RUF threat had not eased during these operations. At about 0930hours, fifty to sixty armed RUF cadres were seen approaching Pendembu. They were effectively engaged by the armed helicopters. Before the area was vacated, RUF bunkers in the basements of buildings as well as their ammunition storage centres were demolished with the help of the engineer battalion.

Phase 5: After the last helicopter took off for Daru, the road columns started to withdraw as well. The mechanised company was told to hold off till the end and bring up the rear of the retreating column after conducting a tactical disengagement. Continuous overwatch and fire support was given by an Mi-35 helicopter till the column reached Daru.

During the withdrawal process, the convoy was ambushed at Kuiva, Bewabu and Mobai – at all these places the rebels were liquidated quickly. The withdrawal was completed by 1730 hours, bringing to an end a successful rescue mission. In this operation seven peacekeepers were injured and unfortunately one of them ultimately succumbed to his injuries. The rebel casualties were estimated to be 34 killed and 150 wounded, though exact numbers are difficult to ascertain.

International Reaction

After the success of Operation Khukri, accolades poured in from all over the world. Kofi Annan wrote a letter to Jetley expressing his gratitude and admiration for the 'thoroughly professional manner' with which the Indian troops planned and executed the extraction of the peacekeepers at Kailahun. He noted that there were only a few casualties on our side and said that that was 'a clear indication of the determination of the force, as well as of its robustness in dealing with any threats emanating from the RUF'. Concluding his letter, Annan said that he was 'particularly pleased that this was a truly international operation with the participation of troops from a number of countries, which all played an essential and vital role in the operation'.[2]

The news of the success was reported around the globe – but described as a UN rescue mission. The importance of the media during military operations cannot be overemphasised. Unfortunately, the Indian media only had a limited presence in Sierra Leone and could not really portray the achievement of our forces. The BBC was the only credible news company covering the operation, but they were focused on highlighting the work done by the RAF and did not really cover the rest of the troops.

The *New York Times* reported, 'In a rare display of force, United Nations troops who picked up a distress signal today rescued all 222 peacekeepers and 11 military observers trapped by rebels inside a peacekeepers' base in eastern Sierra Leone, United Nations officials said.'[3] The action brought relief to the UN and led to a new robust stance for its military force. 'Everyone pulled together, and it worked,' said Fred Eckhard, spokesman for Kofi Annan,[4] while P.J. Crowley, a spokesman for the White House National Security Council, declared that the UN had 'conducted a bold and well-executed operation to free the peacekeepers'.[5]

The UNSC also expressed its satisfaction at the successful outcome of the operation and offered its condolences to the family of Havildar Krishan Kumar, Sena Medal, who gave his life to the cause of peace. In a statement, the council reaffirmed its belief that 'there is now a firm foundation on which UNAMSIL can build as it continues to implement its mandate and work towards a lasting peaceful settlement to the conflict in Sierra Leone'.[6] George Fernandes flew to Freetown to personally meet and congratulate the peacekeepers.

Lessons

Operation Khukri is a good example of the synergy of a multinational effort. The optimum utilisation of all resources and joint planning and execution by the Indian Army, the IAF, UNAMSIL forces and the RAF resulted in a synergy that multiplied the effectiveness of the assets deployed. Commencing operations simultaneously from Kenewa, Daru, Kailahun and Geihun gave us a further advantage by causing confusion among the enemy troops.

The RUF was successfully kept in the dark about the operation. They were led to believe that a battalion was being replaced and that is why there were additional troops coming in. No messages were passed on radio and only satellite phones were used. Code names were used for place names and the Indian troops spoke in their own native tongues to ensure the rebels could not decipher their communications.

The plan was flexible and could be changed at short notice as the situation demanded. The presence of the force commander in person meant that decisions could be taken on the spot. However, the non-availability of aerial and satellite imagery was a big handicap. Instead, real-time use of human intelligence and signal intelligence was used by the artillery and attack helicopters to engage targets. Monitoring of enemy communications over three months helped build a clear picture of their activities, reinforcements and ambush sites. These bits of intelligence were extensively used by our troops.

The dense jungles and the single road between Daru and Kailahun were problems that could be solved by using combat vehicles. Their mobility and powerful weaponry enabled the column to proceed without dismounting at most of the ambush sites. Attack helicopters were also potent assets that proved very effective in breaking ambushes as well denying free movement to the rebels by day. However, the Indian helicopters did not have night-flying capabilities and that added to the problems. We had to optimise the use of British and Russian helicopters, but they flew according to their own rules and their availability was limited and uncertain.

The operations were launched during the rainy season, which seriously impacted the mobility and observation and consequently the logistics support. The bad weather also delayed the movement of troops to their locations by helicopters. However, in operations such difficulties will always take place and have to be managed.

Conclusion

Operation Khukri brought international recognition to the Indian Army and the IAF and demonstrated their professional competence. Without much support from other nations, India carried out an operation 10,000 kilometres away from our shores in an outstanding effort that proved the mettle of our forces. The confidence of our military and political leadership could be seen in their far-reaching decision to carry out this operation.

Deploying such a large force with all its complicated logistics within a short period of time was a remarkable effort. These operations shattered the myth of RUF supremacy and brought them to the negotiating table. It enhanced the international prestige of not just UNAMSIL but also the Indian forces. India also understood that when the chips are down in UN missions, our forces will have to manage on their own. For that reason, the selection of missions must be done very carefully and approved only for places where we have strategic interests.

The greatest reward for the Indian peacekeepers was the rapturous reception given to them by the people of Daru when they triumphantly returned from the battle. It was the welcome of a long-suffering and desperate people who understood that these troops shed their own blood to keep the villagers safe. Out of respect for our forces, they built the Khukri Memorial in the Daru barracks overlooking the Moa River. However, it is an unfortunate truth that not many people in India are aware of this outstanding operation as we failed to publicise our achievement. I hope this recapitulation of the glorious Operation Khukri inspires pride in our forces and our country.

4

The LOC Fence
A Novel Strategy to Control Infiltration in Jammu and Kashmir

'Do not fight the last war.'
Miyamoto Musashi, Japanese warrior and writer

BEFORE BECOMING DGMO, I commanded IV Corps in the Northeast, where I was deeply involved in anti-insurgency operations. After my move, I shifted my focus to the militancy in Jammu and Kashmir. The nature of insurgency in the two places is totally different in intensity and mechanics. In the Northeast, it is a local, low-grade insurgency mainly fuelled by economic dissatisfaction. In Jammu and Kashmir, it is a Pakistan-sponsored militancy in which religion and territorial ambitions are the predominant motivators.

The system of militancy in Jammu and Kashmir saw militants, or jihadis, infiltrating into India from PoK through multifarious ingress points. At the same time, Kashmiri youth were regularly going to Pakistan to train with the ISI. This arrangement ensured that the strength of the militants in the state was invariably retained at optimum level despite attrition by the security forces. Also, the densely forested hills in remoter areas of the state were being used to train militants locally. However, the level of training here was not of the same standard as that being administered by the ISI in PoK and Pakistan.

The hilly and rugged terrain of Jammu and Kashmir makes it difficult to detect the movement of infiltrators. As we saw in Operation Parakram, even when army troops were deployed along the LOC in a densely held defensive posture, infiltration could still continue unabated. It was thus not a question of the number of troops deployed along the LOC. One conclusion, therefore, was well established: it was not possible to control militancy in the state until the infiltration was stopped.

TABLE 4.1 Assessed Infiltration since 2001

Year	No. of infiltration attempts	Estimated no. of infiltration attempts
Years when there was no fence on LOC		
2001	NA	2417
2002	NA	1504
2003	NA	1373
Total (Pre-LOC-fence statistics)	NA	5294
LOC wire fence was almost ready in most areas by August 2004. Notable decline in infiltration is evident in 2004 and the following years		
2004	NA	537
2005	NA	597
2006	NA	573
2007	NA	535
2008	NA	342
2009	NA	485
2010	NA	489
2011	247	52
2012	264	121
2013	277	97
2014	222	65

Year	No. of infiltration attempts	Estimated no. of infiltration attempts
2015	121	33
2016	371	119
2017	419	136
2018	328	143
2019	216	138
2020	99	51
2021 (Up to 30 Nov 2021)	73	34
Total (Post-LOC-fence statistics)	2637	4547

Source: [a]Annual Reports, Union Ministry of Home Affairs (UMHA), quoting Multi Agency Centre (MAC), https://www.mha.gov.in/en/documents/annual-reports, accessed 13 April 2023

[b]South Asian Terrorism Portal (SATP), quoting official records of the Government of India

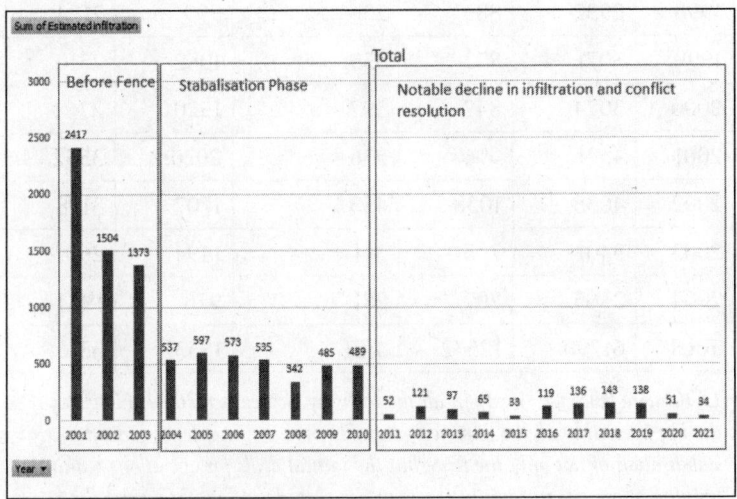

FIGURE 4.1 Assessed Infiltration since 2001

TABLE 4.2 Terrorist-related Incidents and Casualties (1988-2022)

Year	Terrorist-related incidents	Civilians killed	Security force personnel killed	Terrorists killed	Total fatalities
Initial troubled years					
1988	390	29	1	1	31
1989	2154	79	13	0	92
Total	2544	108	14	1	123
Watershed years: Launch of Pakistan-sponsored militancy in Jammu and Kashmir					
1990	4158	461	155	550	1166
1991	3765	382	173	844	1399
1992	4817	634	189	819	1642
1993	5247	747	198	1310	2255
1994	5829	820	200	1596	2616
1995	5938	1031	237	1332	2600
1996	5014	1341	184	1209	2734
1997	3420	971	193	1075	2239
1998	2932	889	236	999	2124
1999	3071	873	355	1082	2310
2000	3074	847	397	1520	2764
2001	4521	996	536	2020	3552
2002	4038	1038	453	1707	3198
2003	3401	795	314	1494	2603
2004	2565	707	281	976	1964
Total	61790	12532	4101	18533	35166

LOC wire fence was ready in all the areas by September 2004. However, the impact could only be expected gradually over the next few years after stabilisation of not only the fence but the tactical drills for operations requiring training to operate in conjunction with the obstacle system. However, the infiltration had clearly declined substantially (as seen in table 4.1).

The LOC Fence

2005	1990	557	189	917	1663
2006	1667	389	151	591	1131
2007	1092	158	110	472	740
2008	708	91	75	339	505
2009	499	71	78	239	388
2010	488	47	69	232	348
Total	6444	1313	672	2790	4775
Notable decline in level of violent incidents and fatalities, as infiltration was already reduced and number of resident militants were also brought down to suboptimal level by constant attrition.					
2011	340	31	33	100	164
2012	220	11	38	50	99
2013	170	15	53	67	135
2014	222	28	47	110	185
2015	208	17	39	108	164
2016	322	15	82	150	247
2017	279	40	80	213	333
2018	417	39	91	257	387
2019	255	39	80	157	276
Total	2433	235	543	1212	1990
Article 370 revoked in August 2019					
2020	244	37	62	221	320
2021	229	41	42	180	263
2022	457	30	30	193	253
Total	930	108	134	594	836

Source: [a]Annual Reports, Union Ministry of Home Affairs (UMHA), quoting Multi Agency Centre (MAC), https://www.mha.gov.in/en/documents/annual-reports, accessed 13 April 2023

[b]South Asian Terrorism Portal (SATP), quoting official records of the Government of India

Tables 4.1 and 4.2 are self-explanatory on the role played by the smart obstacle system (the fence) in dramatically reducing the number of infiltrations (down to approximately 33 per cent in the very first year of establishment). This resulted in reduced numbers of violent incidents and casualties, as security forces could now eliminate the residual militants without them being replenished from across the PoK.

Throughout my tenures as the DGMO and the VCOAS, I had been deeply concerned about our struggle to stop the infiltration from across the LOC. Over a thousand trained infiltrators were crossing over every year to add numbers to the locally trained militants. Even accounting for attrition, the total number of militants at any given time in Jammu and Kashmir remained 2,500 to 3,000. Locally trained militants were arming themselves with weapons and ammunition from caches placed around the state that were being continually replenished, while the infiltrating terrorists came in fully equipped with arms and ammunition. There was a vast established network for supporting the militants that provided them with shelter, food, money and fresh intelligence about security forces. The entire militancy apparatus was working like a well-oiled machine.

The terrorist casualties were between 800 and 1,500 a year, while the security forces suffered 300 to 400 fatal casualties, excluding almost equal numbers being wounded annually. For Pakistan, the loss of militants did not matter much as it continually found cheap cannon fodder in youth it had converted to religious fanatics. The cost of contracting militants or compensation paid to the families of those killed was almost negligible. Besides, the entire operation was funded by proceeds from the illegal drugs market.

However, for India it was becoming unbearable and unsustainable to lose our soldiers in such large numbers. Unfortunately, as long as this infiltration of trained militants continued there was no way to eliminate or even reduce the militancy in Jammu and Kashmir. Therefore, we had to find a new strategy to deal with the situation.

The Problem of Infiltration

During my tenure as the DGMO and then as the VCOAS, I gained a thorough understanding of the ongoing proxy war in the state. I observed the following:

- The key to the Pakistan-sponsored proxy war lay in their ability to keep the flow of infiltrators going and even increasing it every year.
- The gradual radicalisation of the youth in Jammu and Kashmir provided Pakistan with an endless reservoir of resident militants and thus it was not troubled by casualties and losses.
- The infiltrators were getting logistical support and intelligence about the security forces from a widespread network of spies and informants.
- Irrespective of the density of troops on the ground along the LOC, the rugged and hilly terrain provided the infiltrators with enough routes for safe movement.
- The infiltrators were being launched from the forward deployment areas of the Pakistan Army, where they were lodged for a day or two for familiarisation – in both daylight and night conditions – with the terrain they were required to cross.
- As a standard modus operandi, the Pakistan Army carried out small arms firing and shelling elsewhere to divert the attention of our troops while the infiltrators moved across the LOC from other areas.
- Once the infiltrators went past our forward defence line, they had a well-organised guidance system for their movement. They were helped by locals in areas extending northwards from Rajouri–Poonch.
- For our operations to succeed, we needed to eliminate infiltrators at a quicker rate than they could sneak in across the LOC. However, we were unable to match the rapid rate at which fresh militants would replace the ones we eliminated.

Therefore, the only answer lay in creating obstacle systems that would reduce the rate of infiltration to such low numbers that their operations became untenable. To do so, the infiltration had to be checked right at the LOC or within close proximity of it. The terrorists could not be allowed to get into our vast hinterland where anti-militancy operations needed a huge number of troops to achieve optimal density.

As I saw it, the army needed a change of strategy. To bring back normalcy in the state, infiltration of armed terrorists and exfiltration of local youth to PoK for training had to be stopped right at the LOC. Further, 'search and destroy' operations had to be carried out in the hinterland in accordance with well-conceived operational plans to neutralise those terrorists who did manage to infiltrate past the LOC. In addition, the locals who were becoming terrorists had to be stopped and eliminated with the help of better intelligence.

Design of the Obstacle System

In my final months as the VCOAS, I was contemplating the idea of resolving the issue of infiltration once and for all by creating an ingenious obstacle system along the LOC. This fence would aim to deter the infiltrators and channelise them to selected killing areas. It would make infiltration more difficult by stopping or delaying the movement of militants. While they tried to negotiate the obstacle system, we could eliminate them through firepower from our QRTs deployed in the immediate vicinity of the fence.

The obstacle system needed to be a modern smart fence comprising a barrier of triple rows of electrified concertina wire 2.4 to 3.6 metres high. It had to be augmented by a network of motion, laser, magnetic and electronic sensors along with thermal imaging devices. All areas of the fence had to be well-lit and supported with an alarm system. The pillars supporting the concertina wire should be numbered so that identifying the exact location of the breach would be simpler.

The sensors deployed ahead of this obstacle would act as real-time warning systems, with the signal received at the control room of the nearby platoon headquarters. From there, QRTs would be dispatched to the area where the breach was detected. The vast network of secure communications along with additional troops deployed at the fence would make infiltration impossible or a prohibitively risky venture for infiltrators. The fence would be floodlit at night up to Poonch in the South of Pir Panjal Range (SPPR) area. However, in northern areas this was not practical due to the heavy snow in the winter.

Over several months I discussed this idea informally with a number of commanders at different levels, including those in the field. After becoming the COAS, I formally broached this idea in the MO directorate and invited a free discussion. The reaction was of surprise. The VCOAS, Lieutenant General Shantanu Chaudhary, and the DGMO, Lieutenant General Bali Thakkar, considered the idea to be impractical. They thought that it would show a defensive mindset and compared the idea to the Maginot Line created by France, which was bypassed by the Germans during the Second World War.

It is generally very difficult to accept a new idea that is a complete divergence from the existing line of thinking that has been in place for years. Despite the lack of enthusiasm from my staff, I asked the engineer-in-chief to form a study group to suggest a design for the fence I had in mind. I wanted to see a blueprint of the concept that included the fence and the sensors and then discuss the idea further with the Northern Command.

The ditch-cum-bund is a defensive line created to prevent clean runs by enemy armoured formations in the plains of Jammu and Punjab. It had also been dismissed as being too defensive for many years before it was accepted as a sound idea. However, this defensive line is fully manned and would have no gaps in wartime. But the extent to which the proposed LOC fence could be manned depended on terrain considerations and the availability of troops. Even if fully manned, it was inevitable that there would still be gaps.

Offensive operations in the mountains and especially along the LOC do not take place along the entire frontage. They are generally restricted to widely displaced contact points. In other areas along the LOC, the troops continue to remain in defensive mode. The Indian Army knows that our adversary creates diversions by inducting a large number of irregulars prior to an intended conflict. This would necessitate holding the LOC fence with some degree of strength up to a critical moment. The fence would thus prove to be invaluable in interfering both with irregulars and tactical infiltration in such a scenario.

I visited the Northern Command HQ in January 2003 to have a discussion with the commander, Lieutenant General Rostum K. Nanavatty. I was accompanied by the VCOAS, the DGMO and the engineer-in-chief, who was carrying a blueprint of the proposed fence. Also present were Lieutenant Generals V.G. Patankar and Tippy Brar, the commanders of XV and XVI Corps respectively.

During the discussion, I outlined my strategy and pointed out that since all other methods had failed, a new approach needed to be tried. The army and the corps commanders too were vehemently opposed to the idea of a fence for the same reasons as the vice chief and the DGMO – that it was not practical to construct such a fence. Even after a long discussion, I could not get support for the idea.

To assuage everybody's apprehensions, I said that we would take a final decision only after we had constructed a kilometre-long trial fence at Bhimber Gali in Rajouri–Poonch sector. Brar was tasked with overseeing this effort. The engineer-in-chief explained the design of the fence before handing over the sketches. A month was allotted to finish construction of the trial fence, after which we were all to meet at the fence site to determine the pros and cons of the proposal on the ground.

Construction Begins

We met at Bhimber Gali on 8 March 2003. After seeing the trial fence, I was convinced that the full plan should be implemented. We decided that the anti-infiltration obstacle system would be built and installed as soon as possible. The alignment of the fence would not be based on maps, but according to the actual ground position as determined by the battalion commanders and approved by the brigade commanders. This was to take advantage of the intimate knowledge of the terrain at unit and brigade level and also to generate a feeling of ownership and pride for the fence among the commanders on the ground. This approach proved to be very useful.

The cost of construction would not be an overriding consideration because after the Kargil war, the government had given the army (local formation commanders) authority to improve defences and had allocated budget for this purpose. This was a very wise ruling that made it easier to get started. Additional engineer regiments were moved from other commands to assist XV and XVI Corps for expediting the construction work.

By the first week of April 2003, the Northern Command had identified the stretches to be fenced in areas North of Pir Panjal Range (NPPR) and designated 190 kilometres for Phase I. In SPPR, 100 kilometres was designated at that stage. Stretches designated for Phase II were of 110 kilometres and 127 kilometres respectively. The cost per kilometre at the time was estimated at ₹18 lakh for NPPR and ₹21 lakh for SPPR areas. The difference in cost was primarily due to the NPPR fence not being electrified, as it was not considered practical in that area because of snow. If memory serves me right, the total requirement of funds was approximately ₹50 crore. The Army HQ had allotted about ₹20 crore by July 2003.

FIGURE 4.2 Improved anti-infiltration obstable system (IAIOS) – augmenting existing standard AIOS

Extending the Scope

We had another meeting with the corps and divisional commanders in August 2003, by when there had been some changes in the command hierarchy. Lieutenant General Hari Prasad had taken over the Northern Command, Lieutenant General Ashok Kapoor had assumed command of XVI Corps and Lieutenant General Nirbhay Sharma was to take charge of XV Corps the following month.

The Northern Command had considered only those stretches of the LOC that were prone to infiltration for their initial recommendations for Phases I and II of construction. However, during our meeting in August, we decided to build the fence along the entire stretch of the LOC, starting from the Chenab River to Zoji La, a total length of 740 kilometres. The fence would extend from the plains sector to heights up to 3962 metres.

Although my decision was accepted with a certain amount of apprehension and scepticism, Lieutenant General Hari Prasad eventually became the biggest supporter of this idea of a continuous fence. The drive of the new commanders led to the speedy construction of the obstacle system. They also formulated tactical drills and standing operating procedures (SOPs) for troops on the ground to maximise the potential of the fence.

I will be candid enough to admit that I did not have total belief that this fence experiment would definitely deliver, but after four years in Jammu and Kashmir at the apex level, I was convinced that we had no alternative but to try something new to reduce the infiltration and thereby control the militancy. It was enough for me to decide to give it a serious try in an effort to attain our ultimate goal. In the military, commanders sometimes have to take tough and unpopular decisions, because the buck stops with them. Of course, such decisions are not taken whimsically because they could make the difference between success and failure, and the reputations of the commanders depends on the outcome.

I could risk this innovative experiment because I had full faith in our commanders and troops, who could be trusted to put their hearts and souls into any task assigned to them even if they were not in agreement with the decision. This is the ethos soldiers are brought up with and have in their work. I was convinced that our army's high standard of training, regimental pride, enthusiasm and ability to deliver would overcome all odds.

Widespread Acceptance of the Concept

When the construction work on the obstacle system started, there was a general feeling that it was a whimsical idea of the chief. It was only after a year that I found a perceptible change in the mood of the force. During that year, I had visited the construction sites several times to personally oversee the progress and interact with commanders and troops. However, the change of perception among the various units became most evident during the visit of the defence minister, Pranab Mukherjee.

Major General R.K. Mehta, divisional commander of 19th Infantry Division, told the visiting dignitary that when work started on this fence it was known as the 'Chief's fence' but now it was their baby and they were convinced that it would be successful. Mehta added that they were given the freedom to experiment with ideas to increase the efficacy of the obstacle. 'In this experiment,' Mehta concluded, 'we are all together.' The new commanders deserved credit for having generated this kind of drive and sense of ownership among the local troops. Lieutenant General Syed Ata Hasnain, then a brigade commander, recalls that 'units were made to compete in the construction effort' and that the 'enthusiasm by now had become palpable'.[1]

Another instance of enthusiasm among the local units was seen in April 2004, when I accompanied President A.P.J. Abdul Kalam to Bhimber Gali, where the trial fence had initially been erected. We were met by Brigadier Kanwar Vijay Singh Lalotra, who was serving his last day in command. Lalotra said to the president, 'Sir, it is my great satisfaction and pride that a sizeable fence was built in my sector during my tenure. I am convinced about its efficacy.' He continued, 'Sir, it is the Chief's eleventh visit to my Brigade in my tenure. He came to me on the first day of my command and today he is again visiting, which happens to be the last day of my command of the Brigade.' The army had thus convincingly changed their course and methodology of fighting militancy with a new strategy in which the rank and file were totally invested.

During the construction of the fence, I visited formations in Jammu and Kashmir at least once every ten days to evaluate the progress on the ground and encourage the commanders and the troops. When I was a young officer, I had learnt that giving orders was only 10 per cent of the job and 90 per cent was getting the job done. This learning remained with me throughout my military career and I have no doubt that it is applicable at all levels. I came back from each visit more reassured as I saw the fence grow along with the increasing enthusiasm for the concept.

To ensure that these visits did not add to any logistical burden, my standing instructions were that there would be no formal lunches during my visits. Only coffee and sandwiches were to be served during the briefings. At night, instead of dinner, I would have cocktails with the officers, especially the younger ones, so that I could interact with them and get their frank feedback on the fence. These visits thus helped me learn about problems, if any, and gave me the opportunity to resolve them right there.

In Internal Armed Conflict in India, Lieutenant General Rostum Nanavatty writes, 'Whilst no one believed that the "fence" would stop infiltration completely, its effect was instantaneous.'[2] He further writes, 'General N.C. Vij, the then Chief of the Army Staff, was the architect of the concept. He single-mindedly pushed for its creation. He brooked no opposition including from the author and as things turned out, he was proven right.'[3] This reflects the large-heartedness of Nanavatty, who was a true soldier.

Working Together

The portion of the fence between the Chenab and Poonch is floodlit. The lights make it as bright as daylight even in the middle of the night, and it is now a familiar and astonishing sight for fliers crossing air space from Pakistan to India at night. It is terrifying for infiltrators to be caught in those lights for three to five minutes while trying to negotiate the obstacle – if they had not already been killed by the mines and booby traps laid in the approach to the fence. The rapidly reducing number of successful infiltrations is a tribute to the effectiveness of the fence, and many had a role to play in its success.

Infantrymen along the LOC had to not only reorient themselves to operate tactically with this new obstacle system but also learn the computer systems linked to the sensors. Engineer regiments temporarily moved from their peacetime stations in other commands to help with the construction and the laying of sensors and traps. There were many others who helped with electrification, hardware, labour, planning and supervision to ensure that deadlines were never compromised. The commanders always selected the most tactically suitable alignment of the fence and oversaw all the operations at the ground level.

The construction effort was hampered by regular heavy firing including artillery from across the LOC. Our forces retaliated with double the ferocity as the commanders had been given a free hand to respond. Though this response subdued the Pakistani firing, there was still an increased risk while working on the construction of the fence. However, these exchanges of fire could not stop our progress.

Construction work had started in July 2003, but it was not till 26 November 2003 that a ceasefire agreement was reached between India and Pakistan. Until then, we were forced to align the fence more towards our side of the LOC, up to 1,500 metres deep at some places. However, it remained under our observation and domination. These parts of the fence were realigned from early 2004 onward, when it was reasonably clear that the ceasefire was likely to hold for some time. Even though the ceasefire lasted till 2006, one could not trust the Pakistanis to observe it completely even when it was in effect.

While there were many who contributed innovative ideas to augment and enhance the effectiveness of the fence, I would specifically like to mention the efforts of the Dagger Division under Major General Raj Mehta. They began the manufacture of *panjis* (wooden pickets with sharpened points). These were installed near the fence to hamper movements such as crawling and jumping by the terrorists while attempting to cross the fence. Later, Lieutenant General Hasnain replaced the wooden panjis – which had worn out over the years – with steel-planked spikes.[4]

Completion of the Fence

After an agreement on the construction of the fence was reached, it was also decided to create a smart obstacle system. This would include booby traps with improvised explosive devices and sensors. We also agreed on the specifications

'The day I started walking my walk: 4 Dogra, December 1962.'

Major N.C. Vij, Bravo (A) Company Commander, 4 Dogra, which captured Pakistan Post, Chhote Chak, in chicken neck area during the India–Pakistan war of 1971. Also in the picture is Captain Kanaujia

Lieutenant General N.C. Vij, DGMO of the Indian Army, meeting with Major General Tauqir Zia, DMO of the Pakistan Army, in Attari, 11 July 1999

National leadership honouring the armed forces, 27 July 1999. (Left to right) *Air Chief Marshal A. Tipnis, Foreign Minister Jaswant Singh, National Security Advisor Brajesh Mishra, Lieutenant General H.M. Khanna, Lieutenant General N.C. Vij and Air Marshal Vinod Patney*

Lieutenant General N.C. Vij with Prime Minister Atal Bihari Vajpayee, National Security Advisor Brajesh Mishra and Chief of the Army Staff General V.P. Malik, after a briefing at the military operations room, 1999

Indian soldiers performing the last rites of Pakistani soldiers with full honours in conformity to their religious sentiments, during the Kargil war, 1999

General V.P. Malik (left), accompanied by Lieutenant General N.C. Vij (right), addresses troops of the 8th Mountain Division after the victory at Kargil, 1999

Field Marshal Sam Manekshaw and General N.C. Vij during the first Chiefs Conclave, New Delhi, October 2004

Eight former chiefs at the first Chiefs Conclave. (Left to right in order of seniority) Field Marshal Sam Manekshaw, General O.P. Malhotra, General K.V. Krishna Rao, General V.N. Sharma, General S.F. Rodrigues, General S. Roychowdhury, General V.P. Malik, General S. Padmanabhan, General N.C. Vij

President A.P.J. Abdul Kalam and General N.C. Vij at the base camp in Siachen Glacier, April 2004

Wreath-laying at Khukri War Memorial built by the people of Daru in Sierra Leone

The Improved Anti-Infiltration Obstacle System

Night view of a part of the Anti-Infiltration Obstacle System along the Line of Control in South of Pir Panjal Range

The Manekshaw Centre in New Delhi, India

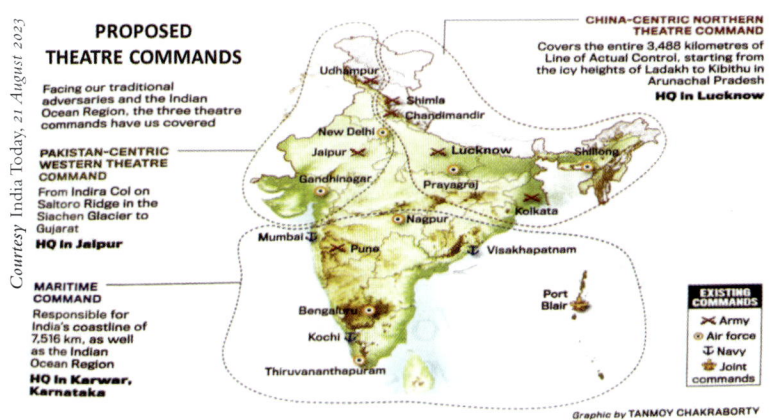

Layout of proposed theatre commands

A road named after General N.C. Vij after his retirement at a civic function organised by the state of Jammu and Kashmir, 2005. It runs along the main arterial route from the state assembly hall to Kachhi Chawni radio station in Jammu

General Vij and Mrs Vij

General and Mrs Vij's family at their house in Texas. (From top left) Son, Nalin Vij; daughter-in-law, Maneerat Tanasarnsaenee; granddaughter, Rhea Vij; and grandson, Nimit Vij

of electrification, lighting and command and control equipment. The mobilisation of resources for a task of this magnitude was one of the biggest challenges.

During the construction, the combat engineers of the Northern Command were supplemented by six engineer regiments (16 Field Companies) from outside the Northern Command by October 2003. These were organised into eight task forces. Approximately forty tippers and fifteen bulldozers were inducted from other commands. It took over a year to complete construction of the entire fence – a total length of 740 kilometres. The initial deadline for the fence to be completed was May 2004. However, it was only completed by 30 September that year.

Nearly 3 lakh tonnes of stories were required for the construction of the fence and it was essential to procure them within a limited timeframe. The mountainous terrain and inclement weather impinged upon construction work during the winter, especially in the NPPR area under XV Corps. Therefore, the bulk of the construction resources were moved to the SPPR area under the jurisdiction of XVI Corps during that time. This effort required over 10,000 porters and 3,000 ponies daily – an astounding task that was managed effectively.

Lieutenant General Hasnain writes in an article that the magnitude of effort that was required to build the fence is difficult to understand. During summer at the LOC water dries up soon, so the troops had to move further down the mountainside each day to get water – not just for cooking and washing but also for curing the cement required in construction. At Gulmarg, the Jammu and Kashmir tourist department came to our assistance by allowing us to use the gondolas of the ropeway during the off-season and even at times during the tourist season. There the snow was so deep that the area had to be dug to align the fence before construction.

Maintenance

Due to the extreme weather conditions in the NPPR area, there is often large-scale damage to the fence. This is especially true after heavy snowfall. The annual damage is approximately 25 per cent of the fence in the NPPR, compared to 8.5 per cent in the SPPR area. Annual maintenance costs range from ₹40 to 50 crore. The maintenance is undertaken by the Northern Command with nine additional porter companies. If required, engineers are brought in from outside the command. From 2016 onward, the government has allocated three additional engineering regiments (Territorial Army) for improving the fence while conducting maintenance tasks.

FIGURE 4.3 Challenges of maintenance of IAIOS

Criticism

One of the criticisms that the fence has received is about its cost-effectiveness. It has been quoted that the annual cost of repairing the fence is approximately ₹150 crore. However, that figure is inaccurate. The actual annual cost for XV Corps to maintain the fence was on average ₹25 crore, and even lesser for XVI Corps. If the fence did not exist, the deployment of an additional number of troops – maybe a division or two – would have been required to achieve the same reduction in cross-border infiltration as was being managed since the fence went up. This would have cost much more in economic terms, not to mention that those troops would have to be redirected away from training for their operational roles and peacetime tenures, and were likely to incur casualties.

More importantly, if the fence did not exist, our losses in fatalities and other casualties would have remained at pre-fence levels. The cost of human life should never be equated in any calculation and our troops cannot be treated as mere cannon fodder. The statistics speak for themselves – the fence has drastically brought down infiltration and thereby militancy. If the fence had not been erected, the situation in Jammu and Kashmir would not have been anywhere as stable as it is today. As per the department of tourism website of the Union Territory of Jammu and Kashmir, nearly 21.18 million tourists visited the Union Territory of Jammu and Kashmir in 2023. This is directly because of the assurance of safety brought about by the improved security situation.

Another criticism of the fence is that its maintenance has had an adverse impact on the winter stocking of forward locations. However, winter stocking is done during summer, and any refurbishment work on the fence is invariably completed well before the onset of the summer season because the infiltration attempts commence at that time. Thus, the maintenance of the fence does not clash with the winter stocking, which commences much later.

There have also been some persisting allegations that the fence is an example of a defensive mentality. Nothing could be farther from the truth. What the armchair critics do not realise is that the presence of the fence has infused a sense of confidence in our troops when it comes to small-team operations, which are inherently offensive.

Some critics have also confused the LOC fence with the IB fence. They are not the same. The latter fence runs along the IB primarily in the plains sector and was constructed by contractors in a non-hostile environment at an exorbitant cost. It took a number of years to complete, unlike the LOC fence that was constructed by our own troops in just over a year, despite being built over a mountainous terrain and in a hostile operational environment.

Improvements

It is important to keep improving our existing systems. The Indian government has approved the establishment of a Comprehensive Integrated Border Management System (CIBMS) for round-the-clock surveillance of all the borders through advanced technology. Several pilot projects were sanctioned under the proposal. Lieutenant General P.C. Katoch, former Director General of Information Systems, Indian Army and a prolific writer on military matters, has said that the Indian Army tried three new designs for a hi-tech modular fence in 2014 — one provided by the Snow and Avalanche Study Establishment (SASE) and two prepared in-house by the army. Testing the efficacy was done by constructing a one-kilometre-long trial fence in Kupwara during winter.

In the new design, strong circular poles were used instead of the traditional iron pickets. Also, it used a new type of concertina coil that had a double-twisted galvanised mesh added to either side. The proposed design was modular, which would make it easier to repair. Due to the improved material used, the new fence was considered to be more robust than the existing fence. It would have the same sensors, traps and alarm systems but with enhanced technology such as visual map displays linked to control rooms.

The entire fence would not be replaced with the improved one. The augmentations would be made during the replacement of broken sections, or where new alignment was required, depending on the availability of funds. The fence would be illuminated by LED lights supported by generators in the NPPR. The government sanctioned three new engineer battalions (Territorial Army) for continuing construction and maintenance of the new fence. The new battalions were inducted in March 2016 after training.

Certain mined areas would need to be refreshed as old mines would have become dysfunctional or displaced. Improvements were also needed in the traps and sensors. There are also some thoughts of changing the position of the fence in certain areas. Since the subject is sensitive and classified, not much data is available in the public domain and it is not possible to know the exact upgrades to the fence and their status.

Conclusion

From 1990 to 2002, we kept trying to tackle infiltration by putting more troops along the LOC but did not get the desired results. Doing more of the same was obviously not the answer. However, when the new idea of a fence with an obstacle system was raised, most felt that the magnitude of effort required to build such a fence was likely to be beyond the capabilities of the troops. There were also concerns about how long it would take and how much it would cost, not to mention the constant firing and shelling by Pakistan that would make the task even more difficult.

However, once the decision was implemented, everything fell in place. The construction was completed in a short duration thanks to the grit and determination of our soldiers and commanders at all levels. But for their immense contribution, this concept could not have become a reality. They truly lived up to the culture and ethos of our great Indian Army.

Since the fence and obstacle system has been in force, the situation in Jammu and Kashmir has moved from the stage of conflict stabilisation to conflict resolution. Matters are improving rapidly. The success of the LOC fence shows that nothing is unattainable once you have made up your mind to succeed.

In challenging decision-making situations like this, commanders feel left alone in the ring, with the burden of responsibility entirely on them.

5

Cold Start Doctrine
Securing India

'Opportunities multiply as they are seized.'
Sun Tzu

Pakistan had always enjoyed the advantage of faster deployment due to shorter distances of its cantonments from the border. India found itself wanting when it wanted to react speedily against Pakistan after the attack on Parliament in December 2001, due to long distances the strike corps had to travel.

Until Operation Parakram, the Indian army's offensive operations doctrine was to employ the massive combat power of its three strike corps. However, deployment took time because of the movement of strike corps from hinterland to operational areas, with all the logistics support. It thus became clear that this was operationally disadvantageous. We just could not afford to have any deployment periods of over ninety-six hours as it would give our adversary the upper hand.

The doctrine in place for operations against Pakistan till then was to advance deep into enemy territory with the aim of quickly destroying one or both of Pakistan's army reserves in the north and south and thereby its war machinery. The philosophy operationally divided Pakistan through the middle by either undertaking offensives in the desert sector or striking at politically important centres. This concept was evolved in 1981 and tested during Exercise Digvijay when General Krishna Rao was the army chief. It was further refined for offensive operations in the plains sector during Exercise Brass-Tacks in 1987, when General Krishnaswami Sundarji was the chief.

It was a strategy of conventional defence comprising two parts. The first part was a dissuasive one entailing a strong defensive position based on ditch-cum-bund, canals and nodal points, which would impose high attrition on attacking Pakistani forces should they manage to pre-empt the Indian action. The second part of the strategy was a counteroffensive at a time and place of India's choosing. The certainty of heavy damage to the strike forces of Pakistan was intrinsically the deterrent part of the operational doctrine.

This doctrine was found to be workable when it was evolved. However, two subsequent developments introduced a new dimension to the warfighting scenario. The first was General Zia-ul-Haq launching a proxy war in Jammu and Kashmir in July 1989 with a view to counter conventional asymmetry by 'bleeding India through a thousand cuts'. The second was Pakistan achieving nuclear capability in 1998. These developments challenged the credibility of a deterrence based on conventional superiority and counteroffensive capability.

The earlier doctrine was thus unsuitable in the changed environment because the enormous size of the strike corps had made them slow to deploy and manoeuvre, leading to a lack of strategic surprise in their deployment. Once the strike corps mobilised, their progress and destination could be easily tracked by Pakistani forces or by their allies such as China. This allowed the enemy to suitably position their reserves to counter the offensive. The lack of integral offensive capability within the holding corps meant that there was a total dependence on the strike corps for any offensive action. This was proving to be a great limitation.

Cold Start Doctrine

The discussions on addressing these limitations started in October 2002 immediately in the wake of Operation

Parakram. We soon realised that apart from the inordinately long time taken for deployment, operations under the then existing doctrine would risk crossing Pakistan's nuclear threshold. A nuclear threshold is briefly defined as 'the point in war at which a combatant brings nuclear weapons into use'. Though the exact contours of Pakistan's nuclear threshold are unclear, in 2001 their former head of strategic planning, General Khalid Kidwai, delineated four generic 'redlines' to define their nuclear policies. These were (i) spatial threshold, determined by the loss of large territories; (ii) military threshold, crossed by the significant destruction of land and air forces; (iii) economic threshold, triggered by economic strangulation; and finally (iv) political threshold, brought into play if there is political destabilisation or internal subversion at a large scale.

However, Pakistan is an unpredictable country whose continual endeavour has been to thwart any Indian counter strikes in retaliation for Pakistan's unabated acts of terrorism. They have been trying to neutralise India's conventional superiority by threatening to use nuclear weapons and having learnt that by projecting irrationality they can leave their opponents uncertain about their intent.

After I took over as the army chief, I constituted a study group under Lieutenant General Bhopinder Singh, who was commanding II Corps at that time. Bhopinder had worked closely with me during the Kargil war. The study group was tasked with examining and recommending (i) practical and operationally feasible solutions aimed at reducing the mobilisation time of all formations, (ii) allocation of additional resources to the holding corps to enable them to undertake multiple limited offensives within ninety-six hours and build shallow bridgeheads up to 10–15 kilometres inside enemy territory. These objectives would be attained while remaining below the nuclear threshold of Pakistan. It was estimated that eight to ten such limited offensives would give India enough territorial gains, which would provide an advantage at the negotiating table later.

Such a scenario would also create a dilemma in the minds of Pakistani leadership as to which bridgeheads would India expand subsequently with its offensive formations and where should they place their reserves to counter our strike corps.

The study group submitted its report three months later. Among its major recommendations was the creation of Integrated Battle Groups (IBGs) that could be speedily deployed. They would go straight for their preselected objectives inside enemy territory while exploiting the element of surprise. These forces would consist of two to three infantry battalions, one or two mechanised battalions and armoured regiments and a medium artillery regiment with air support and defence cover. Thus, each IBG would comprise an overall force of six to eight battalions or regiments – the exact composition was variable and would match the task at hand.

To achieve this, the holding corps needed to be restructured with the additional offensive force potential built into them. Independent infantry and armoured brigades located in corps zones would have to be placed under the command of the holding corps, which would then be redesignated as 'pivot' corps. These could start the operations with their integral resources even while the strike corps were deploying.

From the seven holding corps and three strike corps available along the western borders, we could create up to ten IBGs for the initial attacks. However, for the strike corps to be speedily utilised, many of their elements – especially mechanised forces – should be relocated closer to the borders for much quicker deployment. A similar method of rapid deployment for offensive operations was required for the mountain sectors along our western borders. These formations too needed to be located in the close vicinity of their operational areas. However, the scope of operations by these troops in the mountains would have to be somewhat limited due to the terrain.

After exhaustive discussions with commanders at various levels, these recommendations by the study group were approved for implementation during the Army Commanders' Conference in May 2004.

The establishment of the headquarters of South Western Command at Jaipur and IX Corps at Yol were also approved by the government during a CCS meeting in January 2005 to meet the requirement of forces as per the new doctrine. Being accretional forces, their resources were authorised over and above the existing force level. This was a major development that owed a lot to Pranab Mukherjee, who was the defence minister at that time. It greatly facilitated the overall command and control structure of the army.

The concept and procedure for speedy deployments in the mountain sectors was also developed as a part of this doctrine, which was named 'cold start'. However, we decided to keep the information about the cold start doctrine under wraps and not mention it outside the armed forces to retain its element of surprise. General Padmanabhan, my predecessor after his retirement, had hinted at developing such a doctrine in an interview in which he said, 'You would certainly question why we are so dependent on our strike formations ... and why my holding corps don't have the capability to do the same tasks from a cold start.'[1]

The former defence minister Jaswant Singh once said, 'There is no "Cold Start doctrine". No such thing. It was an off-the-cuff remark from a former chief of the army staff. I have been defence minister of the country. I should know.'[2] No army chief spoke about the doctrine until General Deepak Kapoor hinted at it in 2009. In January 2011, General V.K. Singh all but admitted the existence of the cold start doctrine at a press conference in New Delhi.[3]

In 2017, General Bipin Rawat responded to a question on the cold start doctrine from *India Today*. He was asked, 'Is the Cold Start doctrine instituted after Operation Parakram in 2001 still a choice in response to attacks like the one on Parliament in 2001 or 26/11 in Mumbai?' Rawat replied, 'The Cold Start doctrine exists for conventional military operations. Whether we have to conduct conventional operations for such strikes is a decision well thought through, involving the government and the CCS.'[4]

Between 2004 and 2010 India carried out ten exercises to refine the concept of the cold start doctrine. The first of these exercises was 'Divya Astra' in 2004 and the final one was 'Yodha Shakti' in 2010. These exercises enhanced the Indian military's capability for executing operations based on the cold start doctrine during any contingency. Quick mobilisation both in the mountains and the plains and supply of logistics behind enemy lines were practised to ensure that immediate and unhindered attacks on Pakistan could be executed simultaneously at multiple points. After evaluating the objectives achieved during these exercises, it can be concluded that India has convincingly tested and established synergy and integration among our armed forces for quick and robust offensive operations.

We had also practised and tested fighting capabilities for both day and night operations; surveillance and reconnaissance behind enemy lines; air mobility; logistics buildup; and operations by mechanised armour, artillery and infantry as battle groups. Besides this, we had also conducted exercises in nuclear, biological and chemical warfare and operations involving the navy's maritime commandos and para-dropped troops. All these elements were essential for swift offensive operations under this doctrine.

We are convinced that space exists for a conventional conflict with Pakistan. General Malik has publicly stated that there is a space between proxy war and the nuclear option 'within which a limited conventional war is a distinct possibility'.[5] Remaining within the redlines of Pakistan's nuclear threshold may lead some to label it a 'limited war'. However, since we plan to strike at a number of places, that label may not be correct. Wars are limited only up to the point international borders are crossed. After that, what shape they take and the extent to which they spread cannot be predicted. A lot would also depend on the opponent's reaction and how far they are prepared to go.

After the joint commander's conference in 2004, I had submitted a detailed paper to the government to raise a strike corps for the mountains to enable an 'offensive defence' posture along our northern borders. On 17 July 2013 – nearly nine years later – the CCS approved the proposal. It was a pragmatic move that would send a strong message about our capabilities in the Himalayas. The new XVII Mountain Strike Corps was established in January 2014.

The raising of HQs South Western command and HQs IX Corps were also approved during my tenure to attain a balanced operational posture. My last task on the last day of my office was to issue the execution orders for the raising of these formation HQs. This proposal was approved by the CCS that same morning.

Pakistan's Reaction

Though India had conceptualised the cold start doctrine in the wake of Operation Parakram, it did not formally announce it. When Pakistan eventually got wind of it, it realised that its nuclear posturing through defining nuclear thresholds had been undone by the Indian strategy of opting for multiple shallow offensive thrusts over a wide front. It immediately began to recalibrate its response strategy and carried out four 'Azam-i-Noh' (New Resolve) exercises from 2009. These were Pakistan's biggest drills in twenty years.

General Ashfaq Parvez Kayani, the Pakistan Army chief at the time, claimed that the Pakistan Army 'cannot be caught unawares and is capable of responding to the challenge' of the Indian military's cold start doctrine.[6] Since then, Pakistan has claimed that it is constantly improving its surveillance, reconnaissance and electronic warfare capabilities to carry out swift operations both by day and night. Its National Command Authority frequently meets to enhance the cooperation and understanding between the political leadership and the military. Pakistan is developing inter-service harmony and coordination to handle modern warfare, and its army and air force are primarily focusing on joint operations. It feels that these steps would bring it closer to mitigating the threat of India's cold start doctrine.

Pakistan has also developed tactical nuclear weapons (TNW) for use in the battlefield. Dr Zaffar Khan, the executive director of Baluchistan Think Tank Network, is of the opinion that these weapons have been developed to deter Pakistan's enemy from 'unleashing its juggernaut military aggression against Pakistan'. In an article published in *Express Tribune*, he writes that 'if the rival underestimates the deterring value of these TNWs while attempting to pre-empt these weapons, then such an episode could create potential risk of escalation to strategic instability between the rivals'.[7]

Pakistan believes that its nuclear weapons act as a protective shield against India's conventional superiority. It is convinced that it can use its TNWs to stop India's armoured thrusts and the development of a nuclear-capable short-range surface-to-surface missiles has given it further misplaced confidence. These weapons are not effective in stopping armoured thrusts because they are effective in small target areas and the casualties would be negligible. A large number of weapons would be required by them to neutralise a bridge head of 10–15 kilometres. For this it is important to know that Pakistani stocks of TNWs are somewhat limited. Also, Pakistan needs to factor that even when TNWs are used, these would bring a massive retaliation from India in accordance with our nuclear doctrine.

General Kayani has stated that 'proponents of the use of conventional forces in a nuclear overhang are charting a cause of dangerous adventurism whose consequences can be both unintended and uncontrollable'.[8] Pakistan's misconceived notions and miscalculations can create a hazardous situation in the subcontinent.

Developments since 2020

After developing the cold start doctrine and testing it through various training exercises, the Indian Army has incorporated the lessons learnt by appropriately revising battle procedures. It is known from open sources that many units and formations have been moved closer to the border in new infrastructure built for them. In the absence of a clear political directive in the form of a National Security Strategy (NSS), the armed forces have started military restructuring as they deem suitable. This is, however, still a work in progress.

There have been three major developments during this transition period. The first was the Indian government's decision to appoint a CDS. The post became functional from January 2020. The second was commencement of work on the process of 'Integration' and 'Theaterisation'. The third event was the Chinese intrusion in eastern Ladakh in May 2020, which convinced India that the problem with China is nowhere near settled. It merits greater attention especially given the reality of the China–Pakistan nexus. We should therefore also plan and develop some offensive options against China as it would help us have a strong deterrent posture.

After countless discussions and war games, the shape of the future structure of the armed forces has started crystallising. Of the three services, it is the army that is likely to undergo a major churn. The work is progressing slowly but steadily, though there are still many questions to be answered. We must move deliberately rather than risk unbalancing ourselves in an endeavour to speed up the process.

The Myth of Short Wars

There is a misconception about limited or short wars. For instance, the Kargil war, though confined to a particular sector, had resulted in the entire army being deployed. We were prepared to fight all along the India–Pakistan border if we were not successful in recapturing Kargil heights. The operational strategy of multiple shallow thrusts by IBGs should not be misconstrued as a 'short' war either.

Rear Admiral Sudarshan Shrikhande writes in a *Times of India* blog, that 'wars are rarely short and decisive' especially when seen through 'the prism of political objectives'. He points out that terms such as 'grey zone' or 'hybrid warfare' may have been coined recently, but they are 'age-old realities'.[9]

The present army chief, General Manoj Pande, has stated that 'border-management infirmities can trigger wider conflict' and that 'grey zone aggression' is increasingly becoming the preferred strategy of conflict prosecution with its scope enhanced by technological advancements. 'Self-sufficiency in critical defence technologies and investments in R&D is an inescapable strategic imperative,' says Pande, who believes that India needs to be prepared for a 'full-spectrum conflict' for long durations instead of short wars.[10]

The Role of IBGs

Ever since they were conceptualised in 2004, IBGs (then conceived as battle groups) have been at the heart of the cold start doctrine. They were formed in peacetime as a permanent arrangement by merging independent armoured and infantry brigades with artillery and some elements of strike corps in the vicinity. The operational objectives for the IBGs were predesignated so that they could plan and rehearse for them during peacetime. They were to operate directly under the respective pivot corps.

IBGs will still form the core of the revised structure, though in a somewhat modified shape. There are numerous differing reports on the process of creating and restructuring the Indian Army based on IBGs – including speculation that the entire army will be restructured into IBGs, thereby doing away with brigades and divisions. General Pande is quoted as saying in May 2022 that the purpose of restructuring our existing formations into IBGs was to have forces that are lean and agile. That would afford the commanders flexibility in their deployment.[11] On Army Day in 2023, Pande said, 'We are converting our forces into IBGs, which will contribute effectively to modern warfare.' He added that 'old establishments and units' are being dissolved or 'revamped with suitable changes'.[12]

Reports suggest IX Corps is practising the new formations for operations in the plains on the western borders with Pakistan while XVII Corps is also practising for operations along the northern borders with China. It is certain that the army will test the efficacy of the new IBGs through wargames, exercises and critiques before finalising any reorganisation.

The question of how to best employ the strike corps still remains under debate. Probably I Corps will remain with Northern Command to meet the challenge of Chinese intrusions in eastern Ladakh. The possible mode of employment of the other two strike corps (II and XXI) is still under deliberation.

Conclusion

The belief that even the use of our conventional forces will draw a nuclear response from Pakistan may result into escalation along the nuclear ladder. The responsibility and risks of such a misstep will lie squarely on the shoulders of Pakistan. Both countries have developed second-strike capability. In such a case, Pakistan, being only one-fifth the size of India, would be fully destroyed. Of course, India too would have to face severe consequences. So, it is in the interest of both countries to avoid a nuclear conflict altogether. India would do well to keep our operations below Pakistan's nuclear threshold.

India considered developing TNWs – which is well within our capability – but it was finally considered undesirable because once a nuclear conflict starts, the escalation would become difficult to control. Hence, TNWs would serve no purpose. I believe that India's present nuclear doctrine of no first use but allowing for massive retaliation to inflict unacceptable damage will deter Pakistan from indulging in any gamesmanship and uncalled-for adventurism.

While our nuclear policy is fine, I feel that it must carry a small caveat that should India get verified information of an imminent Pakistani nuclear strike, we would retain the right to pre-empt that strike. The Pakistanis have to be convinced that India means business and that we will not hesitate to put our strong nuclear deterrence to use in case of any mischief by them. Pakistan will have to learn to stop exporting terror to our territory and not be rash enough to use their TNWs, even in their own territory, to ward off an Indian retaliatory response.

India is moving steadily ahead in developing our capabilities for the cold start doctrine to improve our own offensive posture and put off our adversaries. While this restructuring is being progressed, the army elements that are not immediately affected should not be disturbed and continue to function as before in order to retain balance. The changes must be in phases and well thought through. The IBGs concept, which started in 2004, has progressed into now becoming an integral part of the evolution of the Indian Army's process of theaterisation.

6

Jointness, Integration and Theaterisation
Developing Cross-domain Cutting Edge

> 'The only thing harder than getting a new idea into the military mind is to get the old one out.'
> Sir B.H. Liddell Hart, military theorist and historian

AFTER THE FINDINGS OF the Kargil war review committee were published, there was a lot of emphasis and focus on 'higher defence management'. It led to the creation of the post of the CDS, which was a prerequisite for ushering in the institutionalised concept of jointness and integration, because till then all three services were fighting their battles in isolation. In early 2003, there were numerous discussions on the possible roles and responsibilities of the CDS. All three military chiefs were deeply involved in these conversations. This was just after I had taken over as the army chief, so I am completely familiar with the thought processes behind the scenes.

When it seemed that the announcement of this reform was imminent, the proposal was surprisingly shelved. No reasons were disclosed, but rumour had it that a particular political party did not want to implement it. The idea however persisted and has always remained in focus. Incidentally, there was initially not much interest in the post of the CDS because the retirement age was sixty-two at the time, which was also the retirement age of the chiefs. No chief wanted to leave his own service for a truncated tenure as CDS. This anomaly has now been addressed and the retirement age for the CDS has been changed to sixty-five or a tenure of three years, whichever is earlier.

Background

Threats to national security manifest across multiple domains in an orchestrated manner. As a nation, we continue with our efforts to optimally integrate our armed forces and synergise their functioning not only among themselves but also with other agencies handling national security. Addressing this fundamental need rightly tops the agenda of national defence reforms, particularly since the first CDS took office in January 2020.

The Indian armed forces have been operating 'jointly' and have acquitted themselves well in all previous operations, such as the wars of 1965 and 1971, Operation Pawan in Sri Lanka (1987), Operation Cactus in Maldives (1988), Operation Vijay in Kargil (1999) and Operation Khukri in Sierra Leone (2001). However, the realities and challenges of the present-day operational environment highlight the necessity to graduate from mere 'jointness' to an advanced level of 'integration'.

In the Indian context, future external threats are likely to be characterised by multidomain conflicts of varied duration and geographic extent. Other factors to consider would be the use of limited or all-out force within the nuclear backdrop and the increased employment of critical and emerging technologies such as cyber space and artificial intelligence. Such an environment requires swift and dynamic responses entailing calibrated management of the escalation ladder straddling military and non-military verticals. Deeper integration of the armed forces is thus essential.[1]

Ironically, this vital defence reform is receiving focused attention only after over seventy-five years of Independence in a country that laid the foundation of its armed forces on the concept of jointness. After Independence, the joint training of military cadets of all three armed forces was carried out at an interim training academy known as the 'Joint Services Wing' before they proceeded to their respective academies for specialised training.

In December 1954, India was the first country in the world to set up a tri-services military cadet training establishment — the National Defence Academy. This jointness imbibed in the formative years of the nation continues to be seen at various levels of seniority with officers and troops of the three branches of the military attending training courses at various tri-services academies together with paramilitary forces (PMF) and civilian cadres.

These academies include the Defence Services Staff College, which trains officers in operational staff duties; the Military Institute of Technology, which conducts technical courses; the Military Intelligence Training School and Depot that imparts training to all ranks in intelligence and security; the College of Defence Management, which teaches contemporary management concepts and practices; and the National Defence College, which guides flag-ranking officers in the study and practice of national security and strategy. Besides these, each branch of the military has a war college to train officers in higher command responsibilities.

However, despite these career-long interactions between the three branches of the military, jointness has not been institutionalised and has not permeated into the cultures of the individual forces. This is because the structure of the forces allow for very few tri-services appointments, and consequently the three branches do not always have a deep professional understanding of each other. Modern warfare requires enhanced levels of synergy and understanding between all branches of the military and the civil bureaucracy.

Areas of cooperation would include threat assessment, operational planning, wargaming, training, logistics coordination and defence acquisitions, among others. However, the current organisational structures do not lend themselves to synergised operational planning and coordinated utilisation of resources. The forces do not act jointly to achieve national security objectives because each service essentially operates in silos defined by their own threat perceptions and operational doctrines.[1] Thus, there is a lack of a comprehensive and well-rounded perspective among those responsible for planning and formulating strategies for national security.

However, the Indian military has established a few integrated tri-services organisations that draw personnel from all the forces. These include Andaman and Nicobar Command formed in 2001 and Strategic Forces Command in 2003. The latter controls nuclear assets under the nuclear command authority. In addition, we have the Defence Cyber Agency that is responsible for cyber and electronic warfare, the Armed Forces Special Operations Division (AFSOD) for special operations and the Defence Space Agency (DSA) for space warfare and intelligence. These organisations were all established in 2018–19 and have very important and decisive support roles.

The Indian security paradigm has undergone several changes since Independence because the security challenges facing us are varied and complex. We have two unsettled borders where we have fought four major wars – and the undeclared war in Kargil. For the last thirty-five years, India has had to combat terrorism perpetrated by militant and terrorist groups sponsored by our neighbours to the west. These factors mean that we should often take a fresh look at our security requirements and restructuring.

The need for defence reforms to attain a higher degree of jointness has been highlighted by studies and reports from the Kargil Review Committee (2000), Group of Ministers (2001), the Task Force for Review of the Management of Defence, popularly known as the Arun Singh Task Force (2001), the Naresh Chandra Committee (2012), the Shekatkar Committee (2015) and the Defence Planning Committee (2018), among others. There is thus no need to reconsider or hesitate in our efforts to achieve greater jointness and integration. However, what needs to be deliberated upon is how to do it correctly in the Indian context. Another question that merits consideration is how this needs to be done at the apex and theatre levels.

Tense Security Environment at the Borders

India has hostile nuclear-armed neighbours such as Pakistan, where there is a real possibility of radical or fundamental elements gaining access to these weapons of mass destruction (WMDs). It is therefore very important to comprehensively understand the geography and nature of the threats to our national security. These have to be at the core of any conceptual reforms or restructuring of our armed forces.

The primary threats to India are from China and Pakistan, with a great possibility of a combined threat from a Sino–Pak nexus. Both these countries have common and overlapping interests, especially after the construction of China–Pakistan Economic Corridor (CPEC). It is also widely understood that China has been using Pakistan as a strategic tool to keep India tied down and in return has supported Pakistan in every international forum on all issues. As a result of this nexus between them, a combined threat is definitely high on India's list of problems.

The Complex Relationship with China

The Chinese People's Liberation Army (PLA) moved into Tibet in 1950. For the first time in history, the Chinese had a permanent military presence at India's border. Tibet was no longer a buffer state and China became our immediate northern neighbour. In November 1959, the Chinese premier Chou En-Lai made it clear that China disputed the McMahon Line in the northeastern sector and the Kunlun boundary in their western sector and said that his country wanted to renegotiate the entire India–China border. He described the McMahon Line as an illegal vestige of colonialism. The seeds of conflict were thus sown.

While visiting Delhi in 1960, Chou suggested that China might recognise the McMahon Line as a border if India accepted the Chinese claim line up to the Karakoram watershed. If we had agreed to this, the border would have moved from the Kunlun mountain range to the Karakoram watershed and would have given China strategic depth along the Aksai Chin road between Xinjiang and Tibet (now known as the Chinese national highway 219).[2] However, India did not agree to the proposal.

Subsequent developments worsened the relationship and in 1962, the two nations went to war. It is somewhat true that efforts were subsequently made by both sides to return to peace. The question for India was on what basis was peace being offered. Accepting the Line of Actual Control (LAC) appeared to be the only option despite the two nations disagreeing on the LAC at several areas.

China's quarrels with India in the Himalayas has three inter-related dimensions: (i) Disputes over the border; (ii) Disagreements over Tibet; and (iii) Frequent military skirmishes along the perceived boundaries. This has resulted in confrontations in at least thirteen places where the patrolling lines of the two countries overlapped. In 1993, India and China reached the first of five agreements to maintain the status quo along the LAC pending an eventual boundary settlement. India insisted on a provision that both sides would mutually find an agreement on the LAC.

In a follow-up meeting on 29 November 1996, there was an agreement on military confidence-building measures and both countries also agreed on partial demilitarisation of the disputed border. It was reaffirmed that 'neither side shall use or threaten to use force against the other by any means or seek unilateral military superiority'. However, the LAC clarification process for the western sector broke down 'an hour into the meeting' in 2002, according to Sutirtho Patranobis, who wrote in an article in *Hindustan Times* on 29 September 2020 that since then, the process 'has been stalled'. This has also been stated by Shivshankar Menon in his book. He writes that the process of 'LAC clarification has effectively been shelved since 2002' and that India, therefore, does not have an agreement with China over the delineation of the LAC.[3]

A special representative mechanism on the India–China boundary question was constituted in 2003 and has had twenty-two rounds of meetings. The mechanism was to follow a three-step formula for the settlement of the boundary. The first step was to establish the political parameters and guiding principles, and it was completed with the signing of an agreement in 2005. The next step was to establish the framework for a final settlement. This phase started in September 2005, but the talks are still ongoing. Once that is concluded, the final step would be to delineate and demarcate the boundary.

The maps exchanged for the clarification of the LAC were never attended to by China at any stage including during my tenure as the COAS. In hindsight it is clear that it was not interested in settling the border problem anytime soon. Things have become much murkier since then. China published a map in August 2023 that shows the entire Indian state of Arunachal Pradesh as a part of its territory and even giving Chinese names to sixty-two Indian villages over four years in 2017, 2021, 2023 and 2024.

The current Ladakh crisis suggests that India–China relations are darker and more complex than most observers acknowledge. It is tempting to ascribe the current difficulties between the two countries to the memories of previous wars and the unsettled borders. It is true that these two factors affect the thinking in both New Delhi and Beijing and make them suspicious of each other. But why has the conflict between these two nations stubbornly refused to go away? Kanti Bajpai, who is one of India's finest experts on international affairs, has tried to explain this in his book *India versus China*.[4] He identifies four 'drivers of conflict' being the rationale behind the problem.

According to Bajpai, while both India and China had admired the other during various periods until about the fifteenth century, since the late nineteenth century their perceptions of each other have been mostly negative. Here Bajpai is referring largely to the perceptions of the elite in both countries. The influence of colonial thought as well as ignorance and racism on both sides have produced mutual feelings of disdain.

Another driver of conflict is the differing viewpoints on the border lands and Tibet. In fact, this is at the heart of the India–China conflict. Military moves in the Himalayas continue to complicate the relations between the neighbours.

If India and China had been partners internationally, they would have had a history of strategic collaboration to balance out the negative perceptions of each other and their conflicts at the perimeters. They would also have been better placed to reassure each other when disagreements occurred. However, both civilian and military leaderships on either side have lacked robust structures of trust and communication. This pattern looks set to continue. The last issue that Bajpai identifies is that India has increasingly lagged behind China in terms of economic, military and soft power since the early 1980s.

China now feels that it is in a different league. This power inequation can be a possible big trigger for a future conflict. India's increasingly friendly relations with America and Europe is treated with suspicion by China. It aspires to be the number one power in the world and therefore cannot tolerate India standing shoulder-to-shoulder with it in its own immediate neighbourhood. It is unhappy that India is managing to project our strategic autonomy.

There exists a perception that China's primary target is Taiwan. However, given that Taiwan has the explicit support of the US and its regional allies, any move by China on the island nation is unlikely. This possibly makes India the primary target of the Chinese hegemonic design. At the same time, the growing friendship between Russia and China in the wake of the Ukraine war is adding to the concerns for India. These new geopolitical realities appreciably increase the distrust between the two countries.

The Chinese threat can manifest in the continental domain, mostly through our northern borders. In the maritime space, the area of threat includes not only the Indian Ocean but also the South China Sea, through which 60 per cent of India's trade flows. Threats are also likely to manifest through cyberspace. When considering the Chinese threat on land, we often visualise the application of the 'salami slicing' technique (nibling series of small areas, finally adding to a larger gain) that has been the Chinese practice since 1962, but there is every possibility that the war extends over the entire frontage. India would have to generally fight a dissuasive battle at the land borders.

The maritime space of the western Pacific Ocean and the Indian Ocean is together referred to as the 'Indo-Pacific'. The Indian Ocean is now more closely drawn into the US regional security calculus, hitherto confined to the erstwhile Asia-Pacific construct. It is also the primary area of concern for India, because we occupy a pivotal position in the Indian Ocean region dominating the sea lanes across the Malacca Strait – a position that could choke the Chinese navy's access to the Indian Ocean.

While the deployment and effort of the US and their allies would remain focused on the East China and South China seas, they could take advantage of the nucleus provided by our navy in the Indian Ocean should a contingency arise. This is a guiding rational for the US to support India's maritime capability development and for the Indian Navy to develop interoperability with other maritime forces, including those belonging to the European nations now venturing into the region.

China has made great strides in militarising the potential of cyberspace and artificial intelligence and uses them as tools to enhance the potential of the PLA. It has an entire branch of its military devoted to these domains. It is important for India to remember that technology will be the deciding factor in future wars and presently China is way ahead of us in that field.

The Unending Confrontation with Pakistan

What keeps Pakistan in a permanently belligerent mood against India even when we have always wanted peace with them? Pakistan argues that the cross-border terrorism is a consequence of the poor state of India–Pakistan relations. To them Kashmir is the root of all troubles and finding a solution to the Kashmir issue is the magic panacea that will ease all tensions between the two neighbours. To my mind, this conclusion is certainly not sound. Pakistan suffers from an existential threat. For Pakistan, this festering problem with India has been a diversion used by politicians to unify its citizens ever since it became an independent state.

India takes issue with Pakistan's use of cross-border terrorism as an instrument of state policy. Its segmentation of 'good and bad' terrorists is just not acceptable to us. Our relation with Pakistan has been an albatross that has hobbled Indian diplomacy and enabled other powers such as China to gain leverage in the subcontinent.

India sees Pakistan as a failed state. However, according to Menon, 'Pakistan sees India as hegemonistic and expansionist and continues to feel that the partition of the subcontinent is unfinished and Jammu and Kashmir must belong to them.'[5] No matter how much India tries to resolve this issue, this problem is likely to stay for the foreseeable future. With Pakistan almost becoming a vassal state of China, the security paradigm for India is likely to continue being complex.

India has to thus be prepared to fight simultaneously with China and Pakistan. When the ongoing hybrid war in Jammu and Kashmir is added to the mix, India's operational challenge rises to two-and-a-half fronts. India is perhaps the only country in the world that has such heavy operational challenges from unfriendly elements in its neighbourhood.

The Way Forward

There is a definite need to think of all the possible solutions and holistically prepare for a serious problem that is not going to disappear anytime soon. India's policy of peaceful coexistence has always led us to try to resolve these problems diplomatically but firmly. Ideally, we must reach an understanding with both our adversaries. At the very least, we must settle the differences with Pakistan. Serious attempts had been made to do this during the time when Dr Manmohan Singh and General Musharraf were leading their respective countries. However, things did not work out in the end. The issues with China are more complex and will need perseverance and continued political dialogue to find a lasting solution.

For these reasons, there is an urgent need for us to prepare our armed forces to fight wars of the future. The 'power gap' between us and China needs to be reduced. Having said that, the lack of parity between the two nations is reduced in some areas in which India has an advantage over China. For example, in the continental domain, the Indian Army has an edge over the PLA. Our army is battle-hardened and with unmatched standards of leadership, training and motivation. The terrain also provides us with a great advantage as we know how to gainfully exploit it. The confrontation in eastern Ladakh has proved these points.

We are already in the process of improving our jointness, integration and command-and-control structures by introducing theatre commands. The border infrastructure that is so essential for warfighting is also in the process of being improved. These steps will take some time to complete. However, even when all this is in place, there is still much more to be added. We still have to rapidly modernise our armed forces, make up the shortfalls in critical stores, lay emphasis on learning modern warfare and introduce advanced weapon systems.

It is a truism that friendships form only among equals, so India has to reach that position of parity with China to hope for friendly relations with them. Thus, we have no choice but to invest more in our armed forces. Organisational reforms and preparedness will have to be achieved simultaneously as we don't have the luxury of time – especially in view of China not wanting to de-escalate the recent Ladakh confrontation. Only a higher level of preparedness could help us reach a reasonable settlement on the issue.

Jointness and Integration

Though there exists a subtle distinction between 'jointness' and 'integration', the terms are often used interchangeably.

These concepts are a collection of doctrines, platforms and capabilities of the different military services that transcend 'the core beliefs and assumptions of any particular service' and is 'exemplified by the effective integration and employment of the different services capabilities and competencies within a unified command structure'.[6]

Jointness must be ingrained in the minds of military officers as it relies on their understanding of the capabilities of the other services and the potential benefits gained by joint efforts. They have to move beyond the strongly instilled cultural beliefs of their own service and adopt new values and beliefs. The Joint Doctrine of the Indian armed forces states that jointness 'implies or denotes possessing an optimised capability to engage in joint warfighting' with 'a high level of cross-domain synergy'.[7]

Therefore, jointness can be seen more in spirit than in structures. It entails cross-service cooperation in all dimensions. The three military services maintain their respective identities, command and control and yet coordinate their operations seamlessly with each other during operations, planning and training as well as for communications and logistics.

Integration seeks to merge the military services under a single commander but without the loss of their individual identities. It would apply to 'contemporary military across all operational domains of land, air, maritime, cyberspace and aerospace' as per the Joint Doctrine, which also states that 'it does not imply physical integration'.[8] Integration also requires collaboration beyond the armed forces, keeping in mind diplomatic and economic factors at strategic, operational and tactical levels including with partners and allies.

When India successfully liberated Bangladesh during the war of 1971, the land, air and maritime services operated jointly. Despite being operationally successful, it did not lead to better integration among them. This was a factor in operational impediments faced during the Kargil war. The impact of this divergence is likely to manifest more acutely in future wars as each service endeavours to expand its domain and reinforce its primacy in that area.

However, jointness cannot simply be discussed theoretically in peacetime with the hope that it would be successfully practiced during war. While the current environment provides for carrying out joint training when required, the level of jointness achieved would be much greater once an integrated command system is instituted. It must be said, however, that the Indian armed forces are moving deliberately and steadily in that direction.

India's Command-and-Control Structure

Until recent reforms processes were set in motion, the higher defence structure in India had undergone only marginal changes since Independence. The structure is based on a three-tier system, with the top two tiers being the CCS and the defence minister's committee. The third tier controlling military operations is the COSC, which has been headed by the CDS since 2020. In theory, the COSC is the highest authority on operational military matters in the country. However, its major shortcoming – as was also pointed out by the GoM report – is that it still exercises no real power over the individual Services of the military.

Under the current charter, the CDS serves as the chairman of the committee but cannot exercise any military control over the chiefs of the three military services and hence no worthwhile decisions can be taken easily as there is a possibility that each chief may want to protect his turf and reject proposals that would not suit his Service. Therefore, the appointment of a chairman provides no distinct advantage over the erstwhile COSC in operational matters. The three services chiefs are required to advise the defence minister only on matters concerning their respective Service, which results in the lack of a coherent message. Also, the CDS as the chairman of the COSC would have served as the commander of only one of the services and therefore cannot be expected to have complete domain knowledge of other services.

There is currently no clearly defined and structured headquarters tasked with assisting the COSC to exercise integrated operation control. Therefore, it is apparent that as of now the delays in decision-making and its implementation shall continue. Timely decision-making and its implementation can make the difference between winning and losing a war. The COSC needs flexibility and maturity from its members, all of whom must approach the issue at hand with the single aim of achieving integration. The system can work only with open-minded understanding and discussion.

Another thought is that the chiefs' role should be limited to raising, training and sustaining. To my mind this will amount to wasting the immense knowledge that the chiefs carry. The CDS by himself may not be able to strategise, finalise and execute the operational plans.

Beyond the top three tiers of our defence structure lies the fourth rung of command and control – the Command HQs. There are seven such HQs for the army and the air force and three for the navy. Additionally, there are two tri-services commands – the Strategic Forces Command and the Andaman and Nicobar Command – which are led in rotation by a commander from one of the three services. Some more functional commands may also come up in the future as part of restructuring, for example, tri-services training command, defense space command, and tri-services logistics command, etc. The HDs and infrastructure for these shall be found from with the existing command HQs. .

The Command HQs have been created based on geographical operational requirements with all the subordinate field formations required to operate with jointness and in tandem. Interestingly, none of the HQs are co-located in any area, as if done deliberately to avoid intruding on each other's domain. However, with improved communications this may not prove to be a major drawback.

Defining National Security Strategy

As mentioned earlier, India needs to define its NSS to close the gap in strategic planning by defence forces. This shortfall gets further compounded by a lack of clear political direction, as was seen during Operation Parakram. The major military reform of integration is being held back by the absence of an NSS. The varying individual perspectives of the military services leads to many contradictions.

In March 2023, former army chief General M.M. Naravane delivered the General K.V. Krishna Rao Memorial Lecture at Delhi, in which he stated that unless an NSS was in place, 'all talk of theaterisation was simply putting the cart before the horse'. He went on to add that theaterisation is only a means to an end and 'must be specified first in the form of a national defence strategy'.[9] General Naravane was in command until a couple of years ago and was closely involved in the planning of the process of theaterisation.

It will be worthwhile to hear the views of the other chiefs as well. There have been some reports that the Defence Planning Council headed by the current NSA, Ajit Doval, is expected to submit a draft NSS to the government. There is also talk that the government does not want to be bound to any one strategy by committing itself in writing. But all of this is just speculation.

The next steps for integration – and consequently, theaterisation – include assessing national threats and fixing military objectives; empowering the CDS and the COSC and providing the committee with an operational secretariat to manage operations during war; laying down an unambiguous chain of command to control operations, starting from the COSC to theatre commanders and field formations; finalising the numbers of theatres; upgrading other integrated tri-services organisations in non-combat domains, such as AFSOD and DSA; creating tri-services structures for joint logistics, training and human resource management; and ensuring common capability development among the three services. Further to this, all intelligence services must be brought under a single agency at the national level for removing gaps in information during warfare and for real-time collation, synthesis and dissemination of intelligence.

Action on these issues are already being taken, but they need to be refined further. Integration of the three services is just the beginning of improving our nation's security structure from a military point of view. As a next step, there should be integration with the PMF and the CAPF. We need to go beyond the MoD to integrate with other ministries and stakeholders involved in national security affairs.

How Will Integration Further Our Capabilities?

Integration and jointness in the Indian military aims to address the fundamental aspects of doctrinal and operational cohesiveness towards common national military objectives. Organisational restructuring will allow joint capabilities to meet operational demands, while joint training will lead to better understanding of the culture, ethos and functioning of other services. Developing logistics compatibility and prioritising capability development would be the key drivers in the ongoing defence reforms.

Why is integration necessary when jointness exists? In an article, former COAS General Deepak Kapoor writes that 'integration is a step ahead of jointness in ensuring a synergised approach to operations'. In jointness, allocation of resources needs approvals from individual services, but in integration, resources from all three services 'already stand allocated to the appropriate commander'. Kapoor further explains, 'In jointness, the employment of a resource is a subject of debate and discussion at a crucial time, while in integration, its employment is immediate, based on the commander's appreciation of the operational situation.'[10]

There is always a tendency to hold on to old systems that one has been working with for a long time. However, we need to get out of the status quo to overcome the problems in India's current model of jointness. Some issues with the old system are listed below.
- It leads to an anomalous autonomy of each military service with little participation by the other services.
- It stymies interoperability as the geographical zones of responsibilities of the various operational commands of

the three services have no perceptible commonality. In most cases, the command of one service overlaps or is linked with two or three commands of the other services, causing problems in urgent situations.
- It augments inter-services friction, as the commander responsible for execution of the task does not have control over all the forces that are deployed whereas the authority providing supporting forces is not responsible for the success of the operation.

In modern warfare where dynamics and domain may change swiftly, it is imperative for the military services to be interoperable. This is possible only through a secure, reliable and robust defence communication network interconnecting the three services at various functional levels. However, presently the system has no such inter-services communications.

The current system aims to achieve jointness in times of war, but at present this cannot be done because of the lack of commanders and staff trained in a joint-services environment who could function in an integrated manner. The continued inability of the system to impart this training and the lack of integrated staff billets are also impediments to the process of achieving jointness. Military hardware has also become extremely costly, so it is essential that its procurement and induction should follow critical analyses of priorities and cost-benefit considerations. This is only possible under an integrated planning system.

These factors have been debated and considered in various proposals recommending enhanced jointness and integration. The ultimate aim is to take advantage of specialisation in different domains using core competencies, resources and knowledge in an integrated manner to achieve the national military objectives.

Integration Worldwide

United States of America: The US has land borders only with Canada and Mexico, neither of which poses a threat. The

Department of Defense is responsible for military operations through Unified Combat Commands (UCCs) in various geographical theatres around the world. The UCCs are joint military commands consisting of forces from multiple military branches. There are currently 11 UCCs, seven of which are geographical and the rest functional. In addition, US forces have seven combat support agencies.

In 1986, the American armed forces were reorganised by the Goldwater–Nichols Act. Since then, the chairman of the Joint Chiefs of Staff – a committee comprising eight chiefs of their various military branches – does not possess operational authority over troops or other units. Instead, he is the chief military advisor to the president and the defence secretary. Responsibility for conducting military operations goes from the president to the defence secretary and then directly to the commanders of the UCCs, and thus leaves the Joint Chiefs of Staff the task of providing procedural and war-management support.

The primary responsibility of the various chiefs is planning, ensuring personnel readiness and training their respective services for combat. However, as members of the chiefs committee they are also responsible for operational planning. These branch chiefs are also sometimes included in the final decision-making process by the defence secretary or the president.

United Kingdom: The strength of the British armed forces is only two lakh including volunteer reserves. That makes them about one-sixth the size of their Indian counterparts. Being an island nation, the UK does not have hostile land borders. Its command structure emanates from the Crown, but de facto military authority lies with the prime minister and the defence secretary. The CDS is the most senior officer of the armed forces and is the principal military advisor to the defence secretary.

The responsibilities of the CDS include setting strategy for defence, future development and the conduct of operations as a strategic commander. All three military services have their own respective chiefs. The UK has joined hands with

France to create the 'Combined Joint Expeditionary Force' and with seven other countries to create another similar force to conduct operations beyond its territorial areas.

Russia: The Russian armed forces have experimented with command-and-control structures starting in 1992 and then further restructuring in 2010 and 2014. Their branches include the ground forces, the navy and the aerospace forces, among others. The forces are directly controlled by the Security Council of the Russian Federation, a constitutional consultative body of the Russian president. In mid-2010, military districts and the navy's fleets were formed into four Joint Strategic Commands. In 2014, the Northern Fleet was also reorganised as a separate Joint Strategic Command. Thus, Russia has five geographically divided Joint Strategic Commands, besides other functional commands.

China: The most relevant to India of all foreign forces are the Chinese ones. China restructured its armed forces based on the defence white paper it published in 2015. The restructuring focuses on jointness, particularly in view of the rebalancing of US policy in the Indo-Pacific region. President Xi Zinping also holds the post of chairman of the Central Military Commission (CMC), which makes him the commander-in-chief of the PLA. The control runs from the CMC to the Ministry of National Defence and then on to the theatre commanders.

China has optimised its available resources by amalgamating its seven military regions into five theatre commands. Unlike the operations of military regions, the theatre commands no longer directly administer the troops in each region. Instead, they focus on joint command of the forces and are in charge of all non-nuclear operations within their geographical areas.

The Western theatre command primarily focuses on the land borders with India, while Southern – which has the naval component – is responsible for operations in the maritime domain of the Indo-Pacific. The three other theatre commands are Eastern, which is focused on eastern China, the East China Sea and the Strait of Taiwan; Central, responsible for the Mongolian, Russian and North Korean borders; and Northern, which handles north-central China, the capital region and the national strategic reserve. The Western theatre command is the strongest, and the one closest to India.

The PLA Special Strategic Force – complemented by cyberspace and electronic warfare resources – is a major force multiplier which leverages technology to fight the non-contact, asymmetric wars of the future. China's 2019 defence white paper reiterates their intent to further the integrated development of the 'mechanisation and intelligentisation' process and speed up the development of an intelligent and integrated military force structure.

Pakistan: Following military failures in the India–Pakistan War of 1971, a commission led by Hamoodur Rahman, chief justice of Pakistan, recommended establishment of the Joint Chiefs of Staff Committee (JCSC) to co-ordinate all military work and oversee joint missions and their execution during operations. It comprises the Chairman Joint Chiefs of Staff Committee, the chiefs of army, air force and navy, and exercises control over military from the Joint Staff Headquarters (JS HQ). Technically, the JCSC is the highest military body. The chairman, who outranks all other four-star officers, is the principal staff officer to the prime minister. In times of war, he acts as a military advisor to the prime minister for supervision and conduct of joint warfare. Besides, he is the advisor to the president, the Cabinet and the National Security Council. He, however, does not have operational command over the armed forces. The JCSC deals with joint military planning, joint training, integrated joint logistics, and provides strategic directions for the armed forces; it periodically reviews the role, size and condition of the three main service branches; and it advises the civilian government on strategic communications, industrial mobilisation and formulating defence plans. However, it appears that despite this arrangement it is the army chief who rules the roost.

In all cases where militaries underwent restructuring, it has taken approximately fifteen years, if not more, for the new systems to fall in place. India too is likely to take at least five to seven more years to operationalise the proposed theatre commands. We also need to hasten the process, but only with great deliberation and without losing operational balance at any stage whatsoever.

The Integration Process in India

Our lack of integration emerged most glaringly during the Kargil war. In previous wars the services chiefs could make up for this inadequacy, but now there is a need for a proper system to be put in place. The weaknesses in the functioning of the COSC has been highlighted by the GoM report, which also recommended the appointment of a CDS.[11] The primary aim of this appointment was to bring about jointness within the armed forces in all spheres including planning, training, logistics and communications. It was also expected that the CDS would render single-point military advice to political leadership and administer the strategic forces and other tri-services commands.

The hope was that more effective planning would ensure optimal and efficient use of the available resources. The report further stated that the capabilities of the armed forces can be 'enhanced significantly, if rather than operating as three individual entities, they operate with a high degree of jointness and in tandem'. In the two decades since that report was published, the complexities of the modern battlefield have intensified and the need to integrate has increased manifold.

In a continuation of these efforts, the MoD formed the Shekatkar Committee in 2015 and tasked it with recommending steps for enhancing the combat potential of the armed forces and for optimally utilising the defence budget. In its report, the committee recommended the creation of three theatre commands: Northern Theatre Command for the China border, Western Theatre Command for the Pakistan border and National Maritime Theatre for the sea borders.[12] The committee, however, did not dwell on the methodology of this reorganisation, leaving it to the MoD and the services.

Chief of Defence Staff

On 15 August 2019, Prime Minister Narendra Modi announced the new post of CDS from the ramparts of the Red Fort. He said, 'Our forces are India's pride. To further sharpen coordination between the forces, I want to announce a major decision. India will have a chief of defence staff. This is going to make the forces even more effective.' The post was finally established nearly two decades after the initial recommendation.

The formal notification on the appointment of the CDS was issued on 24 December 2019[13] and spelt out the charter, mandate and functions of the CDS. There was also an announcement about the newly created Department of Military Affairs (DMA), which was placed under the CDS. The accompanying press release outlined the aims of the CDS and the DMA, which included promoting jointness in the armed forces for procurement, training and staffing through joint planning and integration of their requirements. It was also to facilitate the restructuring of military commands for optimal utilisation of resources by bringing about jointness in operations, especially through the establishment of theatre commands.

The CDS was declared the permanent chairman of the COSC, with responsibilities for administering and commanding tri-services organisations and agencies. The post was also tasked with implementing jointness within three years of the first CDS assuming office and augmenting the combat capabilities of the armed forces. It is likely that the Andaman and Nicobar command may be subsumed in Maritime theatre command. However the Strategic Forces Command is likely to be retained as an independent entity.

Importantly, it was also declared in the same notification that the CDS will not exercise any military command over the three service chiefs in order to provide impartial advice to the political leadership.

These announcements set into motion further reforms in jointness and integration. Through the establishment of the DMA, the three military services were successfully integrated with the MoD, thereby fixing a long-standing issue. The task for creating integrated structures thus fell on the first CDS, General Bipin Rawat. However, he unwittingly sparked speculation within a couple of months of assuming the position when he prematurely went public with plans that were not yet discussed and vetted.

During an interview in February 2020, about forty-five days after being appointed, Rawat announced, 'We will have theatre commands by 2022.' He went on to add that though he hadn't yet spoken to the service chiefs, the 'decision has to be taken by someone'.[14] However, these plans for integration and theaterisation were stalled when Rawat sadly met his unfortunate end in a helicopter crash near Wellington on 8 December 2021. It took nine months for the government to appoint a new CDS, with Lieutenant General Anil Chauhan taking the chair on 30 September 2022. He is the incumbent as of writing.

Before Chauhan's appointment, the government had revised the criteria for the post of CDS through gazette notifications on 6 June 2022.[15] The revised criteria called for a three-star officer or a retired general under the age of sixty-two. However, positioning such an individual over the serving chiefs is not an ideal arrangement. Whether this policy is a success or not will be determined by the tenure of the present CDS. This should only be an exception and not become a rule.

Likely Theatre Commands

After prolonged discussions, it appears that a decision on theatre commands has been reached by the CDS and the chiefs. Although no official announcement has been made, as per media reports the salient points of the agreement are as follows:

- The Pakistan-centric Western Theatre Command would stretch from Saltoro Ridge at the northern end

Jointness, Integration and Theaterisation

of Siachen Glacier to the mouth of Sir Creek in Gujarat, covering 3,323 kilometres. Its headquarters would be in Jaipur, where the infrastructure of South Western Command already exists.
- The China-centric Northern Theatre Command would cover the entire 3,488 kilometres of the LAC, starting from the heights of Ladakh to Kibithu, the easternmost area of Arunachal Pradesh. The headquarters for this theatre command is expected to be in Lucknow, where the army's Central Command HQ is located.
- The third theatre command would be Maritime Command, proposed to be located at Karwar in Karnataka. The infrastructure for this mostly exists. It will cover the entire coastline of 7,516 kilometres in the Indian Ocean region. However, according to the media reports, the likely location for this HQs may be Combinator. Being away from the coastline, this may not be a suitable place.
- In this case, according to my assessment, the land-based theatre commands would be headed by a commander each from the army and the air force.
- Maritime Command would be led by a naval commander.

Questions Resolved and Unresolved

The biggest impediment in the process of finalising the theatres was the decision on an Air Defence Command, in which even the air force lost their erstwhile enthusiasm. Their present point of view is that most of their aircraft – such as the Mirage, MiG-29, Sukhoi and the newly inducted Rafale – are ideally suited for offensive actions and thus should not be used only for defensive roles. It was further argued that an Air Defence Command would divide limited air assets between defensive and offensive operational roles.

Additionally, in this concept, the close air defence elements of the strike corps would have been placed under the proposed Air Defence Command. This is undesirable as the absence of their own close air defence would have hampered the tasks of the strike corps across the border. Overall, it is a wise decision to discard the concept of an Air Defence Command. Individual IAF commands will now join theatre commands based on their location.

There still remains the question of whether the army's current Northern Command – which looks after the borders with Pakistan in Jammu and Kashmir and tackles the militancy in the erstwhile state – would be able to function efficiently as a part of the vast new Western Theatre Command, which will have four present commands (Northern, Western, Southern, South Western) under it.

The government has resolved issues regarding legal powers of joint services organisations by passing the Inter-Services Organisations Bill, 2023 in Parliament. This legislation bestows powers on the commanders-in-chief – or any other officer heading a tri-service organisation or a theatre command – to take disciplinary and administrative action against personnel under the respective laws of the three services, that is, the Army Act, 1950, the Air Force Act, 1950 and the Navy Act, 1957.

For the theatre commands, there is a need for officers with experience of working across the domains of the three services. To increase the numbers of such officers, a reworking of the human resources policies is currently under way. The military branches have already cross-posted over a hundred officers to other services to enable them to understand how the other services function.

Command and Control Procedure

The government's initial definition of the role of the CDS specifically said that it will not be responsible for operations. However, it was later decided that the theatre commanders will report to the CDS. I believe that it is better if the theatre commanders report to the COSC through the CDS, as it will come with the advantage of the combined knowledge, experience and wisdom of the three chiefs.

The COSC would forward their recommendations to the defence minister's committee, who will further submit it to CCS headed by the prime minister. On all other tri-services matters, other than operational, the CDS as principle adviser, would report to the defence minister, providing a single point of advice. However, if there is a major difference of opinion, all three chiefs should be included in the discussion. The chain of nuclear command authority stays the same, as does the functioning of the operational command headquarters.

Building Blocks for Integration

Defence Acquisition Procedures and Integrated Capabilities Development Plan (ICDP): The fifteen-year 'Long-Term Perspective Plan' has been replaced by the ICDP, which covers a period of ten years. The plan may be divided further into two five-year defence capital acquisition plans or a more immediate rolling two-year acquisition plan. This necessitates a realistic look at India's security threats, the available military budget and the military hardware required to mitigate the threats. The most important step in the process of integration is prioritised capability development that keeps within the defence budget.

The terms for this have been set in the charter of the CDS, who has been tasked with overseeing decisions on prioritised acquisitions for capability development. It may lead to some heartburn when a big-ticket purchase seen as important by one of the military branches is put on the backburner according to the decided prioritisation. This problem will of course have to be resolved amicably.

Department of Military Affairs: The creation of the DMA under the MoD in 2020 was an innovative reform that integrated the military services with the ministry for the first time. With the CDS now vested with the power of the Secretary to the Government of India and placed at the helm of the DMA, the process of integration can be hastened. The

DMA will however have no operational control over the Services. However, another perspective is that the CDS is now burdened with too much administrative responsibility, which leaves him little time for strategic planning. Relieving the CDS of avoidable administrative work would allow him to devote his time to the operational side. Also relevant is the aspect of precedence wherein, CDS on one side is at number 12 in warrant of precedence, but in his dual hat as Secretary DMA he comes at number 23 in the table. This is an anomaly with undesired consequences in functioning. Therefore, the task could be assigned to the Chief of Integrated Defence Staff to Chairman Chiefs of Staff Committee (CISC), who will continue to work under the CDS.

Joint Logistics Nodes (JLNs): The government established JLNs as the first concrete step towards integration of the logistics of the three services. Three such nodes are already operational. These JLNs will provide integrated logistics cover to the armed forces for their small-arms ammunition, rations, fuel, general stores, civilian hired transport, aviation clothing, spares and engineering support.[16] Similar nodes will come up in other parts of the country as the integrated functional and operational theatre commands are established.

Training: The curricula at command and staff level at various military training institutions have already been revised to enhance cross-domain interaction. The next step would be the creation of a joint training command, which could be achieved by upgrading one of the three existing training commands.

Approach to Integration

The GoM report has explained that the introduction of major structural changes in the field of defence 'have to be carefully planned and executed to ensure that there is no disruption of defence capabilities in the process'. It suggests that a 'detailed framework for the introduction and sequencing of the new structures' be drawn up for a smooth transition 'from the existing to the proposed structures'. It should include 'the CDS's precise role, functions and inter-service relationships'.[17] The intent to bring about military integration through the creation of theatre commands can be seen in all three services. General Manoj Pande has declared that the army is fully committed to theaterisation and is supportive of efforts towards evolving integrated theatre commands. 'We are convinced that jointness and better integration is the future,' he is quoted as saying.[18]

Steps for the Introduction of Theaterisation

After finalising the numbers of theatres and their domains and geographic dimensions, the challenge is to work out the nuances of implementation in a reasonable time period without disturbing operational balance. The integration of the three services at the apex level would require the creation of an enabling environment with exhaustive discussions so that decisions are taken after all points of view have been heard. The new CDS has taken the right first step by visiting all the 'Class A' establishments to understand the views of the officers and explain to them his own thought processes. He has also visited command HQs of the three services and held conferences with their commanders to exchange ideas. The services chiefs have been requested to explain the rationale behind integration to their respective staff.

It is also important to work out the arrangements and processes for joint training to overcome the shortage of knowledgeable commanders and staff. Various study groups must put their heads together and come up with plans to implement the transition. The next steps should be to commence integration at the theatre level by establishing theatre HQs at various locations, transferring resources and delineating command and control. The COSC is key in this process.

A theatre command is expected to be self-contained and have all the required combat and logistic resources for integrated force application. To achieve this in entirety right from the beginning seems impractical especially with the presently existing deficiencies, which are more prominent in combat squadrons of the Air Force. Due to budget constraints, army and navy equipment cannot all be upgraded at once. However, this is a phenomenon seen in developing armies all over the world, and thus should not be a restraining factor to commence transition.

We must identify areas within existing resources where integration can begin immediately, then formulate or revise operational and contingency plans at theatre level by assigning the highest priority to the establishment of inter-services communications at all levels. Following this, staffing of all integrated tri-service establishments needs to begin. There is also a view that the theatre commands should not be burdened with logistics responsibilities. However, I believe that all commanders would like to be in control of their operational logistics, as operations are heavily dependent on the same.

The Process Ahead

The ongoing discussion in the public domain generally revolves around the controversies surrounding the number of theatres while ignoring the complexity involved in putting the process in place without creating imbalance. The CDS and COSC now have a mandate to proceed expeditiously with jointness and integration. In the actual implementation process, the following options could be considered:

Option 1: Secure all resources required for the theatre commands before making the theatres operational. This model demands time and budget and all required resources will not be available at the outset. Thus, it is inadvisable.

Option 2: Start work on all theatre commands simultaneously. This would be too disruptive and will certainly create imbalance, especially with the kind of operational challenges present at the moment.

Option 3: Start work on those theatres where the resources already exist. This option makes it easier to implement the necessary changes. This could be applied to Western Theatre Command and Maritime Theatre Command. The experience gained in this process could then be used while establishing the more difficult Northern Theatre Command.

Thus, under the present circumstances, the third option appears to be the most practical. Once the specific theatres and their operational areas have been identified and formalised, the work on establishing the theatre HQs must commence. At the same time, it would be important to continue with the implementation of modernisation plans to make up for the deficiencies.

Once established, the theatre HQs would be required to integrate and update operational plans and carry out a series of wargames and exercises with troops on the ground to identify their own strengths and weaknesses. This would also allow them to test their communications and intelligence, surveillance and reconnaissance (ISR) capabilities as well as their command-and-control structure. Inter-theatre command coordination should also form a part of the process.

At this stage, the necessary deliberations between the military services and other ministries and governmental and intelligence agencies involved in national security plans must be held. This process would be better facilitated by the declaration of an NSS. Using time taken by China as a reference, a minimum of five to seven years would be required to render the theatre commands operational. The processes of modernisation and removal of deficiencies along with improvements in operational logistics would have to run concurrently and are likely to go well beyond this estimated timeframe.

Existing tri-services agencies should be upgraded to command-level organisations and their capabilities intermeshed with theatre assets. The present CDS, General Anil Chauhan and the Air Chief Marshal V.R. Chaudhari have recently dwelt on the importance of space wars. We need to work on this very important domain. There is a need for a joint human resources agency to enable cross-domain postings even while there is a push towards reducing the size of the army in view of the advancement of technology. The size of the army was reduced by 1,20,000 by not recruiting during the COVID-19 pandemic, and the present number of recruitments per year has been reduced to 40,000 from the earlier figure of 60,000. There may be a need to economise, but the ideal way to go about it would be by having an expert group from the three services to work out our overall operational requirements and then work on those figures.

General Pande has said that 'land will remain a decisive domain in warfare, especially in our case where we have contested land borders'.[19] While the planning and coordination process for integration is underway, some concrete actions also need to be initiated to dismantle the existing structures and create new ones.[20] This could happen by transferring existing capabilities and resources from one service to another based on functional need. It is also important to have a coordinated nationwide grid deployment and linking of all ISR assets such as unmanned aerial vehicles (UAVs). Our tri-service institutions could be expanded with the establishment of a tri-service training command and an agency to control joint logistics.

Processes Involving Command HQs

The command HQs of the three services and their formations will continue to play a vital role in maintaining operational balance during warfighting. Reducing the number of operational command HQs is not recommended as that will result in a loss of effective operational functioning. Non-operational commands such as training and logistics may be restructured and additional commanders may be appointed/removed where feasible.

Once the specific theatre commands have been finalised, each command HQ should be placed under a theatre command based on its geographical location. Some realignment of areas of responsibilities of command HQs may be necessary to coincide with theatre boundaries. Theatre commanders should be officers who have inter-services command experience and should derive their authority from the CDS and the COSC. They should however be vested with complete authority to resolve inter-service issues within their theatres. To strengthen the authority of theatre commanders, additional financial powers should be delegated to make them administratively more empowered.

Another issue is the decision regarding the ranks of theatre commanders, and whether they will be of three stars or four stars. At present the CDS and service chiefs are four-star ranked officers. It may not be functionally conducive to equate them with the theatre commanders in our hierarchy conscious military. Ideally the theatre commanders may be more suitable in three-star ranks and given one additional year of service taking them up to the age of sixty-one years, for enhanced continuity and motivation. They may be given the designation of the newly created rank of Colonel General, which will be senior to three stars but junior to a full general. This will reduce the clutter in three star appointments. The other option can be to promote them to a four-star rank. However, the proposals discussed above are still work in progress and have yet not been approved by the government.

Command and Control and Subsequent Phases

The contours of restructuring and reorganisation in the subsequent phases can best be designed by applying the learnings from the first phase of transformation. This should entail assigning operational responsibility to the CDS along with the COSC. The command and control should be on the lines of collective responsibility in which the Services chiefs and the CDS have equal say in the proceedings. An integrated operational HQ should be created in the establishment of CDS from where the COSC can operate. The integrated theatre commands should be placed under the COSC through the integrated operational HQs. The information flow will also continue simultaneously to the respective service HQs. Another important suggestion could be to create the post of deputy chief of defence staff (DCODS), who will look after the operations, intelligence and all types of coordination. His rank could be of three stars. In addition the post of vice chief of defence staff (VCODS) should be established for strategic planning, capability development and procurement. His rank could be of colonel general if theatre commanders are also in the same rank. These posts will be in addition to the post of CISC, who will take over the responsibility of looking after the DMA, under the CDS.

Conclusion

Modern warfare is continuously evolving. Doctrines, concepts, methodologies and weapon systems are constantly being refined to achieve success in the shortest possible time. We have witnessed massive evolution in these spheres since the Second World War. After 1947, we have fought several wars, each with a different dynamic. The biggest lesson that we have drawn from those wars is that our service-specific approach to operations is inadequate for modern-day hostilities. It lends to potentially divisive decisions and delays the response to emerging situations in a rapidly moving battlefield.

A commander controlling the operations in any specified theatre should be self-sufficient in all respects and there should not be any need for constant reallocation of resources. Shifting to the system of integrated theatre commands would, therefore, be a step in the right direction. Given that the resources required for modern warfare are always in limited supply, the theatre commanders are likely to face innumerable challenges. But this shall pave a way for coordinated capability development and optimisation of existing resources. The sooner it is done, the better.

However, immense care should be taken while implementing the integration process and setting up of theatre commands and at no stage should we get operationally imbalanced, even temporarily.

7

Advising against Participation in Iraq War
Nation First

'War creates destruction but solves no problem.'
Prime Minister Atal Bihari Vajpayee,
28 March 2003

Background

On 20 March 2003, the world was shocked and horrified to see the visuals of Iraq under massive aerial bombardment from American and British forces. Thousands of tonnes of explosives were dropped and about 400 cruise missiles fired at locations supposedly housing the Iraqi leadership. This was the 'Shock and Awe' phase of Operation Iraqi Freedom jointly conducted by the US and the UK. It was an unlawful and unjustified attack on a sovereign nation.

During later investigations by their own inquiry committees, the colluding nations were not able to justify their reasons for going to war. Thousands of lives were lost and sufferings inflicted on hapless civilians. The peace of the region was shattered. It was a proof that major world powers can unilaterally act in a manner convenient to them with no justification and without the approval of international forums like the UN.

The coalition of invading nations wanted India to put 'boots on the ground' and participate in the 'stabilisation' of the 'situation' in Iraq after the fall of the Iraqi government. India was in a dilemma about which side to be on as we were faced with our own morals and advocated principles of respecting the sovereignty of all nations on one hand, and our evolving international relations with the US, the regional geopolitical balance and our own national interests on the other. We could not conveniently put aside our long-standing friendship with the people of Iraq.

A national debate ensued, with the saner voices pointing out that the cost–benefit ratio was not in India's favour. The US was putting tremendous pressure on India to send its troops to Iraq, and a few senior political leaders in the cabinet were supposedly in favour of Indian participation. They were supported by some renowned strategic analysts and even a few army veterans. However, the majority of the nation was firmly against us joining the American operation.

An Unjust and Illegitimate Attack

Ever since the events of 9/11, the US had become cynical and paranoid as a nation. It claimed to be vulnerable to an attack from Iraq due to the Central Asian country's alleged possession of weapons of mass destruction (WMDs) and also their support of terrorist groups such as Al-Qaeda. These allegations were based on unconfirmed and unverified reports and twisted to suit the biased intentions of the US. Even before the United Nations Security Council (UNSC) could pass a resolution asking Iraq to readmit arms inspectors, the US and the UK had started amassing their forces in the Persian Gulf with a clear intent to attack Iraq.

It seemed war was inevitable no matter whether Iraq complied with the UNSC resolution or what any inspectors would find if they did. This urge to go to war stemmed from ulterior motives and agendas pushed by strong business lobbies such as the weapons industry, oil companies and post-war reconstruction contractors, among others. The die was thus cast even before international opinion could be formalised.

Hans Blix, chairman of the United Nations Monitoring, Verification and Inspection Commission (UNMOVIC), stated in his report on 14 February 2003 that 'so far, UNMOVIC has not found any such weapons [of mass destruction]'.[1] Despite this statement, all calls by the international community to hold back were ignored by the US and their allies. Mohamed Mostafa El-Baradei, director general of the International Atomic Energy Agency (IAEA), described the US invasion of Iraq as a 'glaring example of how, in many cases, the use of force exacerbates the problem rather than [solve] it'.[2]

On 17 March, the US issued an ultimatum to President Saddam Hussein to leave Iraq within seventy-two hours or face hostilities. However, forcing a regime change hadn't even been mentioned until then. It was an unjust and illegitimate demand and Saddam did not comply. Once the seventy-two hours had elapsed, American and allied forces launched air assaults and cruise missiles from the sea followed by an offensive by ground forces. The violence that followed was broadcast around the world.

By 9 April, merely 20 days into the offensive, the resistance in Baghdad collapsed, and on that same day Basra was finally secured by the British forces. Finally, on 1 May 2003, US President George W. Bush declared that the mission was accomplished and all combat operations in Iraq had ended. But did the operations really end?

A Heavy Price to Pay

The euphoria of the coalition forces soon turned into a nightmare. Casualties had been light in the initial combat in 2003, with around 150 fatalities at the time of Bush's declaration on 1 May. However, the number of deaths of American troops soared thereafter, increasing by approximately 1,000 over the next year. By the time the last of the US troops left Iraq on 31 August 2010, their ranks counted 4,421 dead and nearly 32,000 wounded. The UK lost 179 servicemen, while other coalition countries suffered another 139 deaths. Casualties on the Iraqi side are not clear in any of the studies. However, in 2006, *Lancet* journal published an estimate of 6,54,965 Iraqi deaths including civilians.[3]

The cost assessments of the conflict are varied too. The non-partisan Congressional Research Service estimates that the US spent nearly $ 802 billion on funding the Iraq campaign by the end of fiscal year 2011. However, Nobel laureate economist Joseph Stieglitz and Harvard's Linda Bilmes put the true cost at $ 3 trillion, taking into account additional impacts on the US budget and economy.[4] The UK funded its part in the conflict at the cost of $ 14.32 billion.[5] What is worse is that the US went into this conflict without any defined exit policy. The UNSC eventually recognised the US as an 'occupation power' until an Iraqi-run government could be formed.[6]

Following the collapse of Iraq's government, the nation's major cities erupted in waves of violence. Restoring law and order was an arduous task that soon developed into full-scale guerrilla warfare. However, the Bush administration labelled it as a 'sectarian violence' to cover its failure. Further, the Iraqi army was disbanded by the US and that left the country with no law-and-order machinery. Saddam Hussein was finally captured on 13 December 2003. He was subsequently convicted by an Iraqi tribunal and executed on 30 December 2006.

The Aftermath

Several committees in the US investigated the operation in Iraq. The Senate Select Committee on Intelligence (2004) concluded that the intelligence community's assessments were flawed. The 9/11 Commission (2004) found that the intelligence community had overstated the evidence linking Iraq to Al-Qaeda. The House Committee on Government Reforms (2004) and Senate Foreign Relations Committee (2008) both concluded that the administration had exaggerated the threat posed by Iraq's WMD programme and had made false statements to the Congress and the public to justify the attack.

The UK also investigated the campaign, with the Chilcot Inquiry publishing their findings in 2016. The report concluded that the UK's involvement in Iraq was based on flawed intelligence and that the UK military was ill-prepared for the aftermath of the conflict.

The Indian Position

India initially expressed its reservations about the conflict and emphasised the need for a diplomatic solution. It was not until February 2003 – about a month before the attack commenced – that the issue of Iraq came up in the Indian Parliament. On 12 March 2003, Prime Minister Vajpayee stated that 'the Government of India would strongly urge that no military action be taken that does not have the collective concurrence of the international community'. He further emphasised that 'no ultimatum should be given' because 'war is not an option'. The prime minister was clear that India was only looking 'to find a peaceful solution'.[7]

The day the Iraqi offensive began, the Ministry of External Affairs (MEA) released a press statement that said, 'It is with the deepest anguish that we have seen reports of the commencement of military action in Iraq.'[8] When the Indian Parliament reconvened after its recess on 7 April, one of its first acts was to pass a unanimous resolution deploring (rather than 'condemning', which is the word the Opposition wanted the resolution to use) the military action against Iraq and its attendant aim of a regime change. This resolution set the tone for the position taken by India over the next several months.

Pressure Builds on India

Unable to stabilise the situation, the US was left with no option but to increase their military presence in the country. There were up to 1,50,000 American troops in Iraq at any time through the campaign. British forces had peaked at 46,000 but then fell to 4,100 by May 2009, when the UK formally withdrew from Iraq. Out of the total of 2,97,384 personnel who served during this operation, 99 per cent were from the US and the UK, with Australia (2,000 troops), Denmark (200) and Poland (184) contributing the rest. This total does not include the Iraqi Kurdish soldiers, who numbered over 50,000. Ten other countries offered small numbers of non-combat forces, mostly medical teams or specialists in decontamination.

Faced with a situation akin to a civil war after the collapse of Saddam's government and with increasing casualties, the US started to pressurise India to send troops to help stabilise the situation and establish a new Iraqi government. It requested at least 17,000 Indian soldiers be sent to Iraq. As an enticement during Advani's visit to the US, Bush told him that he would 'do some hard talking with Pakistan to stop exporting terror to India', besides supporting India's aspiration for a permanent seat in the UNSC. British Prime Minister Tony Blair reinforced the US's desire for Indian troops to Advani when the two met in London on Advani's way back to India.

On 16 June 2003, a US state department team arrived in Delhi to 'outline the political and operational context of a possible deployment of troops by India in Iraq'. After reviewing the documents, we found a number of unanswered questions and grey areas. The US did not have the answers and failed to provide a 'defined roadmap for India'. It was keen to get India involved in Iraq primarily to reduce expenses. It stood to save billions of dollars by reducing its troops in Iraq and supplementing them with Indian soldiers.

As per one estimate based on an earlier campaign in Bosnia, it cost $ 250,000 annually to station one soldier abroad, including expenses on arms and transportation. Indian troops would be a much cheaper option even if they were 'compensated' at the same rate as UN peacekeepers, in which each soldier received about $ 1,000 a month.[9] In any case, India would also have not accepted this money as it would project the Indian forces as mercenaries. Thus, for

India it would have amounted to hundreds of millions of utterly wasted dollars in an unjustified involvement.

India's Dilemma

For nearly two months, the Indian government struggled with the issue of how to respond to America's request. US diplomat Albert Thibault Jr was the deputy chief of the US embassy in India at the time. In an interview two years after his retirement, he said that the US came very close to an agreement that would have seen a large Indian contingent sent to Iraq. This claim was at odds with the Ministry of External Affairs (MEA's) view that acceding to the US request for troops 'was not in India's interest'.

There were many that thought India should send troops to Iraq, including some defence analysts who argued strongly that it would be a good opportunity for India to expand our strategic influence and enhance our relationship with the US. We could then ask them to return the favour by helping India become a permanent member of the UNSC.

Others in favour of India sending troops believed the assurances of Bush to Advani that he would put pressure on Pakistani President Pervez Musharraf to halt the cross-border terrorism into Jammu and Kashmir. Bush had also assured Advani that some advanced technology would be shared with India in return for their cooperation. Yet another group saw things from a business viewpoint and believed that sending troops to Iraq would lead to generous reconstruction contracts.

India Decides

The CCS met on 21 June and again on 1 July but left the decision to the Union Cabinet. The chairman of NSAB, C. Rangarajan, was asked by Prime Minister Vajpayee to draft a report on the pros and cons of Indian deployment. Finally, during the meeting of the Union Cabinet on July 14, the prime minister decided to turn down America's request. At a news briefing later that day, US state department spokesman Richard Boucher said that the US had hoped that India 'would have made a different choice'. However, he reiterated that 'India remains an important strategic partner' of the US.[10]

There were several reasons for India to decide not to send troops to Iraq, the primary one being that it was a politically divisive decision that would have received strong objection from almost all segments of the society during an election year. The Indian government believed that the US campaign in Iraq was a unilateral and non-sanctioned action and we anyway did not have a direct stake in the conflict. There were several grey areas in the terms of deployment for Indian troops and casualties would have been inevitable.

Besides these factors, it was also important to protect Indian economic interests – including access to oil and gas resources – by avoiding any disruptions to economic ties with Iraq and other Arab countries. Lastly, the decision also saved the government from the inevitable backlash from the sizeable Muslim population in India.

The Military View

When I returned from a short leave, there was a buzz among the higher echelons of the Indian military about our troops being prepared to be sent to Iraq. I learnt that the formations and units to be sent had already been identified and that deployment was imminent, subject to final approval by the government. From what I gathered; the Indian troops were to be deployed in 'non-conflict' zones. I asked my staff to prepare a contingency plan and operational guidelines for such a mission, just in case this hearsay actually proves to be true.

However, I was very concerned that such an action was even being considered. Why were we doing this? Should the government not seek the views of the military before finalising any decision on this issue? Why should we be fighting a dirty war for another nation? After deliberating on the issue at length, my mind was firmly made up and I decided to share our concerns with the political leadership.

I wrote a detailed letter to the defence minister and the prime minister expressing the army's strong reservations about sending troops to Iraq, so that the same was considered before taking any final decision.

As a nation, we should not fight anybody else's war. In the past, such conflicts have dragged on endlessly. Why would Government not learn from our engagement in Sri Lanka (OP PAWAN), where it was a direct intervention, or even Sierra Leone where we had gone merely as peacekeepers? Besides, the militancy in Jammu and Kashmir was at its peak and at that time we had also started the project of fencing the LOC. Therefore, the army had heavy operational commitments and was not in a position to spare a large number of troops. It would impact our operational efficiency and risk the security along the LOC.

In my letters to the government, I raised some questions to which the answers were in any case essential for formulating operational plans should troops be rolled out anyway. I asked about the command-and-control structure under which our troops would function in Iraq, as I wanted it to be clear that Indian troops should never fight under some other nation's flag. What role was being assigned to the Indian forces? Is the task expected to be maintenance of law and order and peacekeeping? Or would Indian troops be asked to act as an occupational force for quelling any revolts, perhaps even fighting a civil war should one break out? All of these questions needed answering.

Should the Indian government feel compelled to share the responsibility of the US operation, I wrote, perhaps they could consider sending a multi-specialty mobile field hospital instead of sending troops. Another option was to send Indian troops as a peacekeeping force elsewhere to reduce the burden of UN tasks on US and allied troops, which could then be reallocated to Iraq. The concluding message of my letters was that the government should reconsider sending Indian troops to Iraq.

In the CCS meeting held on 1 July, the ministers expressed their views but the NSA did not speak. When I was given the opportunity to speak, I outlined my strong opinions on the matter. The meeting ended with the prime minister saying, '*Abhi chintan karenge* (we will contemplate now).' I recall that after these three words the meeting was terminated without a murmur. After the meeting I immediately wrote to the defence minister reiterating my views. Unfortunately, I have not been able to get these letters traced, even after making due effort. The Indian military has an ethos of obeying the national political leadership. Therefore, we did not express our views publicly. Fortunately, the government's final decision was in line with the views of the armed forces.

India's Internal Decision-Making Process

India's foreign minister at the time was Yashwant Sinha, who later said in an interview that Vajpayee 'liked to work on the basis of consensus'. After Congress party president Sonia Gandhi wrote to the prime minister opposing the proposal to send Indian troops to Iraq, he invited her for a meeting. He then discussed the matter in the Cabinet.

When the consensus in all meetings was that India should not send its troops to Iraq, 'this was the view that was communicated to the Americans'.[11] As to whether the military's recommendations were one of the factors that impacted the government's final decision or not, I cannot say for sure, but we had done our duty.

Conclusion

The military leadership must always present a frank and forthright opinion on matters of national security, and communicate it clearly and precisely to the government, irrespective of whether it is in consonance with the government's views or not. **In this context I would like to quote a few lines from a book written by Lieutenant General H.R. McMaster, who was the National Security Advisor with President Trump in 2017–18. In his book** *Dereliction of Duty***, he called 'Joint Chiefs' as the 'Five Silent Men', because they failed to establish personal** rapport with the civilian leadership necessary to speak their mind. I entirely agree with his views, however I would prefer the words 'professional rapport' in lieu of 'personal rapport' which has a different connotation. If the Indian military did not have a good professional rapport with our government, we too may have ended up in a damaging campaign in Iraq.

The relationship and trust between India's military and civilian leaderships was seen again after the UPA government came into power in 2004. The new government began to reconsider India's continued occupation of Siachen Glacier and was thinking of pulling back from the glacier to ease the tension in the region and improve relations with Pakistan. The military held a meeting with the government in which we explained the strategic importance of the glacier. We asserted that Pakistan was not to be trusted as they may breach the agreement and reoccupy the glacier, which thereafter would become extremely difficult to recapture. We made it clear that the army was not in favour of any pull back or readjustment at Siachen Glacier.

Prime Minister Manmohan Singh said to me, 'General, you are being very hawkish.' I replied that our judgement is based on our professional experiences. The continued infiltration across the LOC and the Kargil intrusion – which had started even while our then prime minister was visiting Pakistan on a goodwill mission – has shown Pakistan to be nothing but treacherous. In view of these observations, we strongly recommend that no readjustments be considered along the glacier as that would make us lose all advantage at that key location.

Dr Singh then retired to the adjoining office to consider our recommendations together with the CCS. After about fifteen minutes, the prime minister re-emerged and declared that they had considered our views and had decided to shelve the idea to pull back from Siachen Glacier.

While the political leadership is required to take the final decision, a good relationship with the heads of the armed forces ensures that the military point of view is seriously considered when it comes to matters of national security.

India's decision not to send troops to Iraq was driven by a combination of strategic, security, economic and domestic factors, and it helped to protect India's interests both at home and abroad.

8

Administrative Reforms
Welfare of the Men behind the Gun

> 'I am a Warrior, defending my Nation is my Dharma...I fight and embrace the consequences willingly...God give me strength that I ask nothing of you.'
>
> The Bhagavad Gita

Introduction

NEARLY A CENTURY AGO, then US president Calvin Coolidge had said, 'The nation which forgets its defenders will be itself forgotten.' That sentiment holds true even today. Indian soldiers believe in the ethos of 'Nation Above All' and derive their strength, pride and motivation from the respect and care that their country provides them. Therefore, the dignity, well-being and honour of our soldiers must be preserved.

The military leadership must strengthen the value systems and manage perceptions to ensure that the personnel feel secure and stay committed. Besides respect and dignity, the areas of concern for soldiers are not much different from any other citizen of the country – career advancement, medical care, education for their children and financial security even after retirement. They have to truly believe that the nation will take care of them and their families if they are ever wounded, disabled or killed in action. The soldiers expect the nation to recognise their sacrifices and value them.

Rajnath Singh, speaking in his capacity as defence minister on the occasion of Armed Forces Flag Day in November 2022, pointed out that our soldiers have risen to 'every challenge with courage'. He said, 'In the process many of them made supreme sacrifices, while many became physically disabled.' The defence minister reminded his listeners that it is the nation's responsibility to 'support the soldiers and their families in every way possible'. He concluded, 'It is because of them that we sleep peacefully and live our lives without fear.'[1]

During my tenure as the army chief, a few major reforms in soldiers' welfare were implemented. These reforms addressed the careers of junior officers, the provision of healthcare for all retired personnel and accommodation for families in military stations, among other matters. While the proposals for many such reforms were already in various stages of discussion with the government, their implementation needed 'vigorous' interactions with the powers that be. These schemes finally saw light of day only after several meetings with the concerned ministers to obtain approvals.

Part I

Improving Career Prospects in the Army

Ajay Vikram Singh Committee (AVSC)

After the Kargil war, the government set up the Kargil Review Committee to analyse the conflict and draw lessons for future. The committee's report was submitted on 28 January 2000 and highlighted several deficiencies in India's security system. As a follow-up, the government set up the GoM to review the national security system in its entirety and formulate specific proposals for implementation. Conscious of the wider scope and extent of its powers, the

GoM reviewed all aspects of the national security system which included both external and internal threats, and internal dynamics for working within the armed forces.

Among many other recommendations, the GoM highlighted that there were problems with the higher age profile of the commanding officers of combat units and the retirement ages of officers. The GoM felt that the armed forces needed to maintain a younger profile to remain fit. Following this, the AVSC was set up with Ajai Vikram Singh – then a special secretary in the MoD – appointed chairman. Other members of the committee were senior officers from the three military services and the department of finance.

The committee was specifically tasked to address the issues raised by the GoM. Among other personnel management issues, the AVSC had to find ways to ensure that officers placed in command of the combat units were in a younger age bracket to compare more favourably with their counterparts in the armies of other nations. It was also meant to ease rank stagnation at the level of majors and lieutenant colonels as part of career management.

The Core Challenge

The Indian Army has had to always deal with a shortage of officers. At one time the shortage was a whopping 26 per cent below target. This deficiency has gradually been reduced but has still not reached the minimum level for effective operational efficiency. There are numerous reasons for this deficit. Two primary factors are the opportunities available in the corporate sector and the rising awareness among aspirants about the quicker rise in hierarchy and ranks in other contemporary government civil services. Those fields have thus attracted talent away from the armed forces.

Additionally, the armed forces have very tough working conditions and therefore are not attractive as a career option unless one has a genuine liking for the military profession. Motivation to work for the armed forces has to stem from pride and the desire to have respect and fame and not from assured career progression. While the military does offer a fair opportunity to rise in ranks, its steep pyramidical structure makes effective management of career progression difficult. The competitive command-and-control hierarchy of the armed forces makes the career curve very steep.

In the army, less than 1 per cent of commissioned officers rise to the rank of major general and only 25 per cent of colonels become brigadiers. From a total of 43,000 officers, only 4,123 can be colonel – that is, less than 10 per cent of the total. Of these, only 1,046 (2.4 per cent) make it to the rank of brigadier and 266 (0.61 per cent) become major general. Thus, officers at the mid-level rank of colonel stagnate at that level for nearly 20 years before being superannuated at the age of 54. If we compare these figures to civilian jobs in government services, we find that over 90 per cent of direct recruits in the 'Group A' cadre rise to at least the level of joint secretary, which is the equivalent of major general in the army.

Deliberations

It was obvious that easier promotions through ranks would be needed. However, there were reservations about these proposals from the navy and air force because they did not face the challenge of their commanders being of advanced age. Presumably they did not want to upgrade rank structure at mid-level, as they felt that it would create a top-heavy force. They also suggested that it would erode the command structure and value of ranks if they had a number of senior officers of the same rank in any single headquarters or organisation.

Notwithstanding the views of the other two forces, it was clear that for the army a considerable increase in the number of vacancies at various ranks was essential for lowering the ages of commanding officers. When asked to consider a substantial increment in the number of senior ranks, Ajai Vikram Singh asked what functions 'flag-rank' officers (brigadiers and above) would perform and what they would do to occupy themselves if their numbers were to be increased. The army's viewpoint was that reorganisation is always possible in any evolving structure, and it should be left to the armed forces to find suitable avenues for gainful employment for these officers. We emphasised that this apprehension should not come in the way of the major objective and mandate of the committee.

Unlike civil services, paramilitary forces and the police, where additional ranks are created to protect the career prospects of their cadre, the armed forces have a strict code of pyramidical appointments. For example, there can only be one commander in a unit or a formation HQ. We needed to be able to offer the respect derived from ranks equivalent to our civilian counterparts.

The army was determined to solve these problems and insisted on pushing through the reforms that they thought would bring a boost to the careers of our officers. Unfortunately, it was difficult to find agreement on this specific issue, especially from the other two services. To explain the army's viewpoint, I sent our adjutant general, Lieutenant General Mohinder Singh, to brief the air and naval chiefs about our specific requirements. Subsequently, I met both chiefs and they were gracious enough to understand our requirements. Both of them agreed to let the AVSC attend to the army-specific requirements in the initial phase while they made up their minds.

The Continued Dilemma

To us in the army, it was obvious that to achieve its objectives, the AVSC would have to implement time-bound progression at lower ranks to ensure that permanent supersession did not take place below the level of lieutenant colonel. Additional posts had to be created at higher ranks to absorb the increased number of promotions at the level of colonel and higher, besides identifying the appointments that could be held by flag ranks.

The ratio of short-service commissioned officers (SSCO) vis-à-vis permanent commissioned officers had to be improved as SSCOs would leave service after curtailed tenures of up to ten years at junior ranks (now increased to fourteen). Lucrative post-retirement benefits and assured post-military career options needed to be created as well as recommendations made for the restructuring of JCOs and other ranks to provide them the right level of motivation and also try to promote them at a younger age.

Despite our best efforts, we were facing unacceptable delays in moving the process ahead at every level. I felt that we would be able to facilitate the decision only by adopting a new strategy. The solution perhaps lay in completing the reform process over two stages. In the first stage, we could restrict the scope of promotions up to the rank of colonel only. The second stage could begin later for the higher ranks. The pressure from the ranks higher than colonel would make identification of vacancies and appointments for the ranks of brigadiers and above inevitable. Otherwise, there would be an unacceptably high level of stagnation at lower levels that would defeat the very purpose of setting up the AVSC.

Unfortunately, I again faced a lot of resistance, this time from my own staff. They wanted to finish the entire process in one go and were reluctant to accept it being spread over two phases. However, from my own experience, I knew that the government would never sanction such a large number of vacancies in all ranks at once. There was also the worry that the government may conveniently hand over the issue to the pay commission, whenever it was constituted.

Our first priority had to be to look after the interests of our junior officers. Coupling proposals for senior and junior ranks together generally drew a negative reaction from the bureaucracy as well as the political leadership. Ultimately, I stuck to my guns and we progressed the case only for the

Administrative Reforms

first stage initially. I feel that helped immensely in hastening the entire process.

Approvals

Having finalised our approach, the army made an elaborate presentation to Defence Minister Pranab Mukherjee. After hearing us out, he agreed with our logic and assessment that there was an issue at the junior levels of officer ranks. This was due to the high level of supersessions in the early stages of one's career until about the age of 37, which was followed by a long stagnation period. Mukherjee was also convinced about the requirement for equivalence between military ranks and their counterparts in civil services.

The defence minister asked us to make a presentation to Finance Minister P. Chidambaram. On my request, Mukherjee agreed to attend the presentation even though the finance minister was much junior to him. It was the defence minister's personal interest and conviction that made the important recommendations of the AVSC see the light of day. I was very lucky to have two of the finest defence ministers of India during my tenure as COAS – George Fernandes in the NDA government and Pranab Mukherjee of the UPA ruling coalition.

During the presentation to the finance minister, it was agreed that while the navy and air force could come out with their proposals in due course, the army's proposals for the first stage should be approved immediately, with recommendations for the second stage followed up later. The proposals were as follows:
- Reduction in minimum service required for promotion to the rank of captain to two years and major to six years.
- Time-based promotion to the rank of lieutenant colonel on completion of 13 years of service.
- Battalions and equivalent units to be commanded by colonels instead of lieutenant colonels.
- 750 posts of colonel to be approved in the first stage.

- Introduction of the rank of colonel (timescale) with a minimum service period of 26 years.

After receiving approval from the government, we commenced our work on the second stage alongside the implementation of the first. This helped us to maintain the momentum and gain advantage of fresh thinking. Subsequently in 2008, the government approved 1,896 additional posts for the army. These included 1,484 colonels (including 750 promoted in the first stage), 222 brigadiers, 75 major generals and 20 lieutenant generals. Similar increases were also approved for the navy and the air force.

Other recommendations of the AVSC in the first stage also included proposals for 'second career' plans, such as retired soldiers having assured opportunities with the CAPF. However, the government has never given these proposals serious thought. To make SSCO a more attractive career option, the service period was increased by four years with additional benefit money for each year served. However, these measures are yet to show positive results.

The work on additional recommendations such as a cadre review of JCOs and other ranks was started in 2009 with a study group being formed. Based on the recommendations of the study group, in 2017 the government approved new posts for 479 subedar majors, 7,769 subedars, 13,466 naib subedars, 58,493 havildars and 64,930 naiks.

Implementation

The government approval for the AVSC recommendations had come in mid-December 2004, to be implemented by 1 January 2005. We had had elaborate discussions about simplifying the promotion procedures in preparation for the day. The military secretary, Lieutenant General Mahesh Vij, was responsible for implementing all the promotion policies for army officers. He was assisted by Colonel Bipin Rawat, who would later become the first-ever CDS.

A number of options and procedures were considered. My emphasis was on simplicity to avoid any confusion during the implementation of such a major reform. Ultimately, we decided that one comprehensive signal would be issued regarding the various timebound promotions like captains, majors and lieutenant colonels. All staff and instructional appointments tenable by majors at that time would thereafter automatically be tenable by lieutenant colonels and all units were to be commanded by colonels.

There was a joke going around that the shops of Gopinath Bazar in Delhi Cantonment ran out of epaulettes on the day the signal was issued for promotions. A total of 19,662 officers were promoted – the largest-ever number of promotions carried out by any army in a single day.

Conclusion

In view of the increasingly complex requirements of modern-day warfare, attracting quality personnel and nurturing leadership are of paramount importance to the armed forces. Therefore, we needed ways to attract bright young talent to a career in the military and then ensure that we retain them. The implementation of the AVSC recommendations was the first major step towards a younger age profile in India's armed forces.

The AVSC recommendations enabled all officers to assuredly rise to the rank of lieutenant colonel in a shorter period. Until then, only about 45 per cent of officers reached this rank. It also provided better financial benefits to the officers, placing them in a higher pay band. The second phase of the AVSC recommendations for cadre restructuring of officers in the forces was implemented in 2008 and gave senior officers more avenues for promotion. At the time, some apprehensions were raised that this would result in a top-heavy army. Time has proven them to be misplaced concerns.

After my superannuation, I was told by some naval and air force officers that orders for implementation of the AVSC recommendations for their services had also been issued. They thanked me for ensuring better career prospects for them and said that it came about only through the army's efforts to have the AVSC recommendations approved. Assured promotion prospects highly motivated the officers cadre and ensured better leadership and performance, thereby increasing combat effectiveness. Better service benefits at all levels have made the armed forces an attractive career option.

Part II

Assured Health Care for Veterans with Dignity

The Backdrop

While in service, military personnel have access to very good medical facilities. Even their dependent family members are taken care of. However, the most difficult period in a soldier's life starts after he retires from service. Most of them are not even 40 (in case of other ranks) when they retire from military service – a time when they are still responsible for shouldering the financial burden of their family. Some have young children while others have dependent parents. The cost of medical treatment for the family invariably becomes the heaviest of all unforeseen expenditures.

This is compounded by the fact that decent medical facilities are usually not available in the villages and smaller towns that most of our soldiers are from. Travelling for treatment adds to the already high medical costs, making it unaffordable for even those of the officer cadre without some form of insurance coverage. Until 2003, retired army personnel could access military medical facilities only for a few specific treatments, and that too up to the limit of the coverage provided by the Army Group Insurance Scheme.

Diseases needing expensive treatments were not covered under the scheme. Even for the treatments that were covered, reimbursement was only partial – in some cases, not even 50 per cent of the actual expense was covered. In addition, there was no facility for cashless treatment and so the medical bills had to be paid in full initially and any reimbursement only came much later. This posed a major problem to veterans with limited income from their pensions.

The navy and air force personnel also faced a similar situation. Our veterans were rightly feeling neglected as they were left to face numerous personal challenges without help. As a result, the headquarters of the respective services were flooded with requests for financial assistance. Only a few of these requests could be met from the limited welfare funds to which each service had access. It was evident that such ad hoc arrangements did not provide any long-term workable solution.

The feeling that the government was not being fair to the armed forces was compounded by the fact that the Central Government Health Scheme (CGHS) – a medical coverage plan for all employees of the Central government and their dependent family members – had been in place since 1954. One could not avoid making the comparison, considering that soldiers who had served under extremely adverse conditions at great risk of injury or death were not being given the benefits that they deserved.

Ex-Servicemen Contributory Health Scheme

It was in 1991 – during General S.F. Rodrigues's tenure as chief – that the Army first started thinking about this problem. For taking up the case with the government, the CGHS was used as a model with specific requirement-oriented modifications incorporated. The first challenge was to establish necessity. The formulation of project details – including the estimated patient load and financial requirements – took a lot of time.

When I was posted to the Army HQ as VCOAS in October 2001, General S. Padmanabhan was the chief. We both agreed that the issue of medical coverage for our ex-servicemen (ESM) should be one of the priority areas of focus and action. The chief asked me to liaise with the government about the proposal together with the adjutant general. Meanwhile, Operation Parakram began and our focus was shifted. However, in between operational imperatives I always took time to follow up with MoD officials regarding the expedited sanction of our proposal.

Fortunately, our efforts were given a push towards favourable consideration by the increased national fervour around the border situation. Finally, on 30 December 2002, the government accepted the necessity and authorised the Ex-Servicemen Contributory Health Scheme (ECHS) in principle. However, approval was just the beginning of the difficulties and challenges ahead. Most government approvals are meaningless until the operating rules and financial aspects have been evolved and addressed. Of course, to reach that point one has to navigate numerous bureaucratic hurdles. The process leading to the launch of the ECHS was no different.

ECHS as a Concept

The primary aim of the ECHS was to provide quality medical coverage to ESM and their dependents through polyclinics established across the country. They would also be allowed full access to military hospitals and specifically empanelled private hospitals. The plan was to offer primary treatment at polyclinics equipped with laboratories and dispensaries, with secondary and tertiary treatment being done at military or private hospitals. This would also serve to reduce the burden on military hospitals.

All types of diseases and treatments were to be covered without any restrictions, and treatment was to be provided on a cashless basis with no cap on coverage. We tried to ensure that the scheme was mostly financed by the government, though some nominal contributions would also need to be made by armed forces personnel during their service tenures.

We conceptualised the ECHS to be managed through the existing infrastructure of the armed forces in order to minimise administrative expenditure. Any spare capacity at military medical facilities was to be used and existing procurement organisations for medical and non-medical equipment would also serve the ECHS. From the very beginning, the ECHS was placed under the COSC and attached to the department of ESM welfare of the MoD.

In order to ensure minimal disruption of the scheme during war and ensuring its continued availability in non-military areas, we began by establishing new polyclinics exclusively for veterans. The existing medical facilities at hospitals in selected military stations was augmented to cater for the heavy ESM load. Following this, civil hospitals and diagnostic centres across the country were empanelled to allow ESM to access specialised treatment or diagnostic facilities not available at the polyclinics.

The Government Approves

When I took over as the army chief on 1 January 2003, my top priority on the non-operational side was to get all governmental clearances to launch the ECHS and make it fully functional at the earliest. Fortunately, I had a very good professional rapport with George Fernandes, the defence minister. Within two days of starting my new position, I requested him to direct his ministry's officials to help us get the ECHS functioning.

I wanted to announce the scheme during my speech at the Army Day Parade on 15 January 2003. I told

the defence minister that getting this approval by then would be a great act of recognition of the sacrifices made by the armed forces in service of the nation. I must fully acknowledge here the minister's sympathetic and action-oriented attitude to this request. Thanks to him, I was successfully able to make the announcement on Army Day as planned. It raised a huge cheer and brought a lot of appreciation from the armed forces.

On Army Day, a traditional 'at home' gathering is hosted in Army House in the evening. The president and prime minister attend the event, as do other ministers, top bureaucrats and diplomats who join serving officers, veterans and their families at this function. During tea, Prime Minister Atal Bihari Vajpayee asked me if we would be able to run the ECHS satisfactorily, as some of the experiences the government had had with the CGHS gave him cause for apprehension. I thanked him for giving us the go-ahead and assured him that we were very confident that we would make it a success story.

The ECHS Is Launched

The work on structuring the ECHS started in earnest immediately after receiving approval. Like in any organisation, it soon became apparent that a project progresses in an expedited manner only if led by the chief himself. Fortunately for me, it had been decided that the effort to operationalise the scheme would be led by the army. This gave me more control over the proceedings.

I started a system of regular review conferences that were initially held every fortnight and subsequently once a month. Besides me, these were attended by the adjutant general, chiefs of staffs of commands, area commanders and the medical heads of the three military services. Where necessary, inputs were taken from the other services. These interactions proved to be productive and useful. Through notable contributions from two adjutant generals – first Lieutenant General A. Natrajan and then Lieutenant General

Mohinder Singh – and support from the MoD, we were able to formulate and finalise the rules and structure of the organisation within three months.

The ECHS was launched on 1 April 2003. Soon we faced teething problems, including a shortage of doctors and trained personnel to run the polyclinics, inadequate quantities of medicines and limited infrastructure and funds. The veteran community in remote areas lacked awareness of the scheme and many reputable hospitals were reluctant to be empanelled. There was also slow progress in getting IT support and fixing accounting procedures. Transition to any new system takes time and the ECHS was no exception. The challenges were overcome diligently and the ECHS would go on to be a comprehensive healthcare scheme that caters to the needs of armed forces veterans and their dependents even in remote areas.

We had planned to make the scheme fully operational within five years of launching, i.e. by 31 March 2008. A network of 227 polyclinics (comprising 104 augmented and 123 new polyclinics) was approved for implementation in the first phase. The scheme was to progressively expand to cover 104 military stations and 123 non-military stations. Within the first year, we had managed to operationalise 95 completely new polyclinics. By the end of my tenure, the total number of polyclinics had increased to 132.

The Current Status

The ECHS currently has over 5.5 million beneficiaries. With around 55,000 servicemen retiring annually, if we assume an average of three dependants per retiree also added as authorised beneficiaries, the ECHS membership is increasing by over 2,00,000 every year. As per information provided by the MoD in Parliament in 2022, the ECHS now provides medical services through a network of 427 polyclinics in India and another six in Nepal. There are 30 ECHS regional centres, and the number of empanelled hospitals has risen to 3,118.

The sheer volume of growth can be judged by the figures shared by the minister of state for defence Ajay Bhatt on 29 July 2022. He stated that 'around 1.65 crore (16.5 million) beneficiaries have availed medical and dental services' through the ECHS from 2019 to 2021. The amount spent by the department of ESM welfare under the scheme in those three years was ₹14,637.89 crore.[2]

The scope and coverage of the scheme has also been expanded over time. On 7 March 2019, the government granted a special sanction allowing Second World War veterans, emergency commissioned officers and premature retirees to be members of the ECHS by waiving the mandatory prerequisites of being ESM and drawing a military pension. These veterans can now avail of the medical facilities at any hospital in an emergency, but in such a case they would have to pay the hospital bills themselves first and claim reimbursement later.

Areas of Concern

Over the past two decades, the ECHS has successfully evolved and expanded to provide necessary services for the welfare of our veterans. However, certain deficits and challenges still remain, which prevent the scheme from reaching the level of satisfaction expected from it. No doubt there exists a constant endeavour to address these issues through periodic reviews and management skill upgrades. However, it is strongly recommended that the areas of concern summarised below be immediately addressed to better meet not only the needs of veterans but also the original goals and expectations of the scheme.

Assured Funding: The scheme is financed by the government from the defence revenue budget. The onus of providing the necessary financial support therefore lies squarely on the government's shoulders. At the time of launch, there were a couple of points of assurance given by the leadership: (i) the quality of treatment provided to the beneficiaries would be of the highest grade; and (ii) funding would be increased in line with an increase in membership and would not ever be a limiting factor under any circumstances. This was a solemn assurance given by the government and it should be adhered to at all times.

Uncertainty of funds is invariably a major source of problems so it is incumbent on the government to support this scheme by finding workable avenues to provision the finances required. However, it should be said that the government does appear to be considering the issue given the marked increase in financial allocation for the ECHS in the financial year 2023–24, with an estimated budget of ₹5,431.56 crore. This had not been so in recent years, as evident from the allotment of ₹3,582.51 crore in financial year 2022–23 and even lesser in preceding years.[3]

To avoid strain on the revenue resources of the military services, the armed forces have asked the MoD to shift the allocation of funds for the ECHS from the 'revenue budget' to the 'defence pension fund', which is a separate entity within the defence budget. However, it is unclear how this proposal will lead to assured allocation of funds for the ECHS. The present system would appear to be a better alternative.

Financial Management and Expenditure Profile: The ECHS needs efficient financial management to reduce operating costs. Given that budget shall always be a constraint, it is pertinent that expenditure is done with the right balance of priorities. This would entail carefully balancing the needs of the beneficiaries, the infrastructure maintenance costs and the employee salaries. Further, there would always be a need to expand the footprint of the ECHS, requiring more capital expenditure. I am hopeful that this will be factored into the budget estimates and the finances allocated proportionately.

Medicine Management: Medicines alone account for almost one-fourth of the ECHS budget. Despite this, medicines are sometimes not available and at other times are of questionable quality. This is a major source of dissatisfaction among ESM. Some steps have been initiated to ameliorate their concerns, like doubling the budgets of polyclinics for procuring drugs and consumables from authorised local chemists. Another proposal is to procure medicines online and arrange delivery directly to the homes of the beneficiaries. Once implemented, this proposal will improve the availability and quality of medicines.

Problems with Empanelled Hospitals: Delays in clearance of bills from empanelled hospitals greatly impact the quality of patient care being provided by these institutions. There are reports that they sometimes deny admission to ESM, citing that the fixed number of beds allotted to ECHS beneficiaries have already been filled. The delays seem to stem from the fact that all hospital bills are required to be vetted by doctors at the polyclinics. The staff and doctors at the polyclinics are already overburdened, so it is thus time to think of outsourcing services to a third party as is done by private insurance companies. These third-party administrators can process the bills and sanction funds speedily while ensuring that due vigilance is maintained.

On the other side of the coin, these private hospitals also need to maintain better standards of probity. Numerous malpractices have been reported, including denial of listed procedures; insistence on cash payments; lack of specialists or investigation facilities; extra charges for disposables, medicines or food; denial of admission to authorised dependents; and medical negligence. These issues seem to have been aggravated by the undue delay in clearance of bills and have become a major irritant.

For an optimum relationship with the empanelled hospitals, we need to review the contract rates periodically to address genuine concerns and ensure strict quality control and vigilance checks. Warnings should be issued to defaulting hospitals, followed by stopping referrals to them and finally imposing the malpractices and unethical conduct code by removing them from the panel.

Modernising Consultations: Doctor consultations over the internet and telephone became very popular during the COVID-19 pandemic. Where feasible these forms of consultations should be resumed and expanded to minimise the inconvenience of travel for patients. An effort in this regard is the Services e-Health Assistance and Teleconsultation (SeHAT), launched by the MoD in 2021. It has a 'home OPD' that enables a patient to consult a doctor through the internet. It is based on eSanjeevani, a similar free OPD service for all citizens from the ministry of health.

Automation: Full automation similar to the Enterprise Resource Planning (ERP) systems of advanced hospitals is also required for the ECHS. It will improve pharmacy inventory management, provide patient medical history to doctors and improve billing and approval procedures, among many other advantages. Automation will also enhance transparency and thereby improve patient satisfaction.

Vigilance: To put a curb on malpractices, effective vigilance mechanisms need to be put in place and continuously upgraded. While the ECHS ensures a structured and transparent approach, there are also instances of patients with no scruples who indulge in unauthorised treatments and others who allow the service to be used by unentitled persons. Such behaviour has had an adverse impact on genuine beneficiaries receiving entitled benefits. The beneficiaries also have an important role to play in maintaining vigilance and carry a major share of responsibility for ensuring the scheme is not being exploited unfairly.

Better Handling of Patients: Ensuring adequate staff would lead to efficient functioning of the polyclinics. This will contribute tangibly towards mitigating the hardships of patients. There are periodic reports of heated exchanges at the polyclinics, both among patients and the staff. The patients need to be handled with dignity and care and their concerns assuaged with the necessary soft skills. For better management, they can consider an app-based service of the kind that modern hospitals use.

Contingency Plans for Emergencies

During the COVID-19 pandemic, empanelled hospitals generally refused to admit ESM, apparently for pecuniary interests. The situation was exacerbated by the fact that the ECHS pays at government rates, while the empanelled institutions are mostly higher-grade private hospitals, where rates surge during pandemics and such emergencies. This resulted in the polyclinics being stretched to the maximum, even though they did not have the capability to handle a pandemic-like situation.

Eventually, the ESM load fell back on the military hospitals. However, there are only 135 hospitals across the three services, with a total bed capacity of 35,000. Even in non-emergency periods, these hospitals have to deal with a severe shortfall of specialist doctors, nursing staff and paramedics. To compound matters, the border skirmishes with China in Ladakh was at its peak at the time. With the heavy troop's deployment, the military hospital load had increased manifold. Thus, they were not in a position to handle the ESM load on top of that. Despite all these problems, the three services somehow created an additional capacity of 9,000 COVID-19 beds of which 3,000 were equipped with oxygen.

We should learn from this experience and equip the ECHS to better deal with a similar situation in the future.[4] A study group should be formed to analyse the likely contingencies and the additional capacity that would be needed. One idea is to set up hospitals for veterans in major cities. It would take up to fifteen years to construct these hospitals from the time the proposal is approved, so the process needs to be expedited. Yes, it is an expensive proposal, but also an essential one.

However, if it proves difficult to get approval, an alternative is to add veterans' wings to the existing military hospitals. These additional wings could be built using prefabricated structures and tented accommodation somewhat akin to field hospitals, which must be procured and kept ready for deployment once an emergency is declared. There should be a provision to automatically sanction the finances required to procure essential medical equipment and supplies and employ additional manpower during emergencies.

In addition to these measures, the facilities in the polyclinics in remote areas must be enhanced to include emergency diagnostic procedures. Like mini hospitals, they need to have the capacity to treat patients until they can be transferred to a bigger hospital. This would entail giving more financial powers to the officers commanding the polyclinics, as also developing better infrastructure for handling emergency situations.

Proposals under Consideration

While the ECHS has been successful, constant reviews of its functioning are a must. One idea to improve the system is through supplementation by private insurance companies. Of course, it is lucrative prospect for the companies, and they will readily step in. But we have to be very careful to adopt such a measure when perhaps the existing system can deliver far better results with a bit more effort.

Notwithstanding any reservations on the matter, some insurance companies were invited to propose a medical coverage package for ESM and their dependents, with the premiums to be paid by the government. However, despite the efforts of these companies to evolve a system, they are yet to produce a seamless model.

Conclusion

The ECHS is a remarkable example of India's commitment to caring for ESM and their dependents. It has helped preserve the dignity of our veterans. The success of the scheme owes lot to the synergy among the three services and the helpful attitude of the government. It also greatly helped that successive service chiefs have kept the ECHS as a major area of their focus.

I am also glad that we have been able to live up to Prime Minister Vajpayee's expectation of doing better than the CGHS. In twenty years, we have a membership of 5.5 million as compared to the CGHS membership of 3.5 million over seventy years. However, this scheme can always be improved and we must keep striving to do better. The dignity of a soldier should remain intact even after retirement.

Part III

Army Welfare Education System

The Context

A job in the armed forces comes with frequent transfers, and that too to remote areas. Therefore, the children of personnel move frequently from one station to another. The positive of having such a childhood is that military children are often highly adaptable, flexible and adventurous. However, the downside is that they often find themselves in places that have very limited educational facilities. In the absence of a good educational infrastructure, the armed forces are left with no option but to create their own facilities to ensure their children don't fall behind in school. The reality of the armed forces not being able to depend on the civil government for educational facilities for their children became clear to the military leadership several decades ago.

Army Schools

In 1980, a decision was taken to establish schools in various regional commands. This led to the creation and registration of the Army Welfare Education Society (AWES), under the aegis of which these schools were to operate. This step was necessary to meet the statutory requirement for affiliation to the Central Board of Secondary Education (CBSE). In the first stage, twenty-eight regimental schools and four high schools were established. Since then, the story of army schools is one of remarkable success.

The schools established under AWES were initially called 'Army High Schools' and later renamed to 'Army Schools' before another change to 'Army Public Schools' (APSs), as they are now known since 1 July 2011. As of 2023, there are 136 APS and 249 army pre-primary schools across cantonments and military stations in India. There are a total of 3.5 lakh students enrolled in these schools with around 8,500 teaching staff. During my tenure as COAS, the army added about 20 APS with an additional 2,000 seats. Six more schools for which work had already started, were added within one year after my retirement.

Higher Education

The success and popularity of the APS was due to the high standards set by them. It emboldened the army to raise the bar and establish higher education institutes such as professional colleges. In 1994, then COAS General B.C. Joshi took the far-reaching decision to offer professional education to military children in our own institutions. This made it possible for many army children to access these otherwise expensive professional programs at very affordable costs. Another major advantage in establishing our own institutes was exclusivity. As admission to such professional institutes was restricted to the wards of armed forces personnel, aspirants had to compete only against their fellow military children.

This initiative initially saw the establishment of one engineering college – the Army Institute of Technology (AIT) in Pune. From that first step, the college system has grown to twelve professional institutions offering degrees in the fields of hotel management and catering technology, law, dental sciences, education, fashion design, engineering and medical studies.

I was personally involved in the development/opening of six of these colleges during my tenure as COAS. These included the Army Institute of Education in Greater Noida (established in 2003); the Army Institute of Management and Technology, Greater Noida (2004); the Army Institute of Fashion and Design, Bengaluru (2004); the Army Institute of Higher Education, Pathankot (2004); the Army College of Nursing, Jalandhar (2005); and the Army College of Medical Science, Delhi Cantonment (2004).

We did not have enough financial resources for the project of establishing the medical college in Delhi. The army owned the land so the formalities regarding permissions for construction were completed without much difficulty. However, the lack of funds was posing a problem. I called for a meeting of all the army commanders in Delhi and sought their suggestions on the matter. It became clear that our own welfare funds were not in a position to spare the money required, so the only possible option was to take a share of the canteen profits from the units in peace stations.

The commanders were not pleased about this and a very animated discussion ensued. I eventually got everyone's agreements on the proposal – but during the lunch break, I found that the commanders were not in a mood to talk to me! I went ahead anyway and now the medical college is very popular. It has also given opportunities to the children of JCOs and other ranks to join this much sought-after stream of professional education as the fee for the programme has purposely been kept well within the financial reach of all ranks.

The Present Situation

It is indeed most satisfying to see that today the armed forces are not only in a position to cater for the education of their own staff's children but are part of the national effort towards higher education. One factor that always has remained constant is the high quality of education in the APSs and our professional colleges. In February 2023, General Manoj Pande talked about the ongoing adaption process under AWES to align the APS and military higher educational institutes with the National Education Policy (NEP) 2020, which has heralded a transformation in education. He highlighted the 'areas of inclusivity, foundational stage development, technology upgrade and teacher's empowerment' as well as the 'flexible, liberal and multidisciplinary ecosystem of higher education'.[5]

It is noteworthy that the board of administration of AWES have been actively pursuing the key welfare objective of shaping the students into responsible citizens and professionals of tomorrow. Another admirable initiative is the army's support of government-aided schools as part of the 'Vidyanjali Project' launched by the education ministry of India. As of today, under this project the 136 APSs have adopted 179 government schools representing every state of India. This number does not include the schools adopted by the navy and the air force.

Conclusion

It is to the credit of the armed forces that they manage to create facilities and fend for themselves in all fields. The professional colleges under AWES are a popular choice for the children of armed forces personnel while the APSs are held in high regard not only among the armed forces but also the civil population. My son studied at APS Dhaula Kuan and recalls that the educational standards were of the highest level, as was the efficiency in administration. The alumni of these institutions are prominent in all walks of life, be it the military or the corporate world. They have found employment in the fields of finance, IT and even the film industry.

Part IV

Manekshaw Centre

One of the major amenities I always felt that we lacked in the army was a sophisticated convention hall with modern infrastructure. I recall that when General Tapishwar Narain Raina retired as COAS on 31 May 1977, he addressed Delhi-based officers at Dhaula Kuan. I was posted in Delhi at the time and so I was present. I remember that he had rued the absence of an auditorium, and it always remained in my mind. So, when many years later I became COAS myself, I decided to work on establishing such a facility.

The location and design of the complex was approved in-house and the financial approvals from the government were also finalised during my tenure. These efforts resulted in the laying of the foundations of the prestigious Manekshaw Centre. One important theme that was always kept in mind was that the building and its décor should befit an army complex and should not be like a five-star hotel. The construction thereafter took a number of years and was completed during General Deepak Kapoor's tenure. It was inaugurated by Pratibha Devi Singh Patil, president of India, on 21 October 2010. This project is entirely self-sustaining with no burden on manpower or finances of the army. The facilities at this centre are provided at nominal costs only within the armed forces. The elegant interior decor of the building showcases the rich ethos and glorious traditions of the Indian Army and also reflects the diverse and remarkable cultural heritage of our country. The facility is a multi-utility and spread over 25 acres of landscaped area. It has multiple auditorium halls, meeting rooms, restaurants, bars, gallery and exhibition spaces. The auditorium halls within Manekshaw Centre host a variety of events, including seminars, conferences, cultural performances and official ceremonies, and the exhibition spaces provide a platform for presentations and artistic expressions. Today the centre acts as an attraction and a versatile venue for the Indian Army and the broader defence community, hosting events, meetings, and cultural programs. Its significance lies not only in its functional aspects, but also in its tribute to the legendary Field Marshal Sam Manekshaw.

Part V

Married Accommodation Project

Fully realising the importance of keeping a soldier and his family secure and also enabling them to stay together, the prime minister in 2001, called for a bigger thrust to construct the deficient dwelling units (DUs) for the defence service personnel. The approved proposal aimed at removing the complete deficiency of married accommodation.

As a step in the right direction, a separate Directorate General Married Accommodation Project (DG MAP) was raised on 31 May 2002. On taking over, I perused the paperwork and within a short time got approval for the same from the government by November 2003. The initial approved plan was for construction of 1,98,881 DUs, combined for three services. The project was to be completed in four phases. In phase 1 and 2, the construction of around 1.3 lakh DUs has been completed ameliorating to some extent long standing deficiency and requirement.

Unfortunately, as per latest indications the project is running behind schedule. According to some reports of parliamentary committee on defence, even after construction of dwelling units over time there still is a deficiency of around 71,000 DUs. Further allocation of adequate funds is a major problem. During the oral evidence in parliamentary committee, it was informed that the ranks and officers who are in the combat wing of the armed forces suffer the most as they spend larger part of their service in the field or difficult areas. Therefore, this needs immediate attention.

Conclusion

Sustained welfare support measures, both in peace and field or conflict, are of immense value. Typically, well-being has been defined as the combination of feeling good and functioning well; the experience of positive emotions, having some control over one's life and having a sense of purpose. Once a soldier relates to the meaning of well-being and methods instituted by leadership of armed forces, his functionality shall automatically improve. The fructification and implementation of some major game changing welfare measures, during my time at helm, still leaves me with a sense of happiness, satisfaction and above all pride to have been part of the most non-demanding and yet high-performing army, operating under varied conditions of terrain and facing operational challenges not seen by any other soldier across the world.

Epilogue

'You are a warrior. Your duty is to stand up and fight against injustice. Nothing is more important for you than this.'
                    Lord Krishna in the Bhagavad Gita

My journey in the Indian Army began on 11 December 1962, when I was not yet twenty. I was very fortunate to be commissioned in one of the army's finest and most decorated infantry regiments, the Dogra Regiment. My unit was to be 4 Dogra, which had fought a heroic battle in Walong against the PLA less than a month before I joined. After over two days of fighting in November 1962, 4 Dogra lost 109 men while 23 were wounded. Additionally, 74 were taken as prisoners. However, the result was that the Chinese aggression was halted at Walong because of the heavy casualties they suffered. For me it was truly baptism with fire.

The army had taken the setback of 1962 very seriously and pledged that never again would they go to battle half-prepared. From then on, we remained in a feverish routine of training and preparation. This has ensured that the army has maintained a high standard of professionalism ever since. It is ironic that at Independence Prime Minister Nehru had announced that we would be a peace-loving country with no enemies, yet we have fought five wars since then.

Besides war, we have dealt with decades of militancy in the Northeast and Jammu and Kashmir, as well as around fifteen years of militancy in Punjab. The years have thrown many challenges at our military, yet India has emerged triumphant in all these operations. It speaks volumes of the bravado and grit of the Indian soldiers and military leadership.

When India is at war, the nation unites and there is a strong spirit of patriotism. The successes of the armed forces have always been greeted with celebration by our citizens. Our nation is extremely proud of our armed forces. One lesson that I learnt at the very beginning of my military career was that when well led from the front, Indian troops can surmount all odds. This confidence has remained with me throughout my service.

Our security situation remains grim. Unfortunately, we are bordered by two countries whose interests are inimical to us. One of them, China, has ambitions to be the sole superpower in the world and cannot tolerate India emerging in the same league. They are most unlikely to settle their borders with India in the foreseeable future. The other one, Pakistan, suffers from an existential threat, wherein it has not been able to reconcile to its own existence.

The Kashmir issue has always served as a rallying point for Pakistan to keep its national unity intact and allow its army to rule over its national affairs. Democracy is a fig leaf of sorts. These countries are more than likely to act in nexus, which adds to the gravity of the situation for us. There is little to no chance of reducing tensions along either the LAC or the LOC as past initiatives to resolve these issues have resulted in unreliable agreements. Hence there is a requirement for us to always remain vigilant and in a state of operational readiness.

When I was commissioned, the strength of the Indian Army was just 5,50,000. There was an enormous shortage of weapons and equipment. The weapons that we did have were obsolete. After fighting three wars in the space of a decade in the 1960s and early 1970s, the national leadership realised the folly of underestimating the challenge to our nation's security.

Ever since, slowly but steadily the army is being transformed. Today, the strength of our army is over 12,37,000. The navy and the air force have also been vastly improved and they are in the process of acquiring fifth-generation weapons and fighters. However, there are still shortfalls. The army lags behind the other forces but is catching up.

Over the past fifteen years we have also started working on indigenisation and manufacturing of war supplies within India. The nation has resolved to acquire high-grade cyber capabilities, artificial intelligence and other cutting-edge technologies and thereby be prepared for the next generation of war. A high degree of indigenisation and self-sufficiency is likely to be achieved within the next twenty years.

Looking back at my forty-three years of service in the Indian Army, I feel that it was a high-octane period right through. The goal was to constantly improve, because irrespective of the rank one attains in the army, one is still only at a point on the learning curve. Fortunately, moving up in rank comes with an expansion of horizon, and one gets the opportunity to deal with national security issues in a decision-making role together with the government.

From my childhood, I have loved the military profession. I suppose it was a calling. Despite the endless periods of high pressure and the frantic tempo of work that rarely slowed down, there was always a desire for more achievements and improvement. It is a profession where you love your comrades in arms. You never lose your faith in each other. There is no other profession in which one would be prepared to lay down one's life on command without a second thought. In the military, it is done in the service of your nation and for the dignity and fame of your units and regiment.

A brief summary of our journey during my tenure is given in Appendix A. Fifteen days before I retired, I addressed a letter to all 30,000-plus officers of the Indian Army in which I reminisced over the milestones that we all had traversed together during my tenure. I wanted to acknowledge that all the achievements of that period were possible only because of their wholehearted support, cooperation and immense hard work. This letter was also a reminder to them that they should remain confident in their abilities to attain even higher goals and face challenges in the years ahead (see Appendix B).

Acknowledgements

It is my true belief that it is an obligation for senior officers in the armed forces to share the knowledge they have gained from their experiences during service to enable future generations to learn from and improve upon the same for overall enhancement of professionalism in the forces. During the journey to recount these experiences, I was encouraged and greatly assisted by many friends, colleagues and, above all, my family.

For this book, great care has been taken to ensure that no sensitive information is included while still recounting events as they actually happened. To do that I have depended enormously on my associates from the army. I would like to express my deep gratitude to those who helped me recapitulate the details of various episodes covered in the book. The manuscript of this book was shared with many colleagues for their analytical comments.

I would like to thank Colonel Vijay Kumar, my former deputy military attaché, for his thorough research work and his help in completing the book. He has been a pillar of strength. My gratitude goes out to Lieutenant General Ravi Sawhney, who was DGMI during my tenure as DGMO and was thus closely involved with the Kargil war and Operation Khukri in Sierra Leone. I have relied upon his advice on many other topics too. I must make special mention of Lieutenant General Mohinder Puri, who helped with the chapter on the Kargil operations. Vital support was received from Lieutenant General Richard Khare, who became DGMI after Lieutenant General Sawhney and was involved with all operational matters after Operation Khukri.

Lieutenant General Ata Hasnain, who was involved with anti-militancy operations in Jammu and Kashmir for a very long time, has also made notable contributions to the book. My thanks also to Lieutenant General Mohinder Singh, who made immense contributions to the chapters on major welfare initiatives such as the AVSC, ECHS and AWES. Lieutenant General Mahesh Vij, who served as military secretary during my time, also made a very valuable contribution in the chapter on the AVSC. I must also acknowledge the advice of Lieutenant General Anil Ahuja on the chapters on integration and theaterisation and the cold start doctrine. It is not possible for me to include the names of everyone, but for their valuable observations it would not have been possible to arrive at a balanced view on the various subjects covered in the book.

I am also thankful to Krishan Chopra, who helped steer this book, and to my publishers, Bloomsbury – especially Nitin Valecha, associate publisher; Anil Ahuja, cover designer; Jaishree Ram Mohan, managing editor; and their team – for encouraging me to write, helping evolve the main structure of the book and editing the same. They were immensely cooperative and provided many useful inputs.

I would also like to put on record my deepest appreciation for my wife, Rita, our son, Nalin Vij, daughter-in-law, Maneerat Tanasarnsaenee, and our grandchildren, Nimit and Rhea, for inspiring me to write this book.

Lastly, I would like to convey my deepest gratitude to all ranks of the Indian Army for their immense contributions and sacrifices, without which our nation would not be as secure as it is today.

Appendix A
Journey Highlights of My Tenure

- Conceptualisation and establishment of a 740-km-long anti-infiltration obstacle system (Fence) along the LOC from River Chenab to Zoji La in just 16 to 18 months, surmounting all odds of terrain and enemy interference. This reduced the infiltration to a trickle (down to 33 per cent in the first year itself).
- Revolutionised health care system for ex-servicemen and their families through launch of Ex-servicemen Contributory Health Scheme (ECHS), a step that brought dignity to the lives of veterans.
- Facilitating approval and implementation of A.V. Singh committee recommendations for early, time-bound and assured career progression of young officers, resulting in promotion of 19,642 officers on a single day in December 2004. Time-scale promotion to colonels was fixed at 26 years.
- Conceptualisation and adoption of 'Cold Start Doctrine' to offset Pakistan's advantage of shorter operational deployment time. The doctrine included creation of Pre- Orbatted Battle Groups located close to the IB, for launching swift offensive in 48 to 96 hours (now termed IBGs).
- Getting approval and issuing operational guidelines for raising of HQs South Western Command and HQs 9 Corps, for acquiring a strategically balanced operational posture. These were accretive forces.
- Carried out a well-coordinated, large-sized operation against insurgents belonging to ULFA, KLO and NDFB groups, crippling their bases and nearly wiping out insurgency in West Bengal and Assam.

- Enhancing the ongoing concept and scope of higher education for wards of Army personnel by setting up eight additional professional colleges under the Army Welfare Education Society, including the Army College of Medical Sciences in New Delhi next to Base Hospital.
- Expedited work on construction of the prime-minister approved Married Accommodation Project (MAP) of 1,98,000 houses to minimise housing deficiency for all ranks.
- Creation of first Directorate General of Information System (C4I2), spearheading the transformation to network centric operations.
- Launch of Non-Commissioned Officers' Academy at Binaguri to train 12,000 NCOs every year.
- Established an Army think tank, the Centre for Land and Air Warfare Studies, in Delhi Cantonment, which has acquired a leading status today.
- Conceptualised a modern multi-facility complex with two auditoriums, conventional halls and an officers' mess with capacity for 800 to 1,000 members. The designing of the structure and financial sanctions were obtained from the government in my tenure and construction work followed over a number of years over the tenure of two of my successors.
- Starting work on setting up of a Defence Services Officers Institute (DSOI), in conjunction with the other two services, in Gurugram. Land was acquired for ₹1, on lease.
- Started the tradition of 'Chiefs Conclave' to seek advice and opinion from the former chiefs about the state of the Army based on their observations. Two clear messages emerged from the conclave – the Army is 'one big family' to which you belong and 'old is gold' in our profession.

Appendix B

Letter to All Officers of the Indian Army

General NC Vij,
PVSM, UYSM, AVSM, ADC

Army Headquarters
New Delhi – 110 011

A/00043/1/COAS   15 January 05

Dear Colleague,

1. I shall soon conclude my innings as your **Chief**; innings which I have found to be exhilarating, challenging and most satisfying at the professional level. I have already conveyed to you that I shall **not** be visiting any formation headquarters for my farewell. I have taken this decision on two counts – firstly, because I have visited you so often that I need not go through a farewell visit merely for the sake of form and secondly, after spending a lifetime in the Army, one can never really bid farewell to this great and unique brotherhood. I shall always **remain attached** to our **Great Army** till I finally fade away.

2. Today is **'Army Day'** and it is also my last one in the present capacity. On this occasion, I can reminisce with you about some of the important events, indeed milestones, which **you** and I have traversed together over the last two years. Generally, messages to the Army are sent by the **Chiefs** on assuming office, **but** I chose not to do so, as I first wanted to chart my course and have you all on board to jointly pursue that goal. Similarly, a Chief's first 'Army Day' message normally highlights future plans. However, this being my last one, it has to necessarily dwell on what you and I have been able to achieve together. What we have achieved **must not** lead to any sense of **complacency** but should promote confidence in your ability to attain yet higher goals in the coming years.

Appendix B

2

3. What did I really aim for :-

"**An inspiring approach towards performing our duty with a sense of direction, confidence and self esteem**".

As to how much did we achieve, we all can draw our own conclusions; but the fact is that **"You all gave Your very best"** and I compliment you for that.

Operations

4. **Tribute**. I would like to begin by paying my most solemn tribute to all those officers, Junior Commissioned Officers and men who have made the supreme sacrifice in the service of our motherland, in keeping with the glorious and high traditions of this Great Army of ours. Ever since independence, our Army has been engaged in fighting several wars and ongoing militancy, including proxy war, for decades with an illustrious and unparalleled record of service to the Nation. I salute all our departed heroes. I also salute the civilian personnel who form an important part of our Army for their devotion and selfless service and for the sacrifices made by them.

5. **Jammu and Kashmir.** Our **three pronged strategy of** combating 'Proxy War' viz, checking infiltration, conducting concerted operations in the hinterland and 'Winning Hearts and Minds' has paid handsome dividends. The **700 Km long fence** created by you all in a record time of less than one year, in the most inhospitable terrain, has brought the **infiltration to a near standstill**. The number of militants has been reduced from 3,500

in January 03 to approximately 1800 now. Consequently, the level of violence in the hinterland has also been brought down thereby **stemming the tide of 'Proxy War'**. **Civic actions** under 'Operation SADBHAVANA' have also been one of **our major thrust areas** with very positive effect. As a result, the current situation holds great promise for **early return of normalcy** in the entire state. **Well done indeed!** I must also compliment commanders at all levels for their sharp focus on upholding the Human Rights of **our people**. Our track record in this respect has indeed been outstanding and has accordingly been commended by the 'National Human Rights Commission'. However, there have been **some aberrations** and we **must** endeavour to **obviate these altogether**. In this regard, our approach towards **transparency** and **speedy dispensation of justice** has been well appreciated and must be pursued with missionary zeal.

6. <u>**North East**</u>. The well coordinated operations between the 'Indian Army' and the 'Royal Bhutan Army' in December 03 - January 04 have appreciably marginalised the KLO, ULFA and the NDFB outfits and brought the insurgencies in West Bengal and Assam to near end. In addition, our thrust on SADBHAVANA like projects has brought about a change in the mind set amongst the people thereby isolating the militants. The Naga peace talks are progressing well and the overall situation is looking up in the North East. The militancy in Manipur continues to simmer, however, it is now being addressed adequately.

7. <u>**Our New Operational Strategy and Doctrine**</u>. Drawing lessons from our experiences in 'Operations VIJAY and PARAKRAM', wherein I was the Director General of Military Operations and the 'Vice Chief' respectively, we have evolved and

Appendix B

4

extensively wargamed the new **'Strategy'** which shall meet our contemporary operational imperatives. Accordingly, we have, in consultation with all Commands, formulated and issued the **'Indian Army Doctrine'** for the first time. You all would have read Part I of this doctrine. Part II, which deals with the operational specifics, is classified and issued to Commands only. Now, we can say with confidence that we shall be able to **respond to** any challenge faced by our country **most expeditiously**. We have also started a **'Centre for Land Warfare Studies' (CLAWS)** headed by a former 'Vice Chief' to act as a sounding board for new thoughts, doctrine and strategy for the Army. This would also serve as a **think tank** with inputs also flowing from our ex-servicemen and other military thinkers.

Modernisation and Management of Revolution in Military Affairs

8. **Modernisation.** Much needed and all encompassing modernisation of Indian Army is well on its way. Many a **State of the Art** weapons and equipment have been inducted and many more are in the pipeline, in synchronization with the 'Revolution in Military Affairs'; to provide **the best to our men in field.**

9. **Revolution in Military Affairs.** We are fully gearing up ourselves to face the challenges posed by the Revolution in Military Affairs. A concerted drive to rapidly develop **"Information Systems"** is going ahead full steam to enable effective conduct of **"Network Centric Operations"**. For this reason, the erstwhile appointment of the **Deputy Chief of the Army Staff (Training and Coordination)** has been replaced by **'Deputy Chief of the Army Staff (Information Systems and**

Appendix B

5

Training)' at the Army Headquarters, with matching organisations at the Command and Corps Headquarters, from within the existing resources.

Improvements in Organisational Structure

10. A case has been projected to the Government to create some additional headquarters albeit without any force accretion. This will greatly facilitate more effective command and control in relation to our new strategy. It should materialise **soon**.

Training

11. **Non Commissioned Officers Academy**. The changing complexities of future wars and Counter Terrorism operations impose even greater responsibility on the shoulders of the junior leaders than ever before. Far more initiative and qualities of leadership will now have to be exhibited by the Non Commissioned Officers. In view of this, we are starting construction of a **'Non Commissioned Officers Academy'** at 'Bengdubi' with an annual capacity of 12,000 to be finally raised to 20,000 Havildars. In the interim, the pilot course will start at 'Binaguri' from 15 April 2005 with a capacity of 700 students per course. The 'Bengdubi Academy' shall be a **unique** model in the world in terms of quality of training and its mammoth training capacity.

12. **Training Courses**. All courses for Officers, Junior Commissioned Officers and Non Commissioned Officers have been rationalised by deleting/amalgamating and suitably modifying

their duration. This has been done through a study over one year in consultation with all Commands and training establishments.

Organisational Aspects and Welfare

13. **Career Prospects of Officers**. The much justified and long awaited upgradation in the career prospects of officers has now been implemented with effect from 16 December 04, when **19,642** officers were promoted in one day as under :-

(a) Lieutenant Colonels to Colonels(Time Scale)- 62

(b) Majors to Lieutenant Colonels - 10,296
(with 13 years service)

(c) Captains to Majors - 3,803
(with 6 years service)

(d) Lieutenant to Captains - 5,481
(with two years service)

(e) **Every one will now retire at least as a 'Colonel'.**

14. Since the 'Ajai Vikram Singh Committee' study was aimed at **lowering the age** of the Commanding Officers and Commanders at all levels and also correspondingly improve the career prospects, **posts of additional '750 Colonels'** have been created by the Government to ensure cadre mobility. The balance of the report for the senior ranks will be processed in due course. With this momentous decision, the Government has done great justice to the officer's cadre. For the men, the same has already

been achieved through the implementation of the **'Assured Career Progression'** scheme since last year.

15. **Shortage of Officers**. Restricted promotion prospects and slow pace of career progression had been acting, as a disincentive for the youth to come forward to join the Army. This had led to grave shortages in the Officer Cadre as also some degree of disillusionment. This aspect has now been **suitably addressed**. A concerted drive was launched in early 2003 to make up the shortfall of officers in the Army. The capacities in Indian Military Academy, Officers Training Academy and Army Cadet College have been enhanced to commissioning of over 2000 from erstwhile 1500 officers per year. The intake of 'women officers' is being increased to 150 per year; their service has been extended upto 14 years and they have now been made eligible for foreign postings. The case for granting them study leave and vacancies on Staff College courses, is under active consideration with the Government. The terms and conditions for all 'Short Service Commissioned Officers', both men and women, will be similar and shall definitely get a **further uplift** in the years to come as part of the remaining recommendations of 'Ajai Vikram Singh Committee Report'.

Transparency in Personnel Matters – Military Secretary Branch

16. This has been one big **thrust area** and many policies have been formulated and communicated to the environment to ensure **transparency**. Broadly, these deal with simplification of redressal procedures and their disposal within six months; free access to Military Secretary's Branch for all officers; Commanding Officers

and formation commanders being consulted by Military Secretary formally to plan officers' postings; and ensuring impeccable fairness in the selection of officers for foreign postings wherein the results are announced on the spot. **'Final Supersession'** has been done away with for the rank of 'Colonel' by introducing the format of **"Special Merit Selection Board"** with 10 per cent of a batch vacancies being reserved for these candidates. The redressal to **'Major Generals'** is now being given through the **"Special Selection Board"**, wherein all Army Commanders and Vice Chief of the Army Staff assist the Chief. I am, however, fully conscious that a lot more can be and **must** be done to bring about even greater transparency in the system.

Education Facilities for Our Children

17. The concept of building educational facilities from within our own resources in the Army was started soon after the 1971 War. A lot has been added on regularly by all my **illustrious predecessors** over the years.

18. We have now undertaken a vigorous drive in this direction. Today we have 116 Army Schools with 1,40,000 children and plans to have ten schools, with modern infrastructure, constructed every year, thereby generating additional annual capacity of approximately seven to eight thousand. We already have **nine professional colleges** of which five i.e., Army Law College at Mohali, Army Dental College at Secunderabad, Army Institute of Fashion Design at Bangalore, Army Institute of Management Training at Noida and B Ed College at Delhi Cantonment have been started **in the last two years. Three more** i.e., **Army Medical College** in Base Hospital at Delhi Cantonment, B Ed

9

College at Mamun and Nursing College at Jalandhar, will take off in the next six months. We have presently 2,000 professional seats for our children and hope to increase these to 4,500 over the next five to seven years. Because of the rapid and considerable expansion in this field, **'Army Welfare Education Society'(AWES)** has been made autonomous and restructured on the lines of 'Army Group Insurance' and 'Army Welfare Housing Organisation'.

Ex Servicemen's Contributory Medical Health Scheme

19. This is the biggest scheme of its kind in the world. After a concerted effort of many of my predecessors, it finally took off in 2003 and with the help of all Commands, we have already established **132 Polyclinics** out of total projection of **227** and empanelled **211 civil hospitals/diagnostic centres**. The process of empanelment of many more such hospitals/centres is underway. From this solid foundation, we can build it up further to entirely fulfil the long standing aspirations of our ex servicemen and their families.

Army Group Insurance

20. The benefits of Army Group Insurance have been expanded with effect from 01 Jan 05 to ensure **better maturity value** and **higher insurance cover** during the service as also to provide **extended insurance cover** upto 25 years of retired period or 75 years of age, whichever is earlier. Details are given overleaf:-

Appendix B

	Officers		Personnel Below officer Rank	
	During Service	Extended Insurance	During Service	Extended Insurance
(a) **Premium**	Rs 1500 (per month)	Rs 31,300 (one time)	Rs 750 (per month)	Rs 15,500 (one time)
(b) **Insurance Cover**	Rs **15 Lacs**	Rs **4 Lacs**	Rs **7.5 Lacs**	Rs **2 Lacs**
(c) **Maturity Value**	Upto Rs **24.62 Lacs** after 34 years of subscription	—	JCOs - Rs **7.72 lacs** Hav - Rs **5.36 lacs** Nk (TS) - Rs **2.67 lacs**	

Married Accommodation Project

21. The Government has sanctioned construction of **1,98,000** houses for the Army over five years to appreciably reduce the waiting period and ensure near 100 per cent availability of accommodation. This scheme has taken off fully and already **7,745** houses are under construction and construction of **52,557** houses will start in the Financial Year 2005-2006.

Army Welfare Housing Organisation

22. Army Welfare Housing Organisation has come a long way since its inception in 1978 and is now a dynamic organisation comparable to the best in the business of construction. A **feedback** was obtained recently from a very large cross section of the officers and men about the **improvements desired** in the quality of

11

houses and terms and conditions being offered by the Army Welfare Housing Organisation. All useful and practical recommendations are already in the process of being **implemented.** It is now being ensured that Army Welfare Housing Organisation colonies provide all modern **amenities** and **administrative support** on the same lines as the best of builders, **albeit at much lower cost** since ours is a welfare organisation. Hereafter, facilities like swimming pools, schools, shopping centres, community halls, gymnasiums and sports facilities like tennis and squash courts will be available in these colonies. The emphasis will also be on providing better construction specifications and an aesthetic environment. The housing complexes will be well located in major cities of the country and provide congenial and healthy atmosphere for living as available in the Army Cantonments.

Chiefs' Conclave – Army A Big Family

23. The first ever **'Chiefs' Conclave'** was held from 22-24 October 2004 to seek the advice and views of the former Chiefs on the state of the Army as they observed it from outside. This was attended by all (eight) former Chiefs and fifteen first ladies. The Government has also approved all **'Chiefs'** to be made **'Honorary Colonels'** of their respective Regiments for life. **Two clear messages** emerged from the Conclave that the "Army is **'one big family'** to which you belong forever" and also **"Old is Gold"** in our profession.

12

Adieu

24. Since I cannot reach out to **everyone personally**, I have shared the major happenings of the last two years with you, through this medium. There are many other important areas like sports and adventure activities where we have made conspicuous progress – the list is far too long to elaborate. **Each one of you** has been **instrumental,** in one way or the other, in achieving these milestones. These are, in fact, just a part of the **continuum** which all my **illustrious and towering predecessors** had established. I am sanguine that there is **so much more** that needs to be done! I am conscious of the fact that, on many occasions, I placed seemingly **impossible demands on you** like construction of the **fence**, but you have always **fully risen** upto it to attain good results. I **compliment** you whole-heartedly for your efforts and unstinted support.

25. I have always maintained that nothing can be achieved by an individual in his tenure unless he is supported by an efficient team. I was singularly fortunate in having **outstanding Commanders and troops,** who enthusiastically supported all our ventures. I looked at my **Army Commanders** as my pool of **'Wise Men'** and all the decisions that we took were as a **collegiate body,** after due deliberations. I am grateful to **each and everyone** of them. At the Army Headquarters, I had **outstanding** Principal Staff Officers and Director Generals, ably led by my **Vice Chief, Lieutenant General Shantonu Choudhry** who silently, and efficiently, created the environment and wherewithal for the organisation to meet the desired goals.

13

26. As mentioned earlier, I had also aimed at **further enhancing self-esteem and pride** in the officers' cadre and the Army through your **excellent** performance and **fulfilment** of your aspirations. I do hope that we achieved that! Ours has always been the **noblest and best** of all the professions and so shall it remain in the times to come. I am proud of having belonged to and having had the **honour** and **privilege** to lead this most **professional Army of the World**, which is also fully poised to soon become one of the best equipped.

27. I now pass on the baton to my very **distinguished successor, General JJ Singh** and I wish **him** and **you all** the very best of luck and success!

28. I think it would only be apt to end my epistle with a quote from Robert Frost which often inspired me **"The woods are lovely, dark and deep; but I have miles to go before I sleep."** I commend this quote to each one of you. As I now say **adieu** to you, I assure you that even after hanging my uniform, I shall **remain with you** in spirit and will look forward to seeing your future achievements with pride and affection.

"Good luck and God bless you all"

(NC Vij)
General

Notes

Chapter 1: The Kargil War

1. 'Musharraf Had Brought Kargil Plan to Me: Benazir', Rediff.com, 25 June 2003, https://www.rediff.com/news/2003/jun/25pak5.htm.
2. General V.P. Malik, 'Indo-Pak Security Relations in the Coming Decade: Lessons from Kargil for the Future', *Indian Defence Review*, January–March 2002, https://www.satp.org/satporgtp/publication/idr/vol_17(1)/VPMalik.htm.
3. General V.P. Malik, *India's Military Conflicts and Diplomacy* (HarperCollins, 2019), 102–103.
4. Benazir Bhutto, *Daughter of the East*, rev. ed. (Simon and Schuster, 2008).
5. Najam Sethi, in a YouTube video 'Kargil War: From Pakistan's Point of View', uploaded 23 November 2013, https://www.youtube.com/watch?v=RZfPOswET78.
6. General V.P. Malik (retd), 'Remembering Vajpayee, Warrior with Will to Win', *Hindustan Times*, 1 January 2024, https://www.hindustantimes.com/cities/chandigarh-news/remembering-vajpayee-warrior-with-will-to-win-101704049395659.html.
7. Air Commodore M. Kaiser Tufail, 'Role of the Pakistan Air Force During the Kargil Conflict', *Centre for Land and Air Warfare Studies*, (2009), https://archive.claws.in/images/journals_doc/1400825199M%20Kaiser%20Tufail%20CJ%20SSummer%202009.pdf.
8. Press Trust of India, 'Soldiers Took Part in Kargil Conflict: Former Pak Gen', *Deccan Herald*, 4 May 2018, https://www.deccanherald.com/world/soldiers-took-part-kargil-conflict-2238119.

9. 'The Kargil Tape that Nailed Pakistan', Newsmobile, 26 July 2018, https://www.newsmobile.in/2018/07/26/the-kargil-tape-that-nailed-pakistan/.
10. Malik, *India's Military Conflicts and Diplomacy*, 129.
11. 'Unless Pakistan Leaves Kargil Alone, No Discussion Can Take Place: Atal Bihari Vajpayee', uploaded 28 September 2017, https://www.youtube.com/watch?v=8OBsHqbNMFE.
12. Bruce Riedel, 'Remembering Sandy Berger and the Day He Saved the World', 2 December 2015, https://www.brookings.edu/articles/remembering-sandy-berger-and-the-day-he-saved-the-world/.
13. 'Kargil War Truth by Pakistani ISI Ex DG: Pakistan Badly Lost with Indian Army in Kargil War', uploaded 7 August 2020, https://www.youtube.com/watch?v=L5ivjjtRxfw.

Chapter 2: Operation Parakram

1. 'Battle against Terrorism Would Be Fought Decisively: PM', Rediff.com, 13 December 2001, https://www.rediff.com/news/2001/dec/13parl11.htm.
2. 'PM Promises Firm Reply to Terrorist Strike', Rediff.com, 14 December 2001, https://m.rediff.com/news/2001/dec/14parl6.htm.
3. S. Kalyanaraman, 'Operation Parakram: An Indian Exercise in Coercive Diplomacy', *Strategic Analysis*, 2002, 478–492.
4. 'Angry India Recalls High Commissioner to Pakistan', *Times of India*, 21 December 2001, https://timesofindia.indiatimes.com/india/Angry-India-recalls-High-Commissioner-to-Pak/articleshow/321558751.cms.
5. Sushil Kumar, 'Operation Parakram after Parliament Attack Lacked Clear Objectives', *Times of India*, 6 November 2011, https://timesofindia.indiatimes.com/india/Operation-Parakram-after-Parliament-attack-lacked-cleared-objectives-Ex-Navy-chief-Sushil-Kumar/articleshow/10625959.cms.
6. Ministry of Defence, Government of India, Annual Report 2002–03, https://mod.gov.in/sites/default/files/MOD-English2003_0.pdf.
7. Kalyanaraman, 'Operation Parakram'.

8   Bruce Pannier, 'The World Waits for Musharraf's Speech on Terrorism', Radio Free Europe, 11 January 2002, https://www.rferl.org/a/1098448.html.
9   'Deployment Completed, Says Delhi', *Dawn*, 3 January 2002, https://www.dawn.com/news/13215/deployment-completed-says-delhi.
10 'JCSC Reviews Counterstrategy', *Dawn*, 2 January 2002, https://www.dawn.com/news/13217/jcsc-reviews-counter-strategy.
11 J.P. Shukla, 'No Weapon Will Be Spared for Self-defence: PM', The Hindu, 2 January 2002, in Alex Stolar, 'To the Brink: Indian Decision-making and the 2001–2002 Standoff', Report No. 68 (The Henry L. Stimson Center, February 2008).
12 Javed Naqvi, 'The Saarc Handshake that Broke the Ice between Pakistan, India', *Dawn*, 28 September 2016, https://www.dawn.com/news/1286661
13 Ibid.
14 Praveen Swami, 'Gen. Padmanabhan Mulls Over Lessons of Operation Parakram', Hindu Vivek Kendra, 6 February 2004, https://www.hvk.org/2004/0204/92.html.
15 Ibid.
16 Praveen Sawhney, 'Bottomline: Jaswant's Butler', Force India, https://forceindia.net/bottomline/jaswants-bluster/.
17 Alex Stolar, 'To the Brink: Indian Decision-making and the 2001–2002 Standoff', *Report No. 68* (The Henry L. Stimson Center, February 2008).
18 Ibid.
19 Ibid.
20 Ibid.
21 Praveen Swami, 'Gen Padmanabhan Mulls Over Lessons of Operation Parakaram'.
22 Sandeep Bhardwaj, 'The 2001–2002 India–Pakistan Standoff (Operation Parakram): A Dangerous Experiment', Revisiting India: Indian History Recounted, 17 July 2013, https://revisitingindia.com/2013/07/17/the-2001-2002-india-pakistan-standoff-operation-parakram-a-dangerous-experiment/.

23 C. Uday Bhaskar, 'No Nation Must Stumble into War: Lessons from Op Parakram Post Uri', *The Quint*, 29 September 2016, https://www.thequint.com/news/india/no-nation-must-stumble-into-war-lessons-operation-parakram-post-uri-attack-pakistan-soldiers-jawans-kashmir-modi.
24 General V.P. Malik, quoted by Brigadier Gurmeet Kanwal, 'Lost Opportunities'.
25 Brahma Chellaney, 'Perils of Crying Wolf', *Hindustan Times*, 27 November 2002.
26 Praveen Sawhney, 'Bottomline: Jaswant's Bluster'.
27 General Padmanabhan, quoted by Brigadier Gurmeet Kanwal, 'Lost Opportunities'.
28 Press Trust of India 'Op Parakram Most Punishing Mistake: Ex-Navy Chief', *Indian Express*, 5 November 2011, https://indianexpress.com/article/news-archive/web/op-parakram-most-punishing-mistake-exnavy-chief/.
29 A.Y. Tipnis, quoted by Brigadier Gurmeet Kanwal, 'Lost Opportunities'.
30 Singh, *A Call to Honour*, 341.
31 General Shankar Roychowdhury, quoted by Brigadier Gurmeet Kanwal, 'Lost Opportunities'.
32 Aditi Phadnis, 'Parakram Cost Put at Rs 6,500 crore', Rediff.com, 16 Jan 2003, https://www.rediff.com/money/2003/jan/16defence.htm.
33 As quoted by Dr Muhammad Sajjad Malik and Dr Pervaiz Iqbal Cheema, 'Media Coverage of Pak-India Standoff 2002: An Analysis', *Journal of Political Studies*, 26 (1), 2019: 309–328, https://pu.edu.pk/images/journal/pols/pdf-files/20-v26_1_19.pdf.

Chapter 3: Operation Khukri

1 Sushant Singh, *Operation Khukri: Hostage Rescue in Sierra Leone* (Juggernaut, 2020), 18.
2 Vijay Kumar Jetley, 'Operation Khukri: The United Nations Operation Fought in Sierra Leone Part II', *USI Journal*, April–June 2007.
3 'Peacekeepers Are Rescued in Sierra Leone', *New York Times*, 16 July 2000.

4 J. Goldman, 'UN Completes Sierra Leone Rescue Mission', *Los Angeles Times*, 17 July 2000, https://www.latimes.com/archives/la-xpm-2000-jul-17-mn-54354-story.html.
5 Ibid.
6 United Nations, 'Security Council Expresses Full Support for Rescue of UN Peacekeepers in Kailahun, Sierra Leone', Press Release, 17 July 2000.

Chapter 4: The LoC Fence

1 Lieutenant General Syed Ata Hasnain, 'Why Fence on Line of Control?', Salute, 19 December 2014.
2 Lieutenant General Rostum K. Nanavatty, *Internal Armed Conflict in India* (Pentagon Press, 2013), 104.
3 Ibid., 127.
4 Hasnain, 'Why Fence on Line of Control?'

Chapter 5: Cold Start Doctrine

1 Ali Ahmed, 'Reopening the Debate on Limited War', Manohar Parrikar Institute of Defence Studies and Analysis, 29 February 2012.
2 Kalpana, 'Cold Start (Military Doctrine)', Alchetron, 3 November 2023, https://alchetron.com/Cold-Start-(military-doctrine).
3 Ajay Shukla, 'Gen VK Singh: "Army Able to Launch Faster Response Against Pak"', *Business Standard*, 13 January 2012.
4 Sandeep Unnithan, 'We Will Cross Again', *India Today*, 16 January 2017.
5 V.P. Malik, 'Strategic Stability in South Asia', panel discussion, Centre for Contemporary Conflict, Monterey, California, 29 June–1 July 2004, quoted by Walter C. Ladwig III, 'A Cold Start for Hot Wars? The Indian Army's New Limited War Doctrine', *Quarterly Journal: International Security*, 32 (3) 2007/08: 158–190.
6 Masood Ur Rehman Khattak, 'Indian Military's Cold Start Doctrine: Capabilities, Limitations and Possible Response from Pakistan', SASSI Research Paper, 31 March 2011.

7. Dr Zaffar Khan, 'Pakistan TNW and the State's Security Paradigm', *Express Tribune*, 31 December 2022.
8. As quoted by Masood Ur-Rehman Khattak, 'Indian Military's Cold Start Doctrine: Capabilities, Limitations and Possible Response from Pakistan', South Asian Strategic Stability Institute, 31 March 2011.
9. Sudarshan Shrikhande, 'There's no Such Thing as a Short War', *Times of India*, 21 February 2023.
10. Rajat Pandit, 'India Needs Capabilities to Tackle Grey Zone Warfare from China, Pakistan', *Times of India*, 23 March 2023.
11. Lieutenant General H.A. Panag, 'Modern Wars Need Technological Edge, Army's Integrated Battle Groups Will Be Toothless Without It', ThePrint, 19 May 2022.
12. Kapil Kajal, 'Indian Army Dissolves Old Units to Develop New Integrated Formations', Janes, 16 January 2023.

Chapter 6: Jointness, Integration and Theaterisation

1. Anil Ahuja and Arun Sahgal, 'A Process-led Approach Towards Integrated Military Commands', DPG Policy Brief, 6, no.22 (2021). https://www.delhipolicygroup.org/publication/policy-briefs/a-process-led-approach-towards-integrated-military-commands.html.
2. Shivshankar Menon, *Choices* (Delhi: Penguin Random House, 2016), 21.
3. Ibid., 30.
4. Kanti Bajpai, *India versus China* (Delhi: Juggernaut, 2021), 4–6.
5. Menon, *Choices*, 109–110.
6. Charles Mark Davis, 'Jointness, Culture, and Inter-Service Prejudice: Assessing the Impact of Resident, Satellite, and Hybrid Joint Professional Military Education II Course Delivery Methods on Military Officer Attitudes' (PhD Dissertation, Old Dominion University, 2017), DOI: 10.25777/fkez-pd25.
7. Joint Doctrine of Indian Armed Forces, April 2017.
8. Ibid.

9. Rahul Bedi, 'Why General Naravane's Criticism of Approach to integrated theatre Commands Is Significant', The Wire, 6 January 2023.
10. Deepak Kapoor, 'Need for Integrated Theatre Commands', Centre for Land Warfare Studies, (2013): 46, https://archive.claws.in/images/journals_doc/1394685182Deepak%20Kapoor%20%20CJ%20Summer%202013.pdf.
11. Government of India, Report of the Group of Ministers on National Security, Chapter 6, Para 6.2, 2001.
12. Sushant Singh, 'Joint Operations versus Integrated Commands: Understanding a New Way to Fight Wars', Indian Express, 10 May 2017, https://indianexpress.com/article/explained/joint-operations-vs-integrated-command-understanding-a-new-way-to-fight-wars-4648574/.
13. Government of India, 'Cabinet Approves the Creation of the Post of Chief of Defence Staff in the Rank of Four-Star General', Press Information Bureau, 24 December 2019.
14. Sandeep Unnithan, 'We Will Have Theatre Commands by 2022: Bipin Rawat', India Today, 17 February 2020.
15. ANI report reproduced in most national dailies.
16. Ministry of Defence, 'CDS General Bipin Rawat Operationalises Joint Logistics Node in Mumbai', Press Release, 1 April 2021.
17. Government of India, Report of the Group of Ministers on National Security.
18. 'Fully Committed to Theatre Commands: Army Chief Gen. Manoj Pande', Hindustan Times, 30 December 2022, https://www.hindustantimes.com/india-news/fully-committed-to-theatre-commands-army-chief-gen-manoj-pande-101672341621287.html.
19. 'Land Will Remain Decisive Domain: Army Chief on Russia–Ukraine War Takeaway', India Today, 17 March 2023.
20. Anil Ahuja and Arun Sahgal, 'A Process-led Approach Towards Integrated Military Commands'.

Chapter 7: Nation First

1. United Nations Security Council, 'Security Council Briefed By Chief UN Weapons Experts on First 60 Days of Inspection in Iraq', 27 January 2003.
2. Jon Boyle, 'Iran Seen to Need 3–8 Years to Produce Bomb', Reuters, 22 October 2007, https://www.reuters.com/article/economy/iran-would-need-3-8-yrs-to-produce-bomb-iaea-chief-idUSL22147111/.
3. 'Iraq War in Figures', BBC News, 14 December 2011, https://www.bbc.com/news/world-middle-east-11107739.
4. Linda J. Bilmes and Joseph E. Stieglitz, 'The Iraq War Will Cost US $3 Trillion, and Much More', *Washington Post*, 9 March 2008, https://www.washingtonpost.com/archive/opinions/2008/03/09/the-iraq-war-will-cost-us-3-trillion-and-much-more/077fd31c-f21b-476e-be59-7c495562d3b0/.
5. 'Iraq War in Figures'.
6. UNSCR, 'The Situation Between Iraq and Kuwait', Resolution 1483, 22 May 2003, http://unscr.com/en/resolutions/doc/1483.
7. Atal Behari Vajpayee, Prime Minister, New Delhi, 12 March 2003, https://www.satp.org/satporgtp/exclusive/iraq/india_gov.htm.
8. Statement by Official Spokesperson on the Commencement of Military Action in Iraq, Ministry of External Affairs, 20 March 2003, https://www.mea.gov.in/Speeches-Statements.htm?dtl/4322/Statement_by_Official_Spokesperson_on_the_commencement_of_military_action_in_Iraq.
9. Praful Bidwai, 'India Must Resist US Pressure to Send Troops to Iraq', Antiwar, 25 June 2003, https://original.antiwar.com/bidwai/2003/06/25/india-must-resist-us-pressure-to-send-troops-to-iraq/.
10. 'India's Decision Not to Send Troops to Iraq Won't Affect Relationship, Says US', Voice of America, 14 July 2003, https://www.voanews.com/a/a-13-a-2003-07-14-43-india-s-66322827/543685.html.

11 Devirupa Mitra, 'How India Nearly Gave in to US Pressure to Enter the Iraqi Killing Zone', The Wire, 19 March 2023.

Chapter 8: Administrative Reforms

1 Swati Luthra, 'Well-being of Soldiers Is a Collective Responsibility:Rajnath Singh', *Mint*, 29 November 2022, https://www.livemint.com/news/india/wellbeing-of-soldiers-a-collective-responsibility-rajnath-singh-11669712964522.html.
2 Ministry of Defence, 'Hospitals Empanelled under ECHS', Press Information Bureau, 29 July 2022, https://pib.gov.in/Pressreleaseshare.aspx?PRID=1846126.
3 Ministry of Defence, 'Defence Gets Rs 5.94 Lakh Crore in Budget 2023-24, a Jump of 13% Over Previous Year', Press Information Bureau, 1 February 2023, https://pib.gov.in/PressReleasePage.aspx?PRID=1895472.
4 Lieutenant General Rakesh Sharma, 'Envisioning Post-pandemic Ex-Servicemen Contributory Health Scheme (ECHS)', Centre for Land Warfare Studies, 16 May 2021.
5 General Manoj Pande, 'Message from the COAS', *Arivoli* (Naveen Printers, 2023).

References

Ahmed, Ali. 'Reopening the Debate on Limited War'. Manohar Parrikar Institute of Defence Studies and Analysis, 29 February 2012.

Ahuja, Anil and Arun Sahgal. 'A Process-led Approach Towards Integrated Military Commands'. DPG Policy Brief 6 (22), 24 July 2021.

Bajpai, Kanti. *India versus China*. Juggernaut, 2021.

Bhardwaj, Sandeep. 'The 2001–2002 India–Pakistan Standoff (Operation Parakram): A Dangerous Experiment'. Revisiting India: Indian History Recounted, 17 July 2013. https://revisitingindia.com/2013/07/17/the-2001-2002-india-pakistan-standoff-operationparakram-a-dangerous-experiment/.

Bhutto, Benazir. *Daughter of the East*. Simon and Schuster, 2008. First published 1988 by Hamish Hamilton.

Bidwai, Praful. 'India Must Resist US Pressure to Send Troops to Iraq'. Antiwar.com, 25 June 2003. https://original.antiwar.com/bidwai/2003/06/25/india-must-resist-us-pressure-to-send-troops-to-iraq/.

Boyle, Jon. 'Iran Seen to Need 3–8 Years to Produce Bomb'. Reuters, 22 October 2007.

Davis, Charles Mark. 'Jointness, Culture, and Inter-Service Prejudice: Assessing the Impact of Resident, Satellite, and Hybrid Joint Professional Military Education II Course Delivery Methods on Military Officer Attitudes'. PhD Dissertation, Old Dominion University, 2017. https://doi:10.25777/fkez-pd25.

Government of India. 'Cabinet Approves the Creation of the Post of Chief of Defence Staff in the Rank of Four-Star General'. Press Information Bureau, 24 December 2019.

Government of India. Discussion on and the Unanimous Resolution Relating to the War in Iraq. Lok Sabha, 8 April

2003. https://www.satp.org/satporgtp/exclusive/iraq/india_gov.htm.

Hasnain, Lieutenant General Syed Ata. 'Why Fence on Line of Control?'. Salute, 19 December 2014.

Jetley, Vijay Kumar. 'Operation Khukri: The United Nations Operation Fought in Sierra Leone Part II'. *USI Journal*, April–June 2007.

Kajal, Kapil. 'Indian Army Dissolves Old Units to Develop New Integrated Formations'. Janes, 16 January 2023.

Kalyanaraman, S. 'Operation Parakram: An Indian Exercise in Coercive Diplomacy'. *Strategic Analysis* 26 (4), 2002. https://doi.org/10.1080/09700160208450063.

Kanwal, Brigadier Gurmeet. 'Lost Opportunities in Operation Parakram'. *Indian Defence Review*, 13 December 2011.

Kapoor, Deepak. 'Need for Integrated Theatre Commands'. Centre for Land Warfare Studies, 2013.

Khattak, Masood Ur Rehman. 'Indian Military's Cold Start Doctrine: Capabilities, Limitations and Possible Response from Pakistan'. SASSI Research Paper, 31 March 2011.

Malik, Dr Muhammad Sajjad and Dr Pervaiz Iqbal Cheema. 'Media Coverage of Pak–India Standoff 2002: An Analysis'. *Journal of Political Studies* 26 (1), 2019. https://pu.edu.pk/images/journal/pols/pdf-files/20-v26_1_19.pdf.

Malik, General V.P. 'Indo-Pak Security Relations in the Coming Decade: Lessons from Kargil for the Future'. *Indian Defence Review*, January–March 2002. https://www.satp.org/satporgtp/publication/idr/vol_17(1)/VPMalik.htm.

Malik, General V.P. 'Strategic Stability in South Asia', Panel Discussion, Centre for Contemporary Conflict, Monterey, California, 29 June–1 July 2004, quoted by Walter C. Ladwig III, 'A Cold Start for Hot Wars? The Indian Army's New Limited War Doctrine'. *Quarterly Journal: International Security* 32 (3), 2007/08: 158–190.

Malik, General V.P. *India's Military Conflicts and Diplomacy*. HarperCollins, 2019.

Menon, Shivshankar. *Choices*. Penguin Random House, 2016.

Ministry of Defence. 'Hospitals Empanelled under ECHS'. Press Information Bureau, 29 July 2022.

Ministry of Defence. Joint Doctrine of Indian Armed Forces. Directorate of Doctrine, April 2017.

Nanavatty, Lieutenant General Rostum K. *Internal Armed Conflict in India*. Pentagon Press, 2013.

Pande, General Manoj. 'Message from the COAS'. *Arivoli*, 28 February 2023.

Pannier, Bruce. 'The World Waits for Musharraf's Speech on Terrorism'. Radio Free Europe, 11 January 2002.

Press Information Bureau. 'CDS General Bipin Rawat Operationalises Joint Logistics Node in Mumbai'. Press Release by Ministry of Defence, 1 April 2021.

Press Information Bureau. 'Defence Gets Rs 5.94 Lakh Crore in Budget 2023-24, a Jump of 13% Over Previous Year'. Press Release by Ministry of Defence, 1 February 2023. https://pib.gov.in/PressReleasePage.aspx?PRID=1895472.

Riedel, Bruce. 'Remembering Sandy Berger and the Day He Saved the World'. Brookings, 2 December 2015. https://www.brookings.edu/articles/remembering-sandy-berger-andthe-day-he-saved-the-world/.

Sharma, Lieutenant General Rakesh. 'Envisioning Post-Pandemic Ex-Servicemen Contributory Health Scheme'. Centre for Land Warfare Studies, 16 May 2021.

Singh, Jaswant. *A Call to Honour: In Service of Emergent India*. Rupa, 2006.

Singh, Sushant. *Operation Khukri: Hostage Rescue in Sierra Leone*. Juggernaut, 2020.

Stolar, Alex. 'To the Brink: Indian Decision-making and the 2001–2002 Standoff'. *Report No. 68*, The Henry L. Stimson Center, February 2008.

Tufail, Air Commodore M. Kaiser. 'Kargil Redux: A Senior Pakistani Air Force Officer's Account of the PAF's Role in Kargil'. *Defence and Security of India* 1 (4), February 2009.

UN Press Release. 'Security Council Expresses Full Support for Rescue of UN Peacekeepers in Kailahun, Sierra Leone', 17 July 2000.

United Nations Security Council Resolutions. 'The situation between Iraq and Kuwait'. UNSC Resolution 1483, 22 May 2003.

Index

IV Corps, 1, 96
XV Corps, 17–19, 22, 107, 112–113
9/11, 61, 163

A Call to Honour, 60
Actual Ground Position Line (AGPL), 3–4
Advani, L.K., 39, 53, 167–168
Afghanistan, 2, 5, 54–55, 57, 74,
    Taliban in, 54, 57
Ajay Vikram Singh Committee (AVSC), 175, 178–183, 206
Akhtar, Javed, 31
Al-Qaeda, 57, 74, 163, 165
Armed Forces Special Operations Division (AFSOD), 132, 143
Armitage, Richard, 63
Army Welfare Education Society (AWES), 196, 198, 206
Arun Singh Task Force, 132
Arunachal Pradesh, 135, 152
Annan, General Kofi, 88, 92–93
Arms and Influence, 70
Atal Tunnel, 6
Attari, 33
Aziz, Lieutenant General Mohammed, 13–14
Aziz, Lieutenant General Shahid, 13–14, 47
Aziz, Sartaj, 12, 30

Baghdad, 164
Bajpai, Kanti, 135–136
Bajrang Top, 20
Bakharwal, 8
Balakot, 70, 75
Baluchistan Think Tank Network, 123–124
Bangladesh, 81, 140,
    liberation of, 2
Banjin, 17
Basra, 164
Batalik, 7, 9, 17–20, 22–23, 25–26, 28, 33–34
BBC, The, 92
Beijing, 135
Berger, Sandy, 30–31
Bewabu, 92
Bhagat, General P.S. (India), 3
Bhandari, Brigadier M.C., 33
Bhimbat, 8–9
Bhimber Gali, 105–106, 109
Bhutto, Benazir, 1, 11
Blix, Hans, 163
Bodhkharbu, 6, 7
Border Area Development Programme (BADP), 44
Brar, Lieutenant General Tippy, 105
Budhwar, Major General V.S., 16–17
Bush, George W., 164–165, 167–168

Canada, 145
Central Armed Police Forces (CAPF), 40, 144, 181
Central Government Health Scheme (CGHS), 184, 187, 195
Chaudhari, Air Chief Marshal V.R., 158

Index

Chaudhary, Lieutenant General Shantanu, 104
Chauhan, Lieutenant General Anil, 151, 158
Chellaney, Brahma, 66–67
Chennai, 48
China–Pakistan Economic Corridor (CPEC), 133
China Study Group (CSG), 43
Chorbat La, 9, 18, 23, 25
Chou En-Lai, 133
Clinton, Bill, 31–32
Coercive diplomacy, 60, 63–66, 70, 73
Cold start doctrine, 121–124, 126, 128
College of Defence Management, 131
Combined Joint Expeditionary Force, 147
Compellence, policy of, 64–65, 67
Comprehensive Integrated Border Management System (CIBMS), 115
COVID-19 pandemic, 159, 192–193
Crowley, P.J., 93

Daru, 79, 89–91, 93–95
Daughter of the East, 11
Defence Cyber Agency, 132
Defence Services Staff College, 131
Defence Space Agency (DSA), 132, 143
Defence Planning Committee, 132
Delhi, 14, 17, 25, 27, 30, 34, 49, 51, 62–63, 74, 86, 88, 121, 133, 135, 143, 167, 182, 197, 199
Department of Military Affairs (DMA), 69, 150, 154–155, 161

Desai, Major, 17
Deterrence, policy of, 64
Directorate General Married Accommodation Project (DG MAP), 202
Disarmament, Demobilisation and Reintegration (DDR), 81–83
Doval, Ajit, 143
Dras, 5–9, 18–20, 22–24, 28, 33–34

Eckhard, Fred, 93
El-Baradei, Mohamed Mostafa, 164
Europe, 31, 46, 136
European Union, 46
Express Tribune, 124
Ex-Servicemen Contributory Health Scheme (ECHS), 185–195, 206

Fernandes, George, 57, 62, 73, 86, 93, 180, 186
France, 104, 147
Freetown, 80, 82, 84–86, 89, 93
From Kargil to Coup: Events That Shook Pakistan, 13

Gandhi, Sonia, 86, 171
Geihun, 90, 93
General Headquarters (GHQ) (Pakistan), 4, 15, 57
Ghana, 81
Godbole, Dr Madhav, 39
Goldwater–Nichols Act, 146
Gorkhum, 17
Group of Ministers (GoM), 39, 40, 175, report, 40, 141, 149, 155
Guinea, 79, 81
Gujarat, 152

Index

Gul, Lieutenant General Hamid (Pakistan), 62
Gulmarg, 112

Harka Bahadur bridge, 8
Hasnain, Lieutenant General Syed Ata, 109, 111–112, 205
Hussein, Saddam, 164–165, 167

India Today, 121
India versus China, 135
Indian Air Force (IAF), 21, 28–29, 38, 52, 82, 90, 93–94, 153
Indra Col, 3
Indus, 5, 7, 9
Integrated Battle Groups (IBGs), 119–120, 125–128
Inter-Services Intelligence (ISI), 2, 4, 13, 47, 62, 66, 96
Internal Armed Conflict in India, 110
International Atomic Energy Agency (IAEA), 164
Islamabad, 54, 74
Iyer, Chokila, 50

Jaipur, 121, 152
Jaish-e-Mohammed (JeM), 49, 51, 59
  See also Lashkar-e-Taiba (LeT)
Jalebi Mor, 7
Jervis, Robert, 70
  'Coercion and the Balance of Power', 70
Jetley, Major General Vijay Kumar, 76, 82, 86–88, 90, 92
Joint Logistics Nodes (JLNs), 155
Joint Services Wing, 130
Jordan, 81
Jubar, 9, 19, 26

Kabbah, Ahmad Tejan, 80
Kailahun, 79, 83–85, 88–94
Kaksar, 8, 20, 23, 26
Kalam, A.P.J. Abdul, 109
Kalia, Lieutenant Saurabh, 26–27
Kaluchak, 61, 73–74
Kandahar, 49
Kapoor, General Deepak, 121, 144, 199
Kapoor, Lieutenant General Ashok, 107
Karachi Agreement, 3
Karakoram Range, 3, 5
Karamat, General Jahangir, 10
Kargil Review Committee (KRC), 38–40, 129, 132, 175
Karnataka, 152
Karwar, 152
Katoch, Lieutenant General P.C., 115
Kayani, General Ashfaq Parvez (Pakistan), 123–124
Kenewa, 79, 89–90, 93
Kenya, 82
Khalsi, 6–7
Khalubar, 9
Khan, Dr Zaffar, 123
Khan, Lieutenant General Abdul Hamid (Pakistan), 3
Khasa, 33
Khattak, Lieutenant General Ali Kuli Khan, 32
Kibithu, 152
Kidwai, General Khalid (Pakistan), 119
Koidu, 82
Kotuma, 91
Kuiva, 85, 88, 91–92
Kukarthang, 9, 17, 26
Kupwara, 115
Kumar, Admiral Sushil, 53
  on Operation Parakram, 68

Index

Ladakh, 5–9, 15–16, 26, 29, 43–44, 125, 127, 135, 139, 152, 193
Lahore, 10–11
Lahore Declaration, 10, 14, 37
Lalli, B.S., 85
Lalotra, Brigadier Kanwar Vijay Singh, 109
Lamayuru, 7
Lancet, 164
Lashkar-e-Taiba (LeT), 51, 59, 61
Leh, 5–8, 24, 44
Liberia, 79–80, 82–83, 87
Line of Actual Control (LAC), 3, 42–44, 134–135, 152, 203
Lomé Peace Agreement, 81–82
London, 85, 167
Lucknow, 152

Magburaka, 83
Makeni, 83
Malacca Strait, 137
Maldives, 130
Malik, General Ved Prakash (*also* General Malik) (India), 1, 32, 66, 86, 122
   on the Lahore Declaration, 10
   on the MO directorate, 1–2
   See also military operations (MO) directorate
Malik, Lieutenant General Abdul Mazeed (Pakistan), 12
Manali, 6
Manekshaw Centre, 199
Marol, 7, 9
Marpola, 8–9
Matayen, 6, 9
McMahon Line, 133
Mehta, Major General R.K., 108–109
Menon, Shivshankar, 134, 138

Mexico, 145
Military Institute of Technology, 131
Military Intelligence (MI) directorate, 18, 54
Military operations (MO) directorate, 1–2, 10, 17–19, 25, 30, 35, 40–41, 47, 56, 104
Military Intelligence Training School and Depot, 131
Mishra, Brajesh, 22, 30–31, 51, 60, 65
Mobai, 91–92
Modi, Prime Minister Narendra, 150
Mujahideen, 12–13, 15, 34
Mukherjee, Pranab, 108, 121, 180
Mulbekh, 7
Musharraf, General Pervez, 10–11, 13–14, 32, 49, 57–59, 61, 63, 66, 138, 168
Mushkoh Valley, 8–9, 18–19, 21–23, 33–34

Nanavatty, Lieutenant General Rostum K., 105, 110
Naravane, General M.M., 143
Narayanan, K.R., 43
Naresh Chandra Committee, 132
National Defence Academy, 131
National Defence College, 131
National Maritime Theatre, 149
National Security Advisory Board (NSAB), 36, 53, 55, 72, 168
National Security Council (NSC), 10, 53, 55, 69, 93, 148
National Security Doctrine (NSD), 36, 72
National Security Strategy (NSS), 36, 72, 124, 142–143, 158

Index

Nepal, 44, 57, 189
New York, 85
New York Times, The, 92
NH-1D, 6–9, 15–16, 23–24
Nigeria, 81
Nimu, 7, 18
NJ 9842, Pt, 3
North of Pir Panjal Range (NPPR), 106, 112–113, 115
Northern Light Infantry (NLI), 13, 15, 22, 24, 34
Northern Theatre Command, 149, 152, 158
Nuclear threshold, 122–123, 127
  definition, 119
Operation Cactus, 130
Operation Iraqi Freedom, 162
Operation Khukri, 76–77, 87–89, 92–95, 130, 205
Operation Meghdoot, 4
Operation Pawan, 130, 170
Operation Topac (later Operation Badr), 2, 14
Operation Vijay, 130

Padmanabhan, General S., 48, 52, 58–59, 61, 121, 185
  on Operation Parakram, 68
Pakistan-occupied Kashmir (PoK), 7, 53, 67, 73, 96, 101, 103
Pal, Lieutenant General Krishan, 21
Pande, General Manoj, 126, 156, 159, 198
Pandit, Rajat, 72
Pannier, Bruce, 57
Paramilitary forces, 131, 144, 178
Patankar, Lieutenant General V.G., 105
Patranobis, Sutirtho, 134
Pendembu, 89–91

People's Liberation Army (PLA), 133, 137, 139, 147–148, 202
Phadnis, Aditi, 72
Poland, 17, 167
Prasad, Lieutenant General Hari, 107
Pulwama, 70
Puniya, Major Rajat, 84
Punjab, 104, 202
Puri, Major General Mohinder, 6, 20, 22–23, 25, 207

Qazi, Ashraf Jehangir, 50
Quick reaction company (QRC), 82, 90

Rahman, Hamoodur, 148
Rao, Abid, 13
Rao, General Krishna, 117
Rao, Nirupama, 51
Rawat, General Bipin, 121, 151, 181
Revolutionary United Front (RUF), 76, 79–80, 82–87, 89–93, 95
Rice, Condoleezza, 54
Royal Air Force (RAF), 88, 92–93
Roychowdhury, former army chief General Shankar, 71
Russia, 13, 46, 82, 136, 144
Russia–Ukraine war, 44–46

Saltoro Ridge, 3, 151
Sando, 8
Sankoh, Foday, 80, 83
Saxena, Girish, 39
Schelling, Thomas, 70
Second World War, The, 104, 161, 189
Security Council of the Russian Federation, 147

Index

Sethi, Najam, in an interview titled 'Kargil War', 11
Sharan, Shyam, 36
Sharif, Nawaz, 1, 10–14, 16, 31–32, 47
Sharma, Lieutenant General Nirbhay, 107
Shekatkar Committee, 132, 149
Sheoran, Colonel Ashok, 33
Sri Lanka, 130, 170
Shrikhande, Rear Admiral Sudarshan, 125
Shyok river, 9
Siachen Glacier, 3, 21, 152, 172
Sierra Leone, 76, 78–80, 82–89, 92–93, 130, 170, 205
geography and terrain, 78–79
Simla Agreement, 2–3, 37
Singh, Ajai Vikram, 176, 178
Singh, Arun, 39,
Singh, Brigadier Surinder, 16
Singh, Colonel Bikram, 41
Singh, Dr Manmohan, 86–87, 138, 172
Singh. General V.K., 121
Singh, Jaswant, 30, 54, 60, 68–69, 86, 121
Singh, Lieutenant General Bhopinder, 119
Singh, Lieutenant General Mohinder, 178, 188, 205–206
Sir Creek, 152
Snow and Avalanche Study Establishment (SASE), 115
Sonamarg, 6
Sood, former army vice chief Lieutenant General V.K., 69
South of Pir Panjal Range (SPPR), 4, 104, 106, 112–113
Srinagar, 6–8, 11, 21–22, 24, 49
Srivastava, D.P., 85
Subsector Haneef (SSH), 9

Suchetgarh, 3
Sundarji, General Krishnaswami, 118
Suru River, 7
Survey, Lieutenant Siddharth, 17

Tactical nuclear weapons, 66, 74, 123–124, 127–128
Taiwan, 136, 147
Taliban, 54, 57
Taylor, Charles, 83–84, 88
Tezpur, 1
Thakkar, Lieutenant General Bali, 104
Thar desert, 59, 73
Theaterisation, 38, 128, 143, 151, 156, 206
Tibet, 133–135
Tiger Hill, 9, 19, 24–25, 27, 31
Times of India, 72, 125
Tipnis, A.Y., 52
on Operation Parakram, 69
Togo, 88
Tololing, 9, 24, 28

Udhampur, 21
UK, 13, 69, 80, 85, 88, 146, 162–167
Ukraine, 46, 82
Umling La, 43
Unified Combat Commands (UCCs), 146
United Nations Mission in Sierra Leone (UNAMSIL), 76, 81–83, 93, 95
United Nations Monitoring, Verification and Inspection Commission (UNMOVIC), 163–164
United Nations Security Council (UNSC), 76–78, 80–81, 93, 163, 165, 167–168

Index

Uri, 70, 75
US Defense Mapping Agency, 3

Vajpayee, Atal Bihari, 10, 12, 30, 32, 37, 48, 50, 57–58, 61, 67–68, 86, 162, 166, 168, 171, 187
Vij, Lieutenant General Kapil, 59
Vij, Lieutenant General Mahesh, 181, 206
Vohra, N.N., 39

Washington D.C., 85
Western Theatre Command (proposed), 149, 151, 153, 158

White House National Security Council, 93

Xinjiang, 133

Yaldor, 17–18, 25

Zia-ul-Haq, General, 2, 11, 14, 118
Zia, Major General Tauqir, 12, 33–35, 37
Zehra, Nasim, 13
Zoji La, 5–6, 8, 18, 107

About the Author

General N.C. Vij, PVSM, UYSM, AVSM, served as the chief of the Indian Army from 31 December 2002 to 31 January 2005. He was also the chairman of the Chiefs of Staff Committee during the Indian Ocean tsunami in December 2004 and was responsible for organising the armed forces' massive rescue and support efforts, including assistance to Indonesia, Sri Lanka and the Maldives. General Vij has the rare distinction of being the only officer who held the posts of DGMO, VCOAS and the Chief, besides commanding two corps – a strike corps and a corps involved in insurgency operations in the North-East.

His tenure as Chief of the Army Staff is remembered for many pathbreaking operational projects, including the anti-infiltration fence along the Line of Control and the cold start doctrine. South Western Command and IX Corps were also sanctioned during his tenure. Among other notable initiatives, General Vij has been credited with launching revolutionary welfare projects such as improvement in career prospects of all ranks and the Ex-Servicemen's Contributory Health Scheme for veterans.

After his superannuation, he was deputed by the government to set up the National Disaster Management Authority with the rank of a Cabinet minister. Subsequently, he became the director of the Vivekananda International Foundation, a think tank based in New Delhi. He is the author of *The Kashmir Conundrum: The Quest for Peace in a Troubled Land*.